FROM DEEP STATE TO ISLAMIC STATE

THE CERI SERIES IN COMPARATIVE POLITICS AND INTERNATIONAL STUDIES

Series editor, Christophe Jaffrelot

This series consists of translations of noteworthy manuscripts and publications in the social sciences emanating from the foremost French researchers at Sciences Po, Paris.

The focus of the series is the transformation of politics and society by transnational and domestic factors—globalisation, migration and religion. States are more permeable to external influence than ever before and this phenomenon is accelerating processes of social and political change the world over. In seeking to understand and interpret these transformations, this series gives priority to social trends from below as much as to the interventions of state and non-state actors.

JEAN-PIERRE FILIU

From Deep State
to Islamic State

*The Arab Counter-Revolution
and its Jihadi Legacy*

OXFORD
UNIVERSITY PRESS

OXFORD

UNIVERSITY PRESS

Oxford University Press is a department of the
University of Oxford. It furthers the University's objective
of excellence in research, scholarship, and education
by publishing worldwide.

Oxford   New York
Auckland   Cape Town   Dar es Salaam   Hong Kong   Karachi
Kuala Lumpur   Madrid   Melbourne   Mexico City   Nairobi
New Delhi   Shanghai   Taipei   Toronto

With offices in
Argentina   Austria   Brazil   Chile   Czech Republic   France   Greece
Guatemala   Hungary   Italy   Japan   Poland   Portugal   Singapore
South Korea   Switzerland   Thailand   Turkey   Ukraine   Vietnam

Oxford is a registered trade mark of Oxford University Press
in the UK and certain other countries.

Published in the United States of America by
Oxford University Press
198 Madison Avenue, New York, NY 10016

Library of Congress Cataloging-in-Publication Data is available
Filiu, Jean-Pierre.
From Deep State to Islamic State: The Arab Counter-Revolution and its
Jihadi Legacy / Jean-Pierre Filiu.

ISBN 9780190264062

Printed in the USA on acid-free paper

'The notion of inviting the army into the country's political life again is extremely dangerous; it could turn Egypt into another Afghanistan or Somalia.'

General Abdelfattah Sisi, Minister of Defence, 15 May 2013, less than two months before his coup against the elected president

'If you are a patriot, you need to shut up and let us do our job, and clean up the mess you made with your revolution.'

Threats from the Egyptian security services reported in January 2014 by former MP Mostafa Al-Nagar*

* Mostafa al-Nagar, born in 1980, is one of the few activists of the Egyptian 25 January 2011 revolution to have successfully joined the political scene. After an early involvement in the Muslim Brotherhood's youth wing—which he left in 2005—he became a vocal defender of human rights and Palestinian causes. (A dentist by profession, he volunteered in Gaza to help the victims of the Israeli offensive of January 2009.) He was jailed four times under Mubarak's regime. In June 2011 he became one of the co-founders of the Adl (Justice) party, and then its only member in the parliament that was elected in November–December 2011, but dissolved by the Supreme Constitutional Court in June 2012.

CONTENTS

FOREWORD

It has been four years now since Mohammad Bouazizi's self-immolation in the Tunisian town of Sidi Bouzid sparked a wave of popular protests against the Arab regimes. President Ben Ali was the first to fall in January 2011, followed by Husni Mubarak the following month. At that time, I was visiting professor at Columbia University, far from my home country and from the Arab world, but close enough to feel the shockwaves of this extraordinary development and to participate in its aftermath.

My background as a historian soon led me to believe that this was only the beginning of a long-term process, itself rooted in the two-century long and complex period known as the Arab renaissance, or Nahda. I was therefore reluctant to use the expression 'Arab spring', anticipating that an 'Islamist autumn' would eventually replace it in the mainstream lexicon. I favoured instead the 'Arab revolution', not because I thought that revolutions would take place in every Arab country, but because I was convinced that a pan-Arab dynamic was nurturing a regional wave of radical protest.

As early as spring 2011, I authored *The Arab Revolution, Ten Lessons About the Democratic Uprising*, published the following summer by Hurst in London and Oxford University Press in New York.[1] Far from being academic landmarks, these 'lessons' were meant to be modest signposts to keep track of a multi-faceted process that would only become more difficult to interpret and to categorize.

This kind of leap in the dark was not the spontaneous attitude a seasoned historian should adopt. Yet I was hoping that Arab historians would benefit from the democratic breakthrough and take a fresh look at their own national narratives. I believed that history was just one of the many scholarly resources that could help us grasp the long-term impact of an event of such profound global importance.

Nearly four years later, I readily confess that my focus on the Arab revolution prevented me from assessing the full potential of the Arab counter-revolution. I thought I had seen it all from the Arab despots: their perversity, their brutality, their voracity. But I was still underestimating their ferocity and their readiness to literally burn down their country in order to cling to the absolute power. Bashar al-Assad has climbed to the top of this murderous class of Arab tyrants, driving nearly half the Syrian population from their homes.

This is how this 'Arab counter-revolution' was conceived: not as a paradoxical sequel, but as a study of the repressive dynamics designed to crush any hope of democratic change, through the association of any revolutionary experience with the worst collective nightmare. In order to describe this systematic war of the Arab regimes against their people, I had to import and scrutinize the concept of the 'Deep State' from neighbouring Turkey. That was a means of explaining how the nucleus of the ruling cliques could strike back with such unbridled violence.

This attempted conceptualization would however have been pretty weak without the parallel use of the Mamluk paradigm to underline how modern 'security' systems were established and empowered. Contrary to previous works about the 'New Mamluks',[2] dealing with the Ottomanized Mamluks of the seventeenth and eighteenth centuries, I am referring to the original Mamluks who ruled Egypt from 1250 to 1517, along with Syria from 1260 to 1516. I draw a parallel between the legitimacy derived by those founding Mamluks from the vulnerable 'caliph' under their control and the one derived by the modern Mamluks from the popular 'votes' held under martial law.

Chapter 1 is dedicated to the Turkish contemporary 'detour' through the Deep State, afer which Chapter 2 addresses the process of state-building in the post-colonial Arab world. My hypothesis is that the Arab renaissance, or Nahda, was consistently contested by two ideologies that laid the foundations for two modern states: Kemalism for Turkey and Wahhabism for Saudi Arabia. In the meantime, it took half a century, from 1922 to 1971, for the colonized Arabs to reach sovereign emancipation. But through this very process, two decades were sufficient, from 1949 to 1969, for military cliques parading as a fighting 'elite' (*khâssa*) to hijack this newly won independence and snatch it from the civilian resistance and from the 'masses' (*'âmma*).

Chapter 3 presents the historical process of power struggles that led to the consolidation of the modern Arab Mamluks, mainly in Algeria, Egypt, Syria and Yemen. Those four countries shared the same characteristics of a reframed nationalist narrative, a populist discourse, a ubiquitous repressive apparatus and a systematic plundering of national resources. More important, they extolled the virtues of the military as the dominant source of legitimacy, while the hegemonic ruling party organized regular plebiscites.

There lies a clear distinction between, on one side, the Arab Mamluks and, on the other, police states (like Tunisia under Bourguiba or Ben Ali) or would-be totalitarian regimes (like Qaddafi's Jamahiriyya or Saddam Hussein's Iraq). Monarchies who had survived the turmoils of the early 1970s ('Black September' 1970 in Jordan and the two failed military coups in 1971–2 in Morocco) were also spared the Mamluk curse.

The 'black decade' of the 1990s in Algeria appears in retrospect as the first attempt of a Mamluk-styled regime to kill the democratic alternative through the unleashing of civil war and the nurturing of the jihadi threat. This is why the 'Algerian matrix' is the focus of Chapter 4, before we turn, in Chapter 5, to the income-generating mechanisms, primarily petrocarbons, that sustain such a level of collective violence. Oil is only part of the equation, contrary again to Libya and Iraq whose regimes could rely on their oil wealth to survive the international sanctions imposed from 1991 to 2003. Geopolitical income, namely a triangular relationship with the USA and Israel, is crucial in the Middle East, while immigration control is more profitable in explaining how the North African regimes deal with Europe.

Chapter 6 explores how the Bush administration's leadership of the 'global war on terror' played directly into the hands of the Arab despots, delaying by many years the democratic uprising that finally took place in 2011. The catastrophic US invasion of Iraq, in 2003, and the subsequent reconciliation between Washington and Tripoli only accelerated the dynastical mutation of the Arab Mamluks, effective in Syria as early as 2000, with Egypt and Yemen ready to follow suit. The Yemeni Mamluks even managed to divert most of the resources transferred by Washington to fight jihadism into the beefing up of family-run praetorian guards.

Egypt represents today the best case study of a successful Arab counter-revolution, through the revamping and the mobilization of a merciless 'Deep State'. Chapter 7 therefore studies in detail how the 2011 popular protests were betrayed and ultimately crushed. A year and a half after the toppling of the first democratically elected president of Egyptian history, General Sisi's regime remains far from stable. The deal offered by the Arab Mamluks, trading oppression for security, is in fact obsolete and the parallel growth of the 'evil twins' of dictatorial denial and jihadi violence, both in Yemen and in Syria, is considered in Chapter 8.

There was no 'Islamic state' in Syria at the start of the anti-Assad demonstrations in March 2011. Now Daesh, the Arab acronym of such infamous 'Islamic State', is controlling one third of the country and by August–September 2014 had dragged a US-led coalition, both in Syria and in neighbouring Iraq, into an air campaign against 'terrorist' targets. In Yemen, the jihadi threat has never been so formidable, and large swathes of the country remain controlled by al-Qaeda. Such a disaster was only made possible by the prevailing confusion about the very nature of the modern Mamluks. This process of Arab dispossession comes full circle, in Chapter 9, with the offensive against Palestinian targets and symbols launched by those supposedly 'nationalist' regimes.

Chapter 10, dedicated to the 'Tunisian alternative', highlights a democratic way out of the Mamluk impasse. The Tunisian transition has been proceeding despite a prolonged economic slowdown and an unprecedented terrorist threat. There is nothing preordained about Tunisia remaining an 'exception', since the Arab people are not doomed to remain pawns, the perpetual victims of a deadly game between their dictators and the jihadis. But it is too early to assess the long-term impact of the sharp fall in oil prices in the summer and autumn of 2014.

In the meantime, my 2011 'ten lessons' might still be of some help, even though they all have to be amended, completed and updated. My first lesson, entitled 'Arabs are no exception', stands firm against all the culturalist and racist reasoning that would exclude the Arabs per se from any democratic evolution. The pugnacity of Arab protesters is testimony to this collective aspiration to freedom. Second, 'Muslims are not only Muslims' is still valid in a region where his or her Islamic faith gives no clue about the political rationale an individual or collective actor may follow.

The fact that 'Anger is power for the young' is still a striking Arab reality, even if this militant 'anger' has failed to materialize into real political and institutional power. The same can be said for the following lessons, 'Social networks work' and 'Leaderless movements can win': the amorphous nature of the Syrian revolution until today, for instance, is key to understanding both its resilience (despite merciless repression) and its impotence (in converting its social capital into political gains).

'The alternative to democracy is chaos' is obviously true in Syria and in Yemen, but also in Libya, where the failure to establish effective institutions fed the militias' warlordism. I am also concerned that the Egyptian military coup will only precipitate more serious disturbances instead of restoring 'stability'. My next lesson, 'Islamists must choose', was a warning against the temptation for the Muslim Brotherhood in Egypt or Ennahda in Tunisia to take their coming electoral victories as a blank cheque, while the Islamist vote was complex, and partly volatile.

President Morsi contributed to the collapse of the democratic transition in Egypt by refusing to choose between his party's internal logic and the national interest. Rashid Ghannouchi was close to falling into the same trap, but the political process was saved in Tunisia by the strong and enduring pressure exerted by the powerful union (UGTT) that imposed an agreement between the Islamist government and the nationalist opposition.

Such compromise between the nationalist and Islamist components of the Arab Nahda is the key to the fulfilment of its historic promises, which I summarized in 'No domino effect in the Renaissance'. This is also why counter-revolutionary forces and powers have a vested interest in exacerbating the polarization between the Islamist and nationalist currents in various Arab societies.

'Palestine is still the mantra' could easily seem out of date in a world where the ordeals of Gaza and the impasse in the quest for a Palestinian state elicit little Arab solidarity or sympathy (the military junta in Egypt has reached unprecedented levels of discursive demonization of Hamas). But the volatility of Arab public opinion during the Israeli offensive against Gaza, in summer 2014, proves that popular feelings still run high when it comes to Palestine, a cause now disconnected from support of Hamas or the PLO.

Finally, 'Jihadis could become obsolete' may sound preposterous when al-Qaeda affiliates dig deep into Yemen and loom over Libya, with a self-proclaimed jihadi caliphate established on both sides of the Syrian–Iraqi border. But the conditional tense was intentionally used in connecting a reverse of the jihadi tide with a breakthrough in the democratic process.

In my book *The Arab Revolution*, I quoted a US intelligence veteran who, in February 2011, confided to me: 'a defeat of the democratic movement would give such a boost to jihadi subversion that the counter-terrorism budget would have to be tripled—not doubled—just to cope with the magnitude of such a threat'[3] This is exactly where we find ourselves today, across the entire Arab world.

The massive surge of the jihadi menace is therefore not to be blamed on the Arab democratic uprising, but on its worst enemies, the dictatorships that played with jihadi fire to deny any substantial power-sharing. More democracy should be the answer, not a new 'war on terror' that would ultimately feed more terrorism. The Arab revolution is only entering its fifth year and its standard slogan, 'The people want change', will echo for many years to come.

The Arab struggle for collective emancipation has been rabidly suppressed by regimes posing as the guardians of regional 'stability' and reaping the associated benefits from their self-appointed fictitious role. Despots will never be part of the solution, since they stand at the very core of the problem. The ubiquitous 'Deep State' eventually nurtured the 'Islamic state' and the Arab Mamluks succeeded in transferring to the rest of the world the responsibility for the monster they had helped to create.

Understanding the dynamic of the Arab counter-revolution is a prerequisite to any decent attempt at containing the jihadi menace. Let us hope it is not too late to grasp this terrible truth: the hundreds of thousands of Arab women and men who fell in their quest for freedom since 2011 were not only fighting for their liberation, but also for all of us to live in a more peaceful world. Apart from any moral consideration, the pathetic error of abandoning the Arab people to their executioners will be an unacceptable price to pay in the future.

Paris, December 2014

1

MEET THE DEEP STATE

The concept of a 'Deep State' (*dawla 'amîqa*) has only recently appeared in the academic and political debate in the Arab world. The notion emerged from the various scandals that shook Turkey in the 1990s, when murky cooperation between state intelligence, corrupt justice and organized crime seemed to 'run' the system behind the scenes. The Deep State, known in Turkish as *derin devlet*, was therefore an irrelevant notion in the Arab world, where the ruling regimes were shamelessly dictatorial.

After the popular Arab uprisings of 2011, the concept of the Deep State became more and more familiar to politicians and analysts. They often attributed to a shadowy Deep State the hurdles facing the various democratic Arab transitions. Many conspiracy theories were built on the assumption that an all-powerful Deep State was striking back and avenging itself on the post-dictatorial regimes. It is therefore crucial, in order to clarify this issue, to return to the Turkish cradle of the Deep State.

A Fateful Car Crash

When reality surpasses fiction, unexpected concepts can take root. This is what happened on 3 November 1996 when a Mercedes crashed in Susurluk, a Turkish town a few hundred km south-west of Bursa. There were four passengers in the car, three of whom died in the crash: a police chief, Huseyin Kocadag; a notorious gangster with extreme-right connections, Abdullah Catli; and Catli's girlfriend. The fourth passenger was only injured and appeared to be Sedat Bucak, an MP representing the south-east Urfa province, where he led local Kurdish militias against the separatist-Marxist insurgents of the PKK (Workers' Party of Kurdistan).

The accident proved beyond the wildest speculation how intimate were the connections between the security apparatus and anti-communist and anti-PKK paramilitary groups, the whole ensemble characterised by a distinct mafia tinge. Kocadag was no less than the director of the police academy in Istanbul. Catli was a wanted criminal both for murders (by the Turkish justice) and drug trafficking (by Interpol, after he escaped from a Swiss jail in 1990). He had been deputy chairman of the 'Grey Wolves',[1] the youth (and combat) branch of the ultra-nationalist MHP (Nationalist Action Party) during the late 1970s.

To make matters worse, five pistols, along with two machine guns fitted with silencers, were found in the wrecked car. Catli was carrying, under a fake identity, a 'green passport', reserved for government officials.[2] And Bucak, whose extended family had been a major target of PKK death squads, was the Urfa strongman for the conservative Party of the True Path (DYP). He had been elected in 1991, and again in 1995, to the National Assembly, where he represented the DYP, the party of the minister of interior (and police general), Mehmet Agar, and of the deputy prime minister, Tansu Ciller.

What has become known as the 'Susurluk scandal' deeply shocked a Turkey that had only thirteen years earlier returned to democracy. The main actor of this restoration had been Turgut Ozal and his Motherland Party (known by the Turkish acronym ANAP). Ozal was able to placate the military leadership that had toppled the elected government in 1980 and had supervised the new 1982 constitution. ANAP won the 1983 elections and Ozal became prime minister until 1989. He died while he was president of the Republic in 1993.

At the time of the Susurluk accident, Turkey was run by a coalition government between the Islamist Welfare Party (*Refah Partisi*, or RP) and the DYP (ANAP and DYP had only managed to collaborate from March to June 1996). Necmettin Erbakan, the Islamist prime minister, spoke dramatically about the scandal:

> The situation is more serious than we think and than the people know. There are military men, police officers, politicians and mafia people involved. Events have taken place that are not known to the public.[3]

But his female deputy, Tansu Ciller, who had been prime minister from 1993 to 1996, chose a sharply different tone. She praised Catli as a 'hero'[4] and, in line with her tough anti-PKK profile, she stood by the minister of interior. It was the genuine outrage of the Turkish public that eventually forced police general Agar reluctantly to resign. From February 1997, millions of people turned out their lights every day at 9 p.m., in an unprecedented demand for more 'light' to be shed on the 'Susurluk scandal'.

A parliamentary commission was set up to investigate the case which published its 300-page report in April 1997. But, in the meantime, the top Turkish generals, regrouped in the National Security Council (MGK), had published a 'memorandum' that was in fact an ultimatum against the Islamist PM. Erbakan was eventually compelled to step down in favour of an ANAP-led coalition, in what has been described as a 'post-modern coup'.[5]

This was only the first blow in a fully-fledged campaign against the Islamist party that ended up outlawed. Erbakan was banned from any political activity for five years. This left the field open for one of Erbakan's protégés, Recep Tayyip Erdogan, who had been the Islamist mayor of Istanbul from 1994 to 1998, before breaking away from his former mentor in 1999.

A State with Many Mansions

The depth of the shameful connections revealed by the 'Susurluk scandal' gave birth to the expression 'Deep State' and to a wide range of conflicting interpretations. It was now established beyond any doubt that the priority given to the armed struggle against the PKK had led to a sustained cooperation between the security forces, both military and police, on the one side, and criminal elements recycled into the 'anti-terrorist' fight, on the other.

But the 'dirty war' waged in the predominantly Kurdish south-east of Turkey had triggered profound changes in the security apparatus and its doctrine. This 'low intensity conflict' was not so much about law and order, but about how to hit the PKK resources through a scorched earth policy and the liquidation of their financiers.[6] Since racketeering and drug smuggling were crucial sources of revenue for the PKK, they became legitimate targets in an underground power struggle that nurtured the expansion of the Deep State.

The number of personnel involved in 'combat' operations reached unexpected heights, whether regular forces or paramilitary groups: the 'special teams', an elite army unit, increased to 23,000; the 'village guards', as local Kurdish militiamen were called, already numbered 36,000 at the beginning of the 1990s and this figure had nearly tripled by the end of the decade; new intelligence networks, parallel to the official National Intelligence Service (MIT), were created to support the various centres of power, providing critical data.[7]

This substantial war effort could have proved to be a terrible burden for the state budget, so it relied increasingly on its own underground war economy. The Deep State could therefore develop as a viable economic model, while it could also boast military victories. From 1992 to 1996, according to government sources, the casualty ratio between the security forces and the insurgents fell from 1 to 2 to 1 to 6.[8] Even if those official figures are questionable, the trend itself is undisputable. And PKK violence had effectively been contained in a peripheral area of the country.

As the French historian and sociologist Hamit Bozarslan put it:

> [even] if the war, and particularly the 'low intensity conflict doctrine', have weakened the PKK, they have created the conditions for the re-emergence or the reinforcement of the paramilitary gangs. The political options in the Kurdish issue have been eliminated, because, among other reasons, for many involved actors, the so-called 'military solution' meant substantial benefits and total independence from the central power.[9]

The 'Susurluk scandal' struck the Turkish public as an electro-shock. The Deep State imposed its reality on the daily debate as a shadowy structure monitoring the prevailing institutions. The main attribute of such an unofficial power structure was of course its absolute unaccountability. But more ominous even was its capacity to influence and, why not, control leaders whose legitimacy came from popular, free and fair elections.

This black hole in Turkish politics could only foster conspiracy theories of all kinds. For example, President Ozal was believed to have been poisoned by the Deep State in 1993 because he favoured a peaceful and negotiated solution to the Kurdish problem with the PKK.[10] The car crash at Susurluk was no longer considered a mere traffic accident, but rather a carefully planned ambush which was in fact targeting the minister of the interior himself.[11]

These were only a small sample of the various 'plots' proliferating in the Turkish press and among public opinion, all of which still linked a fundamental anti-PKK rationale to the burgeoning of the Deep State. However, they missed two main aspects of the post-Susurluk phenomenon that are of great relevance when discussing current Arab politics:

1. The army and the police in Turkey were indeed fighting far-right terrorists during the 1970s, no matter how strongly

anti-communist the security apparatus was. The September 1980 coup was launched against both extremes of the political spectrum and, even though the far-left was struck harder, the 'Grey Wolves' lost some 'martyrs' and many of their leaders ended up in jail. Interestingly, one decade later, the same extremist outcasts were recycled in the all-encompassing struggle against PKK 'terrorism'.

2. Prime Minister Erbakan's robust response to the Susurluk scandal could have paved the way for an understanding between a law-abiding Islamist party and those parts of the military hierarchy that were genuinely outraged by the Deep State's dangerous liaisons. Instead, the scandal only accelerated the showdown between the army top brass and the elected government, with the brutal conclusion, after only a year, of the first Islamist-led cabinet in Turkish history.

3. So the Erbakan government fell as a collateral victim of the Susurluk scandal. It is by definition impossible to assert that the military elites would have toppled the Islamist government without such a scandal (and indeed nothing in the ominous 'memorandum' was connected to Susurluk), but the Refah/Welfare party that had won the 1995 elections was ousted from power shortly afterwards. The idea then prevailed that, no matter how soiled the Deep State was shown to be, the Islamists who opted for the political and parliamentary path would be the ones who paid the price.

It also became obvious that 'crime' and 'terrorism' were relative notions when it came to the Deep State. True, the PKK was relying on its own mafia godfathers or *baba* to finance its guerrilla operations. But they were neither better nor worse than the top gangsters such as Catli, who ran their activities with the protection, and even the collaboration, of the anti-PKK apparatus. Moreover the unbridled dynamics of such a 'dirty war' led to the usual escalation of violence and counter-violence, with each camp accusing the other of being the 'terrorist' villain.

This blend of shadowy warfare, the black economy and conspiracy theories generated, after a while, a ubiquitous perception of the Deep State. Defenders of due process resented it as the most vicious threat facing the Turkish republic. Meanwhile, Kurdish nationalists perceived it as the latest avatar of Turkish armed chauvinism. Islamist activists protested against an illegitimate political machine that they felt was designed to deprive them of their electoral gains. Even the secularist, progressive and leftist militants feared the Deep State's connections with the extreme-right.

Such a complex web of attitudes and interpretations only magnified the ominous aura of the Deep State. Nearly everybody came to believe in its reality without being able to pin it down precisely. But each actor came also to the paradoxical conclusion that the Deep State was working on behalf of the other side of the political or national spectrum. This explains why a consensus eventually coalesced on the pressing need to dismantle the Deep State.

Erdogan Versus the Deep State

We saw above how the military's crackdown against Erbakan in 1997–8 paved the way for the rise of one of his disciples, Erdogan, who freed himself from his political boss in 1999. The way ahead for the former Islamist mayor of Istanbul, who was even jailed for four months in 1999 and banned from politics till 2003, was hardly straightforward,. But this did not deter Erdogan from founding the Justice and Development Party (AKP) in 2001, amalgamating elements of the traditional Islamist movement (the Welfare Party, which had become the Virtue Party, before being also banned) and the conservative wing of the Ozal-founded ANAP.

The AKP insisted on its commitment to 'conservative democracy', to avoid the pavlovian military blowback against any form of Islamism. Erdogan's venture was so successful that, during the general elections of November 2002, AKP won 34.3 per cent of the vote and, more importantly, 363 of the 500 seats in the National Assembly. This two-thirds majority allowed AKP to form the first single-party government in twenty-five years.

This AKP cabinet was first chaired by Abdullah Gül, but he moved to the presidency of the Republic in March 2003, when Erdogan, his political ban now behind him, won a by-election that allowed him to enter parliament and then the government. Erdogan's strength as prime minister was dramatically consolidated when the AKP reaped even more votes (46.6 per cent) in the July 2007 elections (with slightly fewer parliamentary seats, at 341).

At the very beginning of this second term, the so-called 'Ergenekon' case began to unfold. The Ergenekon Valley is a mythical place in Central Asia where a she-wolf is supposed to have rescued the Turkish nation. One of the first documents seized by the police in this case was entitled 'Ergenekon', and detailed a military plot to destabilize the AKP government. (The civilian dimension of this plot was called 'Lobby' in a separate document.)

From June 2007 to June 2009, thirteen successive waves of arrests led to the detention of more than 200 individuals, including the retired brigadier-general Veli Küçük, believed to have established the Gendarmerie Intelligence Branch (JITEM) long before its official founding in 2005. JITEM had often been mentioned during the Susurluk scandal investigations but, while politicians acknowledged its existence as a fighting outfit against the PKK, the military adamantly denied it. Küçük was in fact arrested the same day as Sami Hostan, nicknamed 'Sami the Albanian', well known in the criminal underworld for his past association with Abdullah Catli (it was Hostan who had recovered the dead gangster's body from the Susurluk car wreck).

The indictments against the Ergenekon plotters included the shooting attack on the Council of State (which left one senior judge dead) and three separate attacks against the liberal newspaper *Cumhurryet*, all of these crimes taking place in 2006. The network was also accused of having masterminded certain terrorist attacks, including the murder of the Turkish–Armenian journalist Hrant Dink in January 2007. The manipulation and infiltration of armed groups from the Marxist far-left (DHKP-C) and the Islamist extreme-right (Hezbollah) were also part of this multi-faceted 'strategy of tension'.

The plot literally thickened in the spring of 2009, when an 'Action plan against reactionary forces' was revealed as having emanated from the armed forces' General Staff. Despite repeated denials by General Ilker Basbug, the chief of staff, the authenticity of the document was confirmed. It was an ambitious plan to discredit not only the AKP, but also the latter's political ally, Fethullah Gülen's movement,[12] an Islamic brotherhood (*tarika*) highly active in education, the press and the business world. (Gülen, harassed by the Turkish military, has been living in the USA since 1999.)

But more was to come with the unravelling of the 'Sledgehammer' plot in 2010. In this case, the most senior echelons of the armed forces were accused of having planned, as early as 2003, terror attacks and military incidents in order to foment civilian strife and bring down the AKP government. The explanation that this was only scenario-based forward planning did not hold water, and the three former general commanders of the Naval Forces (Ozden Ornek), of the Air Force (Ibrahim Firtina) and of the First Army (Cetin Dogan) were put on trial.

The June 2011 general elections saw AKP reap nearly half of the votes (49.83 per cent). Erdogan became the first prime minister in the history of Turkey to win three consecutive elections, and each time with a greater share of the votes. AKP gained 327 seats, falling far short of the two-thirds majority that would have allowed it to amend the 1982 Constitution. But Erdogan could with some justification consider his showdown against the

Deep State to have been hugely popular. And there was no reason for him and his supporters to keep their hands tied behind their backs.

In September 2012, harsh judicial verdicts were delivered in the Sledgehammer case. The three convicted generals were each condemned to twenty years in jail (the life sentence initially requested was reduced because the plot was never implemented). Only one in ten was acquitted of the more than 300 officers who were being tried. The defendants denounced a 'witch hunt' against the very pillars of the Turkish republic, branding the trial 'unfair and unlawful'.[13] Observers feared that such a mass conviction would affect the confidence of the Turkish public in their judicial system.

The Ergenekon trial concluded in August 2013, after more than five years of legal argument. Retired General Küçük received two consecutive life sentences. Among the 253 others convicted were renowned officers, nationalist intellectuals, mafia bosses, right-wing lawyers and businessmen, along with opposition MPs and leaders of the 'Grey Wolves'. The severity of the verdicts was supposed to impose the *coup de grâce* on the Deep State.

But the prosecution might have gone too far, and too high, in indicting at a later stage of the trial the retired chief of staff, General Ilker Basbug. He was sentenced to life imprisonment on charges of 'establishing and leading a terrorist organization' and 'attempting to destroy the Turkish government'.[14] The strange irony of Turkey having a convicted 'terrorist' at the top of the state's military apparatus from 2008 to 2010 was not missed. Basbug reacted solemnly to the verdict: 'For those who have been tried under those circumstances, the final say is the people's say. And the people are never wrong and are never deceived.'[15]

The following month, in September 2013, it was now the turn of General Hakki Karadayi, chief of staff from 1994 to 1998, to be tried. The retired general and the other 102 defendants were indicted for the 'post-modern coup' that toppled the Islamist-led government in 1997. The trial was expected to last several years, like the Sledgehammer and Ergenekon cases. But there was a clear 'trial fatigue' in the Turkish public, enhanced by the fact that Karadayi, aged 81, had been unable to attend the hearings on medical grounds. And the fear was mounting that the cycle of retribution against the Deep State could become open-ended.

Erbakan, the Islamist PM at the time of the 'Susurluk scandal' in 1996, had not only been unable to nail down his adversaries in that affair, but had been ousted from power shortly afterwards. Erdogan had learnt this sobering lesson the hard way and had pushed the Ergenekon case to its utmost limits. He could have been satisfied with settling his accounts with the military top brass through the Sledgehammer trial. But adding general Basbug to those on his chargesheet soon appeared counterproductive.

Payback Time

The dismantling of the Deep State through police and judicial measures during Erdogan's second and third terms as prime minister ought to have guaranteed the democratic future of Turkey. This rosy scenario was one where the country, now freed from its shadowy superstructure, could fully benefit from the institutions and the due process of an uncontested democratic republic. But the independence of justice had been repeatedly trampled on during the Ergenekon and Sledgehammer trials. Worse, these cases seemed to reveal an increasingly dark side of the Islamist leader, namely his authoritarian tendencies and the personal vendettas he was waging under cover of the struggle against the Deep State. While more charitable observers were ready to accept this bumpy process of bringing Turkish democracy to adulthood, free from military tutelage, others denounced what they regarded as a 'Soviet-style show trial'.[16]

The European Commission, in its annual report on Turkey for 2012, noted, even before the Ergenekon verdicts, that 'these cases have been overshadowed by their wide scope and the shortcomings in judicial proceedings. Moreover, they tend to contribute to the polarization of Turkish politics.'[17] This was an understated description of a country bitterly divided between AKP supporters and their secular opponents, both claiming that law and the nation were on their side.

The United States had banked heavily on the success of the 'Turkish model'. Barack Obama delivered a vibrant speech in front of the Turkish National Assembly in April 2009, less than three months after his arrival at the White House. The American president lobbied his European allies to promote Turkey's admission into the EU. The AKP democratic record was supposed to demonstrate how Islam and the West could finally reach a win–win relationship, with Turkey serving as a showcase for a harmonious blend between globalized capitalism, the NATO alliance, pluralistic institutions and moral standards.

But the widening crackdown on dissent in Turkey sent shockwaves through Washington. The US ambassador in Ankara, the seasoned diplomat Frank Ricciardone, stated in August 2012 that he had 'heard Turkish leaders in the government and in the opposition expressing their concerns about what needs to be done in terms of access to justice'.[18] This veiled reference to growing dissatisfaction inside the AKP itself only added to the anger of Prime Minister Erdogan, who had previously scornfully called Ricciardone a 'rookie'.[19]

In June 2013, the violent response to a peaceful sit-in in central Istanbul led to widespread protests, including the occupation of Taksim Square in Turkey's biggest city, and demonstrations and incidents in other major urban centres. While eleven people were killed, more than 3,000 were arrested during this wave of protests. Erdogan vilified the demonstrators as mere 'looters'[20] and the pro-AKP media accused Western powers and Israel of a vicious conspiracy to undermine Turkish stability and prosperity.

The parallel between the Turkish Taksim and the Egyptian Tahrir Square (the epicentre of the Egyptian revolution in January–February 2011) was embarrassing for Erdogan: the 'Turkish model' that he boasted was a source of inspiration for the so-called 'Arab spring' was now marred by police brutality and xenophobic propaganda, reminiscent of the worst excesses of the Arab dictatorships. The AKP leadership, worried by the long-term consequences of the prime minister's heavy-handedness, tried a softer approach to placate the protesters.

This volatile context explains why, far from being perceived as the final act of emancipation from the Deep State, the verdicts in the Ergenekon trial in August 2013 were resented by many as another manifestation of Erdogan's authoritarianism. Tensions grew among the Islamist camp itself, with decade-long political allies suddenly at odds over the future of Turkey. Two major trends now seemed to polarize the AKP officials and militants, torn between Erdogan's loyalists and Gülen's affiliates.

This divorce between the two Islamist leaders, one sitting at the head of the government and the other commanding a powerful network from his Pennsylvania exile,[21] fuelled a merciless war by proxy, in the courts as well as in the press. In December 2013, a corruption scandal led to the arrest of forty-seven people, among whom were the sons of three prominent AKP ministers. Erdogan had to cut his losses and substantially reshuffled his cabinet, sacking the three ministers involved, along with seven of their colleagues.

But this was only the beginning of an unsavoury campaign of leaks (in the press and online) of audiotapes, video recordings and various documents, all questioning the public and private integrity of the prime minister, his family and his closest associates. In response, Erdogan and his followers started beating the drums of the international conspiracy again, even though a public threat to expel the US ambassador was never implemented. Dozens of police chiefs were sacked, while the ministries of interior and justice tightened their internal regulations.

Erdogan went a step further, in February 2014, by pushing through the AKP parliamentary majority a law reforming the supreme judicial body (HSYK) that would constrain the independence of judges and prosecutors. He also obtained an unprecedented ban on Twitter and, more generally, a stricter control of the Internet, the Islamist prime minister having accused the social media of threatening Turkish institutions. On both counts he was rebuffed by the Constitutional Court, to the great relief of human rights defenders.

In March 2014, the same Constitutional Court ruled that General Basbug's legal rights had been violated: the former chief of staff was subsequently released after 26 months in jail. Erdogan officially welcomed the decision and even phoned the retired general to congratulate him. The Islamist PM went so far as to cast doubts on the validity of the Sledgehammer and Ergenekon trials. He had a compelling reason to reverse his position on such a sensitive issue: the same judges, often affiliated to Gülen, who had been instrumental against the Deep State, were now going after the prime minister himself.[22]

What had begun as the triumphant revenge of Erdogan against his former foes ended up in a very dubious battle. The prime minister's draft bill to strengthen the National Intelligence Organisation (MIT) was, in April 2014, denounced as the first step towards a *muhaberat* state. (*Muhaberat* is the Turkish version of the Arabic *mukhâbarât*, the generic term to designate the much feared 'intelligence' services, namely the armed elements of the security state whose primary job is suppressing any sign of domestic dissent.)[23]

An opposition MP expressed his fears that this move would 'allow the prime minister to create his own Deep State inside the Turkish state'.[24] The fifteen-year long struggle of Erdogan against the Deep State was no longer portrayed as a legitimate campaign to upgrade Turkey to European democratic standards, but rather as a petty manoeuvre to replace one unruly repressive machine with a docile one more to his own liking.

*

The Turkish Deep State was exposed in the 1990s. At that time, it was intimately bound to the 'dirty war' against the PKK Kurdish guerrillas. Such a mix of unbridled repression, parallel intelligence and the criminal underworld was indeed the trademark of the Deep State. And this patchwork of maverick officers, ultra-nationalist activists and mafia bosses constituted the very fabric of the Ergenekon case.

When the AKP gained power in 2002, a ceasefire prevailed between the Turkish state and the PKK, whose leader, Abdullah Öcalan, had been captured in Kenya in 1999. But the ceasefire collapsed in 2004, with a renewed insurgency that soon reached levels of violence comparable to those of the previous decade. The top brass could then test Erdogan's resolve to defend Turkish territorial integrity with all the might that the police and military could muster.

This trial by fire, jointly experienced by the Islamist government and its military branch, was crucial in forging new bounds of trust, and even loyalty, between the AKP and the security apparatus. Erdogan, while sanctioning the armed strikes against the PKK, launched in 2009 a 'Kurdish initiative', bracing for a grand bargain on the Kurdish question, that had been plaguing contemporary Turkey since its very birth. In 2010, he appointed as head of the National Intelligence Organisation (MIT) Hakan Fidan, who had been involved in secret talks with the PKK.

In March 2013, Erdogan endorsed Öcalan's public appeal for a ceasefire. Kurdish guerrillas started to disarm, before withdrawing into northern Iraq (officially) and north-eastern Syria (clandestinely, since they could rely on the well-established complicity between the PKK local affiliate, named PYD, and the Syrian security services). The road to peace in Turkish Kurdistan remained fraught with dangers, but that was the first attempt at a lasting solution to this three-decade-long conflict, that had claimed the lives of some 40,000 people.

The Islamist prime minister had therefore succeeded in dragging the security apparatus into a peace process with its Kurdish arch-enemy, the PKK. This formidable achievement has to be taken into account when assessing Erdogan's appalling performance on other fronts of Turkish politics during the fateful year of 2013. The June wave of protest and the December corruption scandal eventually jeopardized the very 'Kurdish initiative' that the Islamist prime minister had become so closely identified with.

While the Ergenekon trials were historically linked to the 1996 'Susurluk scandal' and the Kurdish 'dirty war', the Sledge-hammer case stemmed from a different timeline, where the 1997 'post-modern coup' was only the last in a series of three previous military takeovers, in 1960, 1971 and 1980. The 1997 bloodless coup was directed against the first Islamist-led government, while the previous takeovers, even though profoundly nationalist, were supposed to be party-blind.

With the Sledgehammer case, Erdogan chastised the top brass for allegedly plotting against him as prime minister in 2003. He therefore blurred his fight against the Deep State by associating it with the generation-long showdown in Turkey between the Islamists and the military. So, instead of consolidating a national consensus against the Deep State, he fell back on his partisan base to settle old feuds.

The domestic reversal of the popular tides in favour of the self-righteous Erdogan occurred in 2012–13, when the concept of the Deep State became increasingly popular in Arab public debate. The star of the AKP 'Turkish model' had already paled in the various Arab countries undergoing democratic transitions, with mounting opposition against the initially victorious Islamist parties. This was especially true in Tunisia, where the Ennahda party was described as the closest in the Arab world to the 'Muslim–democrat' AKP.[25]

In Egypt, by contrast, there was no love lost between the Muslim Brotherhood and the Turkish Islamists, both vying for the pivotal role in worldwide political Islam. But a ubiquitous Deep State was being blamed for many of the country's problems and, as had been the standard procedure in Turkey, every actor denounced his enemy for manipulating this shadowy structure. When the counter-revolution assumed ferocious proportions in the summer of 2013, observers had not yet adjusted to the real nature and outreach of the indigenous Deep State.

To grasp the specificity (and the perversity) of the Arab Deep State, one has to go back to the process of state-building in these countries. This detour through the founding moments of the Arab states is key to understanding how and why part of those structures do indeed go so 'deep'. Central to this process is the exclusive and patrimonial vision of the nation. Thus Turkey once again offers a comparative approach to highlight the entrenching of the security apparatus at the zenith of the Arab polities.

2

THE MYTHICAL FATHERS OF THE NATION

In the contemporary Turkish debate, the notion of 'parallel state' has sometimes been used as an equivalent to the Deep State. The two adjectives reveal how the very champions of the struggle against the Deep State are accepting some of its basic prejudices. The operatives of the Deep State justify their illegal activities by challenging the very legitimacy of the state, which is accused of being too 'shallow' to fulfil its missions. And the 'parallel state' is mirroring with self-proclaimed efficiency a state that is blamed for being incapable of meeting the public's expectations.

A profound sense of mission and a resolute collective determination are pre-requisites in order to bind together the complex coalition that makes the Deep State work. At the heart of this alchemy lies the firm conviction that acting on behalf of the supreme interests of the nation who elected their politicians and civil servants may be too weak a conjunction to defend earnestly. This absolute belief is reinforced by an unquestionable equivalence between the interests of the nation and those of the Deep State.

To achieve this equivalence, being more patriotic or even xenophobic than the 'shallow state' is not enough. What is needed is a patrimonial approach to the country and a paternalistic vision of its people. And it is being rooted in the historical process of state-building that led key elements in the Deep State to claim an innate right to decide what is good for the country they served, and therefore deserve more than any others. The Turkish example in that regard is only of partial relevance to the Arab world.

No Turkey without Kemalism

The roots of contemporary Turkey are commonly traced back to the 1908 Young Turk revolution. Stirred by Sultan Abdulhamid II's repressive policies and by the string of humiliations suffered by the Ottoman Empire, this revolution resulted in the reinstatement of the 1876 Constitution (that Abdulhamid II had suspended after only fourteen months) and the convening of a new parliament. The main force in this revolution, as well as in the National Assembly (with 60 seats out of 275), was the Committee for Union and Progress (CUP), whose appeal went far beyond ethnic Turks (the founding seat of CUP was the Greek city of Salonika).

In 1909, the CUP managed to crush a counter-revolutionary coup in Istanbul, which led to the deposition of Abdulhamid II and his replacement by the more docile Mehmed V. But the Ottoman defeats, first against the Italian invasion of Libya in 1911, and then in the Balkan wars of 1912–13, sealed the fate of the pluralistic CUP. A military triumvirate, composed of Enver, Talaat and Djemal (the so-called three Pashas), seized power in 1913 and put an end to the constitutional era.

The 'three Pashas' shared a passionate Turkish nationalism (with the dream of Pan-Turkism substituting for the Ottoman ideal), a fascination for German militarism and a strong antipathy towards Christian minorities, who they resented as a 'fifth column' in the very bosom of the Empire. In the context of the First World War, they joined forces with the Central Empires in

1914 and launched the following year a mass deportation of the Armenian population, one that culminated in genocide. The disastrous collapse of the Ottoman army in 1918 forced the 'three Pashas' to flee into exile where they were eventually killed by Armenian avengers (Talaat and Djemal) and the Soviet military (Enver) respectively.

The Ottoman Empire was forced to sign in 1920 the Treaty of Sèvres that instituted French, British, Italian and Greek zones of influence, while opening the way for an independent Kurdistan. Mustafa Kemal, a former CUP officer, raised the flag of resistance against such a treaty. The liberation struggle, starting from central Anatolia (where nationalist Ankara was defying Ottoman Istanbul), rolled back the occupying armies, before the Sultanate was abolished in 1922.

The Republic of Turkey was established in 1923, with most of its present borders recognized the same year in the new treaty signed at Lausanne. (Armenia had become a Soviet republic in 1920; the boundary with Iran had been defined in the sixteenth century between the Ottoman and the Safavid empires; the British Empire would negotiate in 1926 the border with the Iraqi province of Mosul; and the French Republic would offer the Syrian province of Hatay/Iskenderun in 1939 in order to placate Turkey in the run-up to the Second World War.)

Mustafa Kemal, who raised modern Turkey from the ruins of the Ottoman Empire, had all the attributes of an 'enlightened despot': his one-party rule mercilessly crushed all dissent in order to promote his ambitious vision of progress (abolition of the Caliphate, unification of the school system, Latinization of the alphabet, a new civil code, the imposition of civil marriage and the extension of voting rights to women). He also defeated three major Kurdish revolts between 1925 and 1937. In 1934—four years before his death—the National Assembly bestowed upon him the title of Atatürk, Father of the Turks, acknowledging his achievements.

Exalted by such a legacy, it was certainly hard for the Kemalists, as Atatürk's followers came to be known, not to view themselves as the only true nationalists and patriots. In their candid tautology, Turkey was what Atatürk had made of it. Thus, stating that Turkey was Kemalist was just another way of acknowledging that Turkey was Turkish.

The ominous coalition that wanted to carve up Turkey had indeed been defeated in 1922, but the Kemalists considered it their duty to wage an endless fight against the domestic enemies that still threatened Turkish integrity: Kurdish rights were therefore perceived as an existential threat—and fought against as such; while any expression of Islam in the political sphere was deemed as blatant subversion—and dealt with as such.

Turkey stayed neutral during the Second World War, but its rallying to the Western camp in the Cold War facilitated the loosening of political constraints: the Democratic Party (DP) was authorized in 1946, along with the Kemalist Republican People's Party (CHP) and, after four years of painstaking transition, DP was voted into forming the new government. The DP power decade of the 1950s ended brutally with the military coup of 1960, followed by the trial and hanging of the deposed prime minister, Adnan Menderes.

The army, under Atatürk and his successors, could henceforward focus on its mission to defend the sovereignty of Turkey, because it knew that the CHP one-party system and the attached bureaucracy, often staffed with former military officers, were upholding the principles of Kemalism (*atatürkçülük*). But the DP's resolve to submit the military to civilian rule had traumatized the top brass, who decided to supplant the declining CHP on the domestic front with a martial, and even ruthless, response.

The military intervened twice again: in 1971, they toppled the government to replace it with a technocratic cabinet with a strongly Kemalist flavour; but in 1980, a military junta assumed direct power, dissolved the parliament and banned all political parties. Terrorist violence, from both the extreme-right and the far-left, had reached the unprecedented level of ten deaths a day. This allowed for true popular support for the coup.

In 1982, 92 per cent of the electorate voted in favour of a Constitution drafted by the military, with General Kenan Evren, chief of the National Security Council (MGK), acting president of the Republic. This 'security-oriented constitutionalism', as the French political scientist Jean Marcou described it,[1] was a desperate attempt to turn the clock back to the golden age of Atatürk's rule. But such a top-to-bottom approach lacked the modernist vision that had animated Mustafa Kemal.

Turkey had changed, forcing the military to withdraw reluctantly to their barracks. This is when the Deep State started to develop, as a belated response to the challenges of Kurdish separatism and political Islam. The 'post-modern coup' which the MGK executed in 1997 was the last public manifestation of this kind of self-righteous interference. After that ultimate show of strength, the Deep State went deeper.

But the military contingency planning never excluded the possibility of a direct takeover. As the *New Yorker* put it, commenting on the Sledgehammer case, 'however close the generals came to removing Erdogan in 2003, their casual tone makes it clear it was not the first time they'd had the conversations'.[2] The AKP era mass trials clearly signalled that Turkey had moved to a different era. And that happened in sharp contrast with the Arab world and its own Deep State.

From Ottoman Arabs to Colonized Ones

From the second half of the sixteenth century until the end of the eighteenth, the Arab lands were under Ottoman rule, with the notable exception of independent Morocco, of the Algerian port of Oran/Wahran (most of the time under Spanish occupation) and peripheral Oman (the Ottomans controlled Muscat only from

1581 to 1588). More than two centuries of Ottoman domination extended from 1574, when Tunis was re-conquered by Spain, to 1798, when the then General Bonaparte invaded Egypt.

In 1705 Hussein ibn Ali established a dynasty of Tunisian 'beys' that garnered a substantial degree of autonomy from Istanbul. And in the central Arabian province of Nejd, the pact concluded between the Saud family and the preacher Ibn Abd al-Wahhab had consolidated a 'Wahhabi' fiefdom, controlled after 1776 from Riyadh. But from Algiers to Basra, as the historian Eugene Rogan eloquently framed it, 'the Ottoman sultan was universally accepted by the Arabs as their legitimate sovereign. They prayed in the sultan's name on Friday, they contributed soldiers for the sultan's wars, and they paid their taxes to the sultan's agents.'[3]

The French occupation of Egypt was short-lived, but this Western invasion laid bare the shortcomings of the Ottoman Empire and stirred in reaction the Arab renaissance, or Nahda. Mohammad Ali seized power in Cairo in 1805, on behalf of the Ottoman sultan, but eventually founded his own dynasty of 'khedives'. The Tunisian beys and the Egyptian khedives embarked on an ambitious programme of tax reform and military upgrading, with an emphasis on industrialization in Egypt and on constitutional rule in Tunisia.

This top-to-bottom Nahda was accompanied, and sometimes welcomed, by a new intellectual class that fed on the relative democratization of the Arabic language (through the printing press) and of the educational curriculum (through the opening of new teaching institutions). The Nahda thinkers and agitators hoped to achieve freedom from Ottoman rule and to resist Western imperialism.

In order to take up this double challenge, some Arabs favoured the promotion of a European-style nationalism, anchored to the principle of one people, one land and one language. Others considered an Islamic revival was the key to confronting colonialism and reversing Ottoman decline. Today, the first trend would be called 'nationalist' and the second one 'Islamist', yet these notions were not at that point relevant in the nineteenth century (those two political families were then far from distinct from one another).[4]

The French invasion of Algeria in 1830 marked the beginning of the colonial moment in the Arab world. The British, more interested in controlling the sea route to India, started their expansion with the occupation of Aden in 1839, before securing agreements and 'truces' with the various sheikhs ruling on the southern shore of the Persian Gulf. The two Western powers struck a fatal blow to the Nahda-driven modernizing dynasties, with France imposing its protectorate on Tunisia in 1881, and Britain occupying Egypt the following year (the British protectorate of Egypt was only proclaimed in 1914).

Rivalry between the European states eventually sharpened their colonial impulse. In 1906, France and Spain formalized their ambitions in Morocco, with Paris establishing a fully-fledged protectorate over most of the country in 1912, while Madrid controlled its northern and southern margins. Italy, eager to carve out its own imperial domain, invaded Libya in 1911. The Ottomans were only left with Hejaz, Iraq and what the Westerners called Greater Syria and the Arab *Bilad al-Sham* (the 'country of Sham', Sham being the name of Damascus, in Arabic and in Turkish).

The 1908 Young Turk revolution had nurtured high expectations among the pro-Ottoman Arabs, and 60 of the 275 deputies of the new parliament were Arabs. But the 1913 military coup and the ethnic chauvinism of the three Pashas antagonized even the Arab officers of the Ottoman army, who began plotting against what they resented as Turkish oppression. When the Istanbul triumvirate aligned with Germany and engineered a Sultan's call for 'jihad' against France, Britain and Russia in 1914, such a call fell on deaf ears in the Arab world (except, paradoxically, among the Iraqi Shias).

On the contrary, the 'nationalist' and 'Islamist' components of the Nahda rallied around Sherif Hussein of Mecca, the Ottoman governor of Hijaz, but more importantly a descendant of the Prophet Mohammad from the Hashemite lineage. This genealogy convinced 'Islamists' that the Sherif would be a far better qualified caliph than the Turkish sultan. And the 'nationalists' saw the Bedouin leader as the champion of Arab values, honour and identity (as stated above, the contemporary notions of 'nationalist' and 'Islamist' were not used at that time).

In 1916, Sherif Hussein launched his 'Arab revolt' (in Arabic *thawra*, literally, revolution). The Turkish novelist Nedim Gürsel has described in his much debated *Daughters of Allah*[5] the absolute shock of the Turkish officers, besieged in Medina and devastated by what they loathed as an Arab treason. The Turks reacted with such violence that Djemal Pasha, one of the three rulers of the Ottoman Empire, now in charge of the Arab provinces, was called in Damascus *Al-Saffah*, the Blood-shedder.

Britain had promised Sherif Hussein that an 'Arab kingdom' would be established after the Ottoman defeat; but London also secretly agreed with Paris to share the coming spoils of the Arab provinces. And the British Foreign Secretary, Arthur Balfour, endorsed in 1917 the Zionist plan for a 'Jewish national home' in post-Ottoman Palestine. Those contradictory commitments could never be reconciled once the First World War was over, as the Paris Peace Conference demonstrated in 1919.

France and Britain divided the region from which the Ottoman forces had been expelled into 'mandates' of the newly created League of Nations. France got Syria and Lebanon, while Britain got Palestine and Iraq. London believed that a buffer state would be needed between its two possessions, which gave birth to the new entity of Transjordan. Sherif Hussein watched his Arab dream collapse in total impotence. His son Faysal, who had entered Damascus as a victor in 1918, was expelled by the French military in 1920 but received the throne of Iraq as compensation from the British. His older brother Abdullah settled in Amman, the most parochial capital of the young emirate of Transjordan.

At the end of the First World War, the collapse of the Ottoman Empire led not to the emancipation of the Arabs, but rather to their subordination to Western imperialism. Arab independence had disappeared between the Atlantic Ocean and the Persian Gulf and there remained only two enclaves free from colonial domination: in central Arabia, a Wahhabi kingdom, led by Abdelaziz Ibn Saud, had challenged the Ottomans, and now defied the Europeans; in North Yemen, Zaydism, a local offshoot of Shiism, was officially upheld by Imam Yahya, whose absolute power in Sanaa had deterred all the Western incursions into 'Arabia Felix'.

Formal Independence

It took half a century, from 1922 to 1971, for the Arab world to regain its independence. This painful process was initiated in Egypt, when a nationalist revolution (*thawra*) shook the country during the spring and summer of 1919, in protest against the Paris Peace Conference and its negation of the right to self-determination. More than 800 Egyptians were killed by the British armed forces, despite the non-violent nature of this uprising, many of the messages from which were to find an echo in the 2011 Tahrir revolution.[6]

Such levels of repression failed to quell the nationalist upsurge and Britain had to terminate the Protectorate in 1922, recognizing the Egyptian King Fuad as a sovereign head of state. But London had restricted independence in the four areas of communications, defence, Sudan policy and, in an ominous link, protection of minorities *and* of British interests. This imperial sword of Damocles would weigh heavily on Egypt's fate through the following three decades, during Fuad's reign, and even more so during his successor Farouk's (1936–52).

In Iraq, the British Empire amalgamated under its mandate the previous Ottoman governorates of Baghdad, Basra and Mosul. London chose its new ruler: Faysal, the frustrated 'King of the Arabs', who had been based in Damascus from 1918 to 1920. A referendum was organized by the British administration to legitimize the new king; and given the ban on rival candidates, Faysal was approved through a one-question plebiscite by 96 per cent of voters. This Hashemite kingdom, with no indigenous roots, relied heavily on an army built around the former officers of the Ottoman armed forces, most of them Arab Sunnis (while the majority of the population was Shia, with a strong Kurdish irredentism in the north).

In 1932, Britain granted independence to Iraq, with far fewer strings attached than in Egypt, even though the imperial power pursued its close monitoring of Iraqi domestic affairs, with regular, and generally unpopular, interference. This same year saw the proclamation of the Kingdom of Saudi Arabia. This was the culmination of the state-building process led by Abdelaziz Ibn Saud since the re-occupation of Riyadh on behalf of the Al-Saud family in 1902.

Ibn Saud had succeeded in controlling first the central province of Nejd, then, in 1913, the coastal region of Al-Ahsa on the Persian Gulf. Conspicuously neutral during the anti-Turkish 'Arab revolt' of 1916–18, Ibn Saud turned against Sherif Hussein in 1925, expelling him from the Hijaz. The Wahhabi conquest of the holy cities of Mecca and Medina sent shockwaves through the Muslim world.

Ibn Saud then decided it was time to rein in the *Ikhwan* (literally the 'Brothers', a Wahhabi militia of settled Bedouins) whom he had unleashed until then against his successive Arab enemies. An operation coordinated with the British forces in Iraq concluded with the destruction of the *Ikhwan* in 1929 at the Battle of Sabilla. Ibn Saud was now free to establish a country so closely identified with the ruling family that their people became known as 'Saudis'.

Lebanon and Syria fell in 1920 under a French Mandate that was so eager to dismantle the 'Arab kingdom' that it designed the Lebanese borders far beyond the traditional limits of Mount Lebanon, before carving up Syria into five different entities. France was therefore planting the seeds of future crises, including the major 'Arab Revolt' that shook Syria in 1925–6. It took the Second World War (and the 1941 conflict between the armies loyal to Pétain's Vichy or to de Gaulle's Free French) to cripple imperial rule. Syria and Lebanon became independent republics in 1943, but they both had to wait for the ultimate French withdrawal in 1946 to gain full sovereignty.

The League of Arab States, generally known as the Arab League, was launched in Cairo in 1945. Its founding members were Egypt, Saudi Arabia, Syria, Lebanon, Iraq and Transjordan, soon to be joined by Yemen. The emirate of Transjordan, a buffer state created by Britain between its mandates over Iraq and Palestine, would achieve its formal independence only with the Treaty of London signed by the now King Abdullah with Great Britain in 1946. Even then, the Soviet Union vetoed its admittance to the United Nations, considering that Transjordan was still too intimately tied to Britain.

The proclamation of the state of Israel in May 1948, one day before the end of the British Mandate in Palestine, led to the first Arab–Israeli war. Eight months of conflict concluded with the incorporation of 77 per cent of mandatory Palestine into the territory of Israel. Of the remaining 23 per cent, 1 per cent became the Gaza Strip, under Egyptian administration; but the remaining 22 per cent, called the West Bank (of the Jordan river), was soon absorbed by Abdullah's kingdom.

This 'union of the two banks' (the Palestinian West Bank and Transjordan) was the founding act of the Hashemite kingdom of Jordan (the annexation of the West Bank was only recognized by Britain and Pakistan). And Abdullah did not live long enough to enjoy his newly expanded kingdom: in July 1951 he was assassinated in Jerusalem, during Friday payers at the Al-Aqsa mosque. The murderer, a Palestinian nationalist, sought revenge for Abdullah's dealings with Israel.

The Italians, who had occupied the Libyan territory since 1911 (and had named their colony "Italian Libya" in 1934), were defeated by the Allies in 1943. Britain started to rule the coastal provinces of Tripolitana and Cyrenaica, while France governed the Saharan Fezzan. The emir Idris al-Senoussi, who had wisely sided with the British during the war, could also rely on his strong support among the nationalist militants, often members of the Senoussi Sufi order. A UN-sponsored process led to the proclamation in 1951 of the independence of Libya, with Idris as its constitutional monarch.

In North Africa, France accepted a loosening of its colonial grip only after its humiliating 1954 defeat in Indochina. The Moroccan Sultan Mohammad had been exiled in 1953 to Corsica, then to Madagascar, and popular protest against this harsh French diktat nurtured two years of violent disturbances. The 'revolution of the King and the people', as the nationalists celebrated it, forced France to accept the triumphal return of Mohammad in November 1955. Four months later, France officially recognized the independence of Morocco.

King Mohammad V, as he was known after 1957, secured his sovereignty over Tangier, where Spain relinquished any authority. But 'Spanish Sahara' remained beyond his reach, despite the 'Ifni War' that nationalist guerrillas waged (and lost) in 1957–8. Hassan II, who succeeded his father after his death in 1961, managed to negotiate the Ifni enclave back from Spain in 1969. But in his ambitions over the remaining Spanish territory, he had now to compete with Polisario, a liberation movement of the 'Western Sahara', strongly backed by Algeria.

Tunisia became independent shortly after Morocco, in March 1956. But the six months preceding the end of French rule were marred by a violent power struggle between the two leaders of the nationalist Neo-Destour, Habib Bourguiba and Salah Ben Youssef. The path of negotiation chosen by Bourguiba was denounced as treacherous by Ben Youssef. The two camps probably lost far more militants in their bloody feud than during the whole campaign against French colonialism.[7] But Bourguiba prevailed and forced Ben Youssef to flee to neighbouring Libya.

The Algerian struggle for independence was certainly the most tragic in the entire Arab world. Such violence was intensified by the duration of the French occupation (132 years), the importance of the European colonial population (sometimes settlers whose families had been there for several generations) and the fiction of 'French Algeria'; while their administrative incorporation into the French republic never yielded the expected rights for the indigenous population.

The armed resistance launched in November 1954 by the National Liberation Front (FLN, to use its French acronym) only succeeded in ending French rule in July 1962. While nationalist propaganda hailed the 'million martyrs' of Algeria, historians consider the toll of the 'liberation war' to be around 250,000 killed, 80 per cent of them by the French military.[8] Even those revised figures prove that no other Arab country had experienced such trauma to achieve its collective freedom.

Last but not least, Britain had to fulfil its pledge to abandon its possessions east of Suez. Kuwait was the first protectorate to gain its independence, in 1961, with Iraq abandoning its claims over the new state two years later. In 1967, the constellation of sheikhdoms that Great Britain had coalesced into a 'Federation' and a 'Protectorate' of South Arabia merged, after the British withdrawal, into a 'Democratic and Popular Republic of Yemen' (DPRY), commonly known as South Yemen. In 1971 London finally severed all its ties to the sovereignty of Bahrain, of Qatar, of Oman and of the seven emirates of the Trucial Coast, who established the federation of United Arab Emirates.

The four new members joined the United Nations the same year. The painstaking process of Arab emancipation was now completed, with one major caveat: Palestine, a full member of the Arab League, remained in a diplomatic limbo, with a 'declaration of independence' adopted by the PLO in Algiers in 1988, and the admission of Palestine by the UN as a 'non-member state', with observer status, in 2012. The two-state solution between Israel and Palestine seems now even less attainable than at the beginning of the peace process in the 1990s.

A Dictatorial Hijacking

It took half a century for the Arab countries to rid themselves of Western domination. But it took only two decades, from 1949 to 1969, for the military cliques to reap the fruits of this hard-won Arab independence. There was no battle over the political regression to region-wide dictatorship, often because the viciousness of colonial repression had extracted a heavy price on civilian resistance and the liberal camp: they arrived at independence often exhausted by the liberation struggle, while armed plotters were waiting in the wings, legitimized by a 'Third World' discourse.

The Arab–Israeli conflict was also crucial in strengthening anti-democratic forces who claimed their dedication to the anti-Zionist cause, even though their main focus was the silencing of domestic opposition. It is therefore no surprise that the first coup of this regressive cycle occurred in Syria in 1949. As the late journalist Patrick Seale described it:

> It is in Syria that the post-war impotence of classic nationalism is most clearly demonstrated. Out-dated by their own success against the mandatory power, they were incapable of diagnosing the problems posed by independence and were ousted by younger, more radical groups.[9]

In March 1949, the Syrian chief of staff Colonel Husni Zaïm seized power in a bloodless coup that was a direct consequence of the military humiliation inflicted on his country during the recent war with Israel. In neighboring Iraq, the army had in the past repeatedly interfered in state politics, but had never dared to challenge the monarchy itself, while Zaïm had rid himself in Syria of all constitutional obstacles. It was not long before he dissolved all political parties.

Zaïm was the only candidate in the June 1949 presidential election, where he officially received 99.4 per cent of votes cast. This pattern of authoritarian plebiscite would soon become a standard feature in the Arab world. And Zaïm's eagerness to sign a ceasefire with Israel, effective in July, stemmed from his urge to deploy his armed forces on the domestic front,[10] another distinctive feature of the coming dictatorships.

This move however came too late to save Zaïm from one of his subordinates, Colonel Sami al-Hinnawi, commander of the southern region. In August 1949, armoured battalions took control of Damascus. Hinnawi's associates executed the president and his prime minister on the spot. But Hinnawi's experience was even more short-lived than his predecessor. In December 1949, Colonel Adib Shishakli, commander of the first brigade, took over. Hinnawi fled to Beirut where he was assassinated by those avenging Zaïm's murder.

The new military leader, Shishakli, pledged to restore civilian rule first. A new constitution was drafted and adopted. Six cabinets would be formed in the following two years, half of them with minority participation on the part of the Muslim Brotherhood (operating then as the Islamic Socialist Front).[11] The Baath party, established in Syria in 1947, and the Communist party were vocal in their opposition to any alignment with the Western powers. Political instability reached such a level that, in November 1951, Shishakli assumed total control of the republic (parliament was dissolved and parties were banned).

In Egypt also, the humiliation of the Israeli victory had sent shockwaves through domestic politics. Militia from the Muslim Brotherhood had fought alongside the Egyptian army: they accused King Farouk and his government of having betrayed 'jihad' in Palestine. In December 1948, a Muslim Brother assassinated Prime Minister Mahmoud Nuqrashi. Four thousand Islamists were jailed in retaliation, before the founder of the Brotherhood, Hassan al-Banna, was murdered in February 1949, most probably under official orders.[12]

The Egyptian monarchy was nevertheless able to absorb this shock because it had lived through nearly three decades of a parliamentary system. The Wafd party, heir to the 1919 revolution, had won all the succeeding elections, but other nationalist or progressive parties were challenging its dominance. The press still enjoyed a fair amount of freedom, while unions were developing. But it was the brutality of British unilateralism that brought down King Farouk.

In January 1952, British forces crushed the nationalist protest in the Suez Canal area, killing dozens of Egyptian police officers in their barracks when they refused to surrender. This led to widespread anti-Western riots in Cairo, with schools, cafés and foreign institutions looted and destroyed. Muslim Brothers actively contributed to this 'Cairo burning' and opened secret channels with a clandestine group of Free Officers, through one of their founders, Anwar Sadat.

Six months later, led by Gamal Abdel Nasser, the eighty Free Officers took control of the army. All generals were arrested, except Mohammad Naguib and another who had endorsed the coup. King Farouk, holed up in his summer palace in Alexandria, was soon deposed and exiled. In the same choreography that had already been enacted three times in Syria, armoured units took control of strategic points and a 'communiqué number one' was broadcast on the radio to herald the coup. Sadat was chosen to read the declaration:

> We have undertaken to clean ourselves up and have appointed to command us men from the army whom we trust in their ability, their character and their patriotism. It is certain that all Egypt will meet this news with enthusiasm and will welcome it.[13]

The self-righteousness of such an opening salvo is impressive. For Nasser and his partners, it was not only the monarchy, but also the parliamentary class, starting with the Wafd, that were condemned. The 'blessed revolution', as the officers celebrated it, was supposed to fulfil the frustrated promises of the 1922 independence.

The Syrian dictator Shishakli had found welcome soulmates in the Egyptian Free Officers. He had outlawed all parties except his own Arab Liberation Movement, just as Nasser would grant a monopoly to the Arab Liberation Rally. A cheerful Shishakli visited Cairo in December 1952, just after an unprecedented military parade in Damascus. This demonstration of force, designed to mark the first anniversary of the military regime, was marred by the skidding of a tank into the crowd, killing 52 people. What other symbolism could more vividly and accurately illustrate the dangers of unchecked military rule for a vulnerable civilian population?

Following in Husni Zaïm's steps, Shishakli ran in July 1953 as the only candidate in a presidential 'election' where he officially amassed 99.7 per cent of the votes. The irrelevance of such a farcical plebiscite was demonstrated seven months later, when a general mutiny of all the commanders in the provinces forced Shishakli to flee to Brazil (where he was murdered in 1964 by a vengeful Druze).

Contrary to Egypt, where the Free Officers effectively killed the parliamentary system, the Syrian military restored free and fair elections in 1954, with the Baath party gaining 22 out of the 142 seats (many of the 64 'independent' MPs were in fact backed by the Muslim Brotherhood). Political bickering resumed, amid a quite vibrant press and militant union activism. But Nasser's aura outshone that of any Syrian leader, especially after the failure of the 1956 'tripartite aggression' of Israel, France and Britain against Egypt.

The Baath party had won the foreign affairs portfolio for its leader, Salaheddine Bitar, and his pan-Arab creed led him to push for union with Egypt. Disgruntled officers went to Cairo in January 1958 and threw themselves upon Nasser's mercy: 'Do with us what you will. Just save us from the politicians and from ourselves.'[14] This Baathist and military joint action caused, the following month, the unconditional surrender of Syrian independence to Egypt, with Nasser now presiding over the United Arab Republic (UAR).

In July 1958, the Iraqi Free Officers overthrew the monarchy, shooting the king and many of his family. Nasser believed that the new ruler in Baghdad, Abdelkarim Qasim, would soon join the UAR. But Qasim was an Iraqi nationalist at heart and he preferred to rely on the Communist party rather than the Iraqi branch of the Baath. He suppressed with merciless violence the pro-Nasser uprising of Mosul, in March 1959. The numerous plots uncovered in Iraq in the following years consolidated Qasim's own dictatorial tendencies.

In UAR 'northern province'—as Syria was now called—Egyptian arbitrary rule also left deep scars. Military intelligence and security operatives became increasingly intrusive. Parties had been banned, in a clear breach of the promises made by Nasser to the Baath. Discontent was so pervasive in the Syrian public that the bloodless coup of September 1961, restoring the independence of Syria, was celebrated as a new liberation. Even the disillusioned Bitar welcomed such a move.

The three and a half years of UAR authoritarianism had nevertheless struck a terrible blow against the capacity of the Syrian political class to live up to their patriotic pretences. The army had restored their power, but the political environment was swamped by murky intrigue. Baathist and Nasserist plotters competed in the shadows. In February 1963, Qasim was overthrown in Baghdad by a Baathist coup (he was executed, along with thousands of his followers). The next month, the Baathists echoed this success by taking over Damascus, and then Syria.

The coups that had toppled the monarchy in Egypt, in 1952, and in Iraq, in 1958, were irreversible. The royal families that had reigned since independence were accused of being too lenient towards Britain, the former colonial power. They were therefore liquidated, symbolically in Egypt, and physically in Iraq. The resulting power struggles among the plotters themselves prevented any relaxation of the constraints on the political scene, with its intrusive intelligence and one-party system. In Syria, the frequency of the coups and the tragic experience of the UAR proved paradoxically how entrenched was the pluralistic political legacy that even the French Mandate had been compelled to cope with. It would need a militarized version of the Baath to annihilate this specifically Syrian trait.

The nine founders of the National Liberation Front (FLN) had launched the Algerian emancipation struggle against France in 1954. When independence was achieved in July 1962, through negotiations between Paris and the Provisional Government of the Algerian Republic (GPRA), three of those 'founding nine' had already been killed by the French military. The six survivors were Krim Belkacem, vice president of the GPRA; Ahmed Ben Bella, Mohammad Khider, Hocine Aït Ahmed, Mohammad Boudiaf and Rabah Bitat; also formal members of the GPRA, but released from French jails only in March 1962.

The GPRA, supported by the French federation of the FLN and the domestic resistance, soon faced a formidable contender: the 'army of the frontiers', led by Colonel Houari Boumediene, had escaped the French offensives in its safe havens of Morocco and Tunisia; it was probably three times stronger than the FLN networks in Algeria proper, devastated after seven years of fighting. The ambitious Ben Bella sided with Boumediene in order to achieve supreme power.

Soon after the proclamation of Algerian independence, Boumediene's army moved from Tunisia to crush the GPRA in the eastern city of Constantine. In September 1962, the military entered the capital Algiers, after at least a thousand people died in this fratricidal fighting. The GPRA was replaced by the newly founded 'Political Bureau' of the FLN. Ben Bella, the self-appointed prime minister, rewarded Boumediene with the defence portfolio.

During the following year, 1963, the five remaining members of the 'founding nine' all turned their efforts against Ben Bella: Belkacem, followed by Bitat, went to France, Khider fled to Geneva, Boudiaf was put under house arrest in Southern Algeria, while Aït Ahmed organized armed resistance against the new regime in the mountainous ranges of Kabylia. In their opposition to Ben Bella and Boumediene, obviously weakened by the lack of any coordination between them, they were adamant in denouncing the betrayal of the anti-colonial struggle by what had now become the Popular National Army (ANP).

The last sequence of this military cycle was completed in September 1969 when Colonel Moammar Qaddafi deposed the Libyan King Idris in a bloodless coup. Qaddafi candidly admitted he had joined the army, six years before, in the hope of staging such a putsch.[15] This was the first time that plotters had joined the military in order to seize power, and not the reverse.

Crown Prince Hassan Reda (Idris' nephew) was swiftly arrested, along with the main decision-makers. Idris, who was then undergoing medical treatment in Turkey, was rendered powerless. Qaddafi himself read the usual 'communiqué number one' from Benghazi's radio station, proclaiming the establishment of the 'Libyan Arab Republic'.

Before the 1922–71 cycle of Arab independences was even completed, military rulers had replaced the nationalist leaders in most of the countries from Algeria to Iraq. The fact that the new power cliques often had dubious or disputable resistance credentials led to an escalation in nationalistic rhetoric and an obsessive focus on regime security (with the famed 'foreign agents' as standard bogeymen). The ubiquitous 'intelligence' services, or *mukhâbarât*, interfered blatantly in the lives of millions. While the struggle for independence had been closely tied to demands for increased freedom, this dictatorial hijacking did indeed prove terminal for individual and collective liberties.

Fathers and Pretenders

This sketchy overview of centuries of Ottoman/Turkish/Arab history may read like déjà vu for some. However, it is useful in underlining an unexpected parallel between the only two 'fathers of the nation' of the post-Ottoman twentieth century: Mustafa Kemal Atatürk and Abdelaziz Ibn Saud. No matter how blasphemous such an association may appear to many, the facts are self-evident: these two leaders are the only ones who actually shaped their own country (including its boundaries, polities and ethos) through their politico-military struggle, their personal vision and their overwhelming charisma.

Kemalism and Wahhabism are both state ideologies that deliver to the ruler and their clique undisputed authority, social mobilization and a legitimizing discourse. The repression of 'unorthodox' practices in 'cosmopolitan' Hijaz was no less ruthless than the fight against 'reactionary' Islam in the Anatolian countryside. Shia culture was no more recognized in the 'kingdom of Nejd and Hijaz' than Kurdish culture was in nascent Turkey.

There was one more attribute shared by Kemalism and Wahhabism: both ideologies were fiercely opposed to the Arab Nahda. Kemalism rejected it as one of the fateful Ottoman legacies that accelerated the Empire's decomposition and challenged Turkish identity. Wahhabism developed in the Nejd hinterland that remained out of reach of the Nahda. And the Saud's followers waged their jihad exclusively against other Arab Muslims, thus obliterating any possibility of joining the Nahda, even in its Islamic revival dimension.

King Mohammad V had sometimes been celebrated in Morocco as 'the father of the nation'. But he was exiled to Madagascar when the Moroccan liberation struggle was at its most violent.

He was certainly a source of inspiration for the anti-French activists: his Alawi dynasty had reigned over Morocco for three centuries, deterring any Ottoman encroachment, and this identification between king and country was unparalleled in the Arab world.

The first king of independent Morocco was nevertheless unable to substantiate his claims over 'Spanish Sahara'. The nationalist guerrillas were defeated in the 1957–8 'Ifni war'. Mohammad V's son and successor, Hassan II, eventually regained Ifni in 1969, but that was not enough to placate the military who tried twice to liquidate him, in July 1971 and in August 1972. The 'Green March' that Hassan II launched in November 1975 was a master stroke, since this human wave was not resisted by the departing Spaniards; and the armed forces, now focusing on their fight against the Sahraoui guerrillas of the Polisario front, had ceased to be a threat to the throne.

King Abdullah I could hardly be described as the 'father of the nation', since Transjordan was conceived as a buffer state by the British Empire rather than a nation. The Hashemite dynasty also had to face the deep parochialism of the local Bedouins, who never forgot that their king was originally a Hijazi outsider. Interestingly, it was through his secret dealings with the Zionists[16] that Abdullah tried to emancipate his kingdom and himself from British tutelage. This dangerous gamble brought him the Palestinian 'West Bank', but also precipitated his brutal death.

Abdullah's grandson Hussein escaped a dozen attempts on his life during his 1953–99 reign. He lost the West Bank to Israel in 1967, but kept claiming those Palestinian territories as his own, which was one of the main reasons behind the conflict with the PLO in 1970, the so-called Black September. It was only reluctantly, and under the Palestinian intifada pressure, that King Hussein agreed in 1988 to sever his symbolic ties with the West Bank. This was a paradoxical way of acknowledging the identification between his dynasty and the original Transjordan, now the 'Hashemite Kingdom of Jordan'.

The monarchs of Morocco and Jordan were no match for Ibn Saud as 'fathers of the nation', but Bourguiba clearly had the ambition to stand as the Tunisian equivalent of Atatürk. He therefore had to erase from collective memory and official history the mark of his nationalist arch-rival, Ben Youssef (eventually assassinated by Bourguiba's agents in Frankfurt in 1961). Another challenge Bourguiba had to face in his Atatürkian metamorphosis was the strong attachment of the Tunisian public to constitutional monarchy and to the 'benevolent father' figure of the Bey.

The Tunisian sovereign, whose dynasty had reigned over Tunisia for two and a half centuries, nominated Bourguiba as prime minister in April 1956. However, 'the Supreme Fighter',[17] as his supporters lauded him, could not be satisfied with less than absolute power. When the constitutional assembly, elected just after independence, elaborated a draft of a British-style parliamentary system in January 1957, Bourguiba squashed the proposal. Then he waited only six months before launching a merciless attack on the very principle of monarchy, obtaining the instant proclamation of the Tunisian republic.

It took two more years of manoeuvres and intrigues for Bourguiba to impose a presidential constitution with basically no countervailing power, in June 1959. Yet such a shrewd politician made a tragic mistake when he issued an ultimatum to de Gaulle in July 1961 requesting the immediate evacuation of the French base in the Tunisian northern port of Bizerte. De Gaulle flatly refused and, in the ensuing confrontation, at least six hundred Tunisians were killed compared to two dozen French soldiers.

The armed forces resented Bourguiba's disastrous gamble with their life and honour. Bizerte would be evacuated by the French as planned by de Gaulle, after the independence of Algeria, underlining how futile had been the sacrifice of the Tunisian military in 1961. Inspired by a shared hatred of Bourguiba, a network involving Ben Youssef's supporters and implacable officers (including the president's aide de camp) started to plot Bourguiba's death.

The conspiracy was uncovered in December 1962. Soon a tribunal with sessions broadcast live rapidly issued the verdicts. Ten defendants (five military and five civilians) were executed by firing squad. The location of their mass grave was kept secret.[18] Bourguiba accused Ben Bella and the Algerian regime of supporting the plot. He then consistently downgraded the army, favouring instead the state police and the one-party apparatus to control Tunisia. In 1975, he felt strong enough to be proclaimed 'president for life', a title no other Arab autocrat had dared to assume.

*

The absence of authentic 'fathers of the nation' paved the way for the series of military takeovers that set the dictatorial tone of the Arab world. Bourguiba escaped the regional wave by preempting an army coup, which gave to its own 'enlightened despotism' a distinct police-state flavour. Nasser was gallant enough to let the deposed king flee into exile. His self-proclaimed disciple, Qaddafi, instigated his coup while the Libyan king was abroad, but he had the crown prince tried and jailed. In Iraq, the military junta that liquidated the royal family, in 1958, established an enduring pattern of bloody vendettas and brutal retribution.

It took a decade and a half of alternating coups (some bloodless, some violent) and parliamentary interludes before Syria fell prey to the Baath party. In Algeria, it was the progressive elimination or marginalization of the FLN founding nucleus that cemented the power of Boumediene, and then Bendjedid. In Yemen, it was the overlap between the civil war (in the north) and the decolonization process (in the south) that led to a unique blend of military rule, as we shall see in the next chapter.

No matter how forcefully their state propaganda beat the drums of patriotic bravado, all those military plotters knew better than anybody else how shallow their nationalist legitimacy was. They had diverted the country's development in order to maximize the benefits of their ruling elite. The more they feared a counter-coup, the louder they screamed against 'Zionism' and 'imperialism'. Their paternalistic (at best) and often deprecatory approach towards their own people was devastating. Meet the modern Mamluks.

3

THE MODERN MAMLUKS

It was Napoléon Bonaparte who introduced the Mamluks to the West. After he invaded Egypt in July 1798, his army slaughtered thousands of them near the Pyramids, a disaster that opened the road to Cairo to the French. When General Bonaparte sailed back to France the following year, he took some Mamluk renegades back with him, even promoting one of them to be his faithful bodyguard for the next fifteen years.

Emperor Napoléon I had a Mamluk squad incorporated into his own Imperial Guard, and Francisco Goya left vivid memories in Madrid of the Mamluk subjugation of the patriotic uprising of 2 May 1808. The Mamluks of the Imperial Guard, despite numbering fewer than two hundred, came to embody the worst of the French Empire in the eyes of its enemies. The end of the Napoleonic saga coincided with their liquidation in the Cairo citadel by Mohammad Ali, the founder of modern Egypt.

The Mamluks were then reduced to a nostalgic footnote in Orientalist folklore. That was not a fitting way to honour their millennium-long history. In Arabic, Mamouk literally means slave; Abbassid caliphs, in Baghdad or in Samarra, sometimes opted to recruit Turkish slaves into their personal guards, so their loyalty as absolute outsiders would be less questionable during local power struggles.

This system became an institution in the last part of the twelfth century, when Saladin's heirs established their dynasty of Ayyubid sultans in Egypt and Syria. Slave traders were selling captives from the Black Sea, the Caucasus and even Central Asia on the markets of Aleppo, Damascus or Alexandria. Selected individuals were sent to military school (the most famous of which was inside the citadel of Cairo) under the undisputed guidance of one sole master. Once their training was completed, they were emancipated and started a new life as free soldiers.

In 1249, the French King Louis IX led the Seventh Crusade into Egypt. He was defeated and captured at Mansura, but the Mamluks considered this victory as theirs and toppled the Sultan. The French monarch had to pay a hefty ransom to be released. With the Crusaders' threat out of the way, the Mamluks could face the far greater menace of the Mongols, who devastated Baghdad and killed the Caliph in 1258. Two years later, the Muslim victory at the Battle of Ayn Jalut, near the Palestinian city of Nablus, brought a dramatic halt to the Mongol invasion.

A hero of the battles of Mansoura and Ayn Jalut, Baybars killed the last Ayyoubid ruler and had the Mamluk Sultan Qutuz assassinated in order to seize his throne. This dark side of his military bravado was absent from the florid epics that have celebrated his reign (1260–77) until today. Baybars' stroke of genius was to take under his protection, in Cairo, a member of the Abbassid family who had survived the massacre and proclaim him a 'Caliph'. This powerless Caliph was transferring his legitimacy as a descendant of the Prophet to the non-Arab rulers of Cairo and Damascus, who often spoke very poor Arabic.

Such an emasculated Caliphate continued to develop as a dynasty, while the very dynamics of the Mamluks forbade them to follow such path. The Mamluks were banned from marrying outside their ethnic group and their sons were not supposed to take up civilian or military office. Family networks were regularly fought by the Mamluks as a group, no matter how divided the personal loyalties could be. This Darwinian logic offered the key to power to the most ruthless of competitors, with a permanent tension between the winner's temptation to establish a dynasty on behalf of his scions and the collective resolve of the Mamluks to maintain a balance among the various factions.

The Mamluk world functioned as a counter-society, with its own codes and rites (such as the game of polo, horse races and archery competitions), alienated from local Arab societies. Civilians were generally despised by the ruling class, but peace and order were widely popular after the tribulations of the Crusades and the Mongols. The Islamic classical divide between the ruling elite or *khâssa* (the 'special' ones) and the masses of the *'âmma* (the 'ordinary' ones) reached unprecedented depths.

The government was militarized and the vizier was downgraded to being a mere treasurer. With the notable exception of Baybars, nor did Mamluks interfere in religious affairs. The ulemas therefore respected the tacit agreement through which the Islamic credentials of the former slaves were never questioned. Mamluk rulers were also celebrated as the 'Sultan of Islam and of the Muslims' (*Sultan al-Islâm wa al-Muslimîn*), with an emphasis on their leading the jihad.[1]

Mamluk rule lasted two and a half centuries. The Ottomans, who conquered the Middle East in 1516–17, wiped out the Mamluks from Syria, but allowed the surviving ones to serve them in Egypt. The local population feared most the periodic quarrels pitching one military clan against another, since they could escalate into fully-fledged battles in vulnerable cities. Long before Bonaparte's invasion and Mohammad Ali's massacre, the Mamluks' star had waned.

The reader may well wonder why the Mamluk paradigm should be resurrected in this analysis of the contemporary Arab militarized state. As this chapter unfolds, the parallels between the two historical sequences will I hope emerge. The modern Mamluks, like their medieval predecessors, lacked the legitimacy of century-long dynasties, but compensated for this shortcoming with their strong belief that might was right. They were not emancipated slaves, although they often came from the lower social strata, where the army was the only route to social promotion.

Modern Mamluks loathed the traditional elite; they yearned for populist revenge, even when their revolutionary impulse was fed by an urge to grab the spoils of the ancien regime. They soon constituted a *khâssa* world apart from the rest of the *'âmma* population, with its privileges, protocol and ceremonies. But their deep attachment to Baybars and his successors was the Darwinian sanction of a recurring power struggle.

Nasser, Boumediene and Assad were far from being the most talented rulers, but they were ruthless survivors in an implacable environment of intrigues, coups and treachery. They learnt to kill before being killed. Their obsession with security defined the fate of the nation. After hijacking the gains of independence, they made a whole population hostage to their ambition. And, like Baybars in his time and afterwards, they found many people ready to join in such a quest for glory.

An Insecure Nasser

The hagiographic narrative depicts Nasser as a brave officer, outraged by the 1948–9 humiliation in Palestine, who in 1952 led a band of Free Officers to restore Egypt's dignity. He had to confront a multi-faceted domestic 'reaction', with two major Muslim Brotherhood conspiracies against him in 1954 and 1965, while fighting through two imposed 'imperialist' wars, in 1956 and 1967. Despite the magnitude of the task, he vied consistently for Arab unity and collapsed from exhaustion in 1970 after having restored peace in Black September Jordan.

This narrative has been basically maintained under Sadat and Mubarak, because both dictators knew how dearly they would pay for uncovering the founding crimes of their political predecessor. While it is true that Nasser faced a dozen attempts against his life and regime, these mostly came from within his own military establishment. But Nasser, as a former Muslim brother himself,[2] owed much to his talent at engineering coups; he spent his life in power in a world of plots, often posing real threats.

The Free Officers who ousted King Farouk in July 1952 established a fourteen-member Revolutionary Command Council (RCC) that Nasser chaired and controlled through his close aides Abdelhakim Amer and Zakaria Mohieddine. But they needed a public figurehead to embody and legitimize their coup. They turned to General Mohammad Naguib, whom they believed offered the best combination of popularity and docility. Naguib was named prime minister in August 1952 and became their first president, following the proclamation of the Republic (and the dissolution of the parties) in June 1953.

The Liberation Rally, a loose organization vibrant with nationalism and populism, was launched as the political arm of the Free Officers (and the only legal party). Nasser became deputy prime minister; and Amer, a lowly major in 1952, was catapulted to the chief of staff of the armed forces (a ministerial-level post). Zakaria Mohieddine, promoted to minister of the interior, soon strengthened the security apparatus: the Special Branch, founded by the British in 1911, was expanded into the General Investigations Service (GIS/*Mabâhith 'âmma*).

The Military Intelligence Directorate (MID/*Mukhâbarât 'askariyya*) was re-oriented towards a political operation; and some of its most loyal (and effective) members went to create the Presidential Bureau of Information (PBI)—under Nasser's direct supervision—and the General Intelligence Department (GID/*Mukhâbarât 'âmma*).[3] GIS, part of the ministry of the interior, was supposedly civilian, but all intelligence agencies were militarized under the Free Officers' regime.

Such obsession with security was from the outset a hallmark of Nasser's and his successors' regimes. The fact that supposedly civilian intelligence was grounded in military expertise and leadership is another example of this Deep State in the making. Nasser was well aware that his own popularity could not match Naguib's. The first Egyptian president could furthermore rely on the democratic commitment of most of the armed forces, who echoed the banned parties' call for free elections and a new constitution.[4]

In true Mamluk style, Nasser decided to plunge Egypt into crisis in order to neutralize Naguib: a ring of provocative explosions preceded the dramatic legalization of political parties in March 1954, in order to associate public strife with political pluralism. Then the military police engineered a transport strike that brought the country to a standstill, while Liberation Rally agitators demonstrated in Cairo shouting: 'No parties! No parliament! No elections!'[5] Naguib turned to his minister of the interior, Zakaria Mohieddine, who demanded written orders to suppress the protest and warned of a bloodbath. Caught between the Free Officers and the street troubles, Naguib escaped the showdown and agreed to back down. Though now powerless, he was still the nominal president. In April 1954, all trade and student unions were banned.

Six months later, Nasser killed two birds with one stone after the failed (and most probably staged) attempt on his life in Alexandria by a Muslim Brother. Naguib was accused of being part of the plot and was put under house arrest for the next eighteen years. The crackdown on the Muslim Brotherhood sent some 20,000 of their members to jail (with only one in twenty standing trial).[6] This cleared the way to absolute power for Nasser and his circle, who banked on their land reform and the anti-monarchy rhetoric (and trials) to burnish their revolutionary credentials.

The transition from coup to 'revolution' (in fact, Nasser's dictatorship) was complete in June 1956: the new constitution and Nasser's presidency were approved by 99.9 per cent of voters.

The RCC was dissolved but, as had always happened with the Mamluks, Nasser could not rest on his laurels. Indeed, he would have to face a formidable rival from within his own circle during the next decade: Abdelhakim Amer was promoted to the unprecedented rank of Field Marshal in 1957.

To grasp the perversity of such a power struggle, one has to realize that military rank had nothing to do with the appointees' actual fighting capacities and performance. Amer nearly broke down during the November 1956 'tripartite aggression' by Israel, France and Britain against Egypt. Nasser took over the operational initiative and, even though his army was clearly defeated, he was celebrated as the political victor of the crisis after the unconditional withdrawal of the invading forces under US pressure.

But Amer knew intimately the paranoia of his former fellow plotter and repeatedly unveiled new conspiracies, starting in April 1957, to keep the president off his guard. More importantly, the commander in chief had transformed the officer corps into the largest 'patronage network' in Egypt, as the sociologist Hazem Kandil aptly put it, commenting: 'for the army, the field marshal had become something like a Santa Claus'.[7]

When the Syrian leadership pushed an initially reluctant Nasser into accepting union with Egypt,[8] in 1958, the president of this new 'United Arab Republic' saw the opportunity to get Amer out of his way: the field marshal was appointed governor of the 'Northern Province', just as unruly Mamluks were sent to Damascus when they became too much of a threat to the Sultan in Cairo. But the union was short-lived and collapsed in 1961, partly because of the military brutality unleashed by Amer in his own fiefdom.

The field marshal came back to Cairo. In autumn 1962, Nasser tried to force Amer out of the military high command, prompting the army boss to denounce the president's 'fear of democracy'.[9] The Egyptian intervention in Yemen also played into the hands of Amer and his top brass protégés.[10] Eventually, Nasser became the supreme commander of the armed forces, but had to cope with Amer shadowing him as first vice president and deputy commander-in-chief. Nasser could then bitterly complain to Anwar Sadat, one of the founding Free officers: 'I am responsible as president, but it is Amer that rules.'[11]

In June 1963, unable to dislodge the field marshal from the military leadership, Nasser established a Vanguard Organization (VO) inside the newly formed Arab Socialist Union (ASU), the avatar of the long-gone Liberation Rally as the only legal party. The Egyptian president was too much of a despot to trust the people, but the clandestine VO offered him a powerful intelligence arm that could even spy on Amer's supporters in the military.

The field marshal retaliated by having his Military Intelligence Directorate (MID) uncover a Muslim Brotherhood plot (with thousands detained and at least 250 deaths under torture) in the summer of 1965. Amer lashed back at Nasser, accusing the rival civilian GID of incompetence, at the least, and demanding its dissolution. This war by proxy on intelligence only sharpened the anti-Islamist campaign, with Sayyid Qutb being hanged in August 1966. After the 1954 'plot', a more confident Nasser had chosen to jail, rather than execute, the Muslim Brotherhood's senior leadership.

The Nasser/Amer constant feud was critical to the comedy of errors leading Egypt into the trap of the 5 June 1967 war, with eyes wide open. (One third of the armed forces were pinned down in Yemen, which made any chance of victory against Israel seem ludicrously implausible.)[12] Everybody in Cairo was bluffing to outwit their rivals, but Israel wisely used this verbal escalation to deliver a nearly fatal blow to the Egyptian military. On 9 June, Nasser announced the collective resignation of the country's leadership (including Amer's and his own) in a dramatic speech. ASU engineered mass demonstrations all over Egypt to beg Nasser to stay in power.

In a carefully staged move, Nasser retracted his resignation on 11 June. After five years of strife, the Egyptian president had finally ousted Amer. A smear campaign was soon underway, each camp blaming the other for the 'Six Day War' humiliation. Two months later, Amer was taken into GIS custody where he either swallowed poison to commit suicide (the official version) or was swiftly executed (the accusation of his faithful followers who would from then on be relentlessly targeted and purged by Nasser's intelligence services).

It had taken the 1967 disaster for the Egyptian dictator to rid himself of his military nemesis. Nasser would eventually focus on the re-conquest of the Sinai he had so painfully lost, with the 'war of attrition' flaring on the Suez Canal. He was also forced to court the heroes of the time, those Palestinian guerrillas he had harried in the previous decade. The Palestine Liberation Organization (PLO), launched in Cairo in 1964 under Nasser's auspices, had to be conceded to the Fatah movement and its leader, Yasser Arafat, in 1969.

Unable to restore Egyptian territorial integrity, Nasser could no longer claim to champion the Palestinian cause. He opted for damage control, sanctioning the PLO's encroachment on others' sovereignty: the October 1969 Cairo agreement between Lebanon and the PLO, whose violation of Lebanese sovereignty was so blatant that it had to remain secret; and the ceasefire between Jordan and the PLO ending Black September in 1970. This was Nasser's last achievement, just before he died from a heart attack.

From Sadat to Mubarak

The security triumvirate that ruled the country on behalf of Nasser was caught off guard by his unexpected death: Ali Sabri ran the ASU, Shaarawi Gomaa handled the Vanguard Organization (VO) as well as being minister of the interior, and Sami Sharaf was the head of the Presidential Bureau of Information

(PBI). They settled on Anwar Sadat as Nasser's successor, since they were convinced the new president would only be a transitional one, giving them time to prepare their takeover (and settle their tripartite accounts).

Sadat nevertheless outwitted his supposed allies, since he benefited from his familiarity with Nasser's dirtiest secrets. In April 1971, he proclaimed the union of Egypt with Syria and Libya, dissolving the mighty ASU into a wider entity. In July, he was informed of the details of a conspiracy involving Sabri, Gomaa and Sharaf. He offered Sharaf a deal if he would turn against his fellow plotters. Sharaf miscalculated and refused, then was sacked with the other ringleaders.[13] The whole counter-coup was proudly labelled Corrective Revolution, in echo, as we shall see later, of the 'corrective' coup Assad had waged in Damascus in November 1970.

The project of the tripartite union with Syria and Libya had served its purpose and Sadat now dropped it. But he purged and revamped the GIS profoundly, restructuring it into the State Security Investigations Service (SSIS, *Mabâhith Amn al-Dawla*). For Sadat the intelligence dimension of the PBI had become useless and the service was downgraded to a presidential briefing structure. The brutal expulsion of the Soviet advisers in July 1972 signalled a significant switch in intelligence cooperation from the KGB to the CIA. Sadat could also rely on his old friend Kamal Adham, now the head of Saudi intelligence.

The Egyptian and Syrian presidents began secretly preparing a combined offensive against Israel. But, while Assad had hoped through waging war to regain the Golan Heights, Sadat was envisioning a political war to break the deadlock with Israel, before turning to the USA and their mediation to recover the Sinai. The fact that Sadat had no combat experience added to the unlikelihood of such a scenario coming to pass.

On 6 October 1973, the Egyptian army crossed to the eastern bank of the Suez Canal in a coordinated move with a brazen

Syrian assault on the Golan. But Sadat decided unilaterally to halt the offensive on 9 October, leaving the Syrians to face alone the full might of the Israeli counter-offensive. Then the Egyptian president resumed the military offensive on 14 October, opening a breach that the Israelis soon sneaked through to advance on the western bank of the Canal.

Sadat's final decision to accept a ceasefire in place, on 22 October, was the last straw that broke the military's endurance, despite its brave battlefield performance. The popular and strong-willed chief of staff, Saadeddine Shazly, was blamed for all the shortcomings of the war and exiled as military attaché to London. Shazly was different from Amer since, contrary to what had happened in 1967, this time the army had been consumed with its patriotic duty, neglecting the domestic power struggles.

The vice president chosen by Sadat was Husni Mubarak, chief of the air force and the least inclined of senior officers to coup temptations. Sadat launched the Opening (*Infitâh*) policy to reach out to Western and Gulf investors. State employment continued to grow at the same alarming rate of a yearly minimum of 8 per cent as during Nasser's years, in order to nurture networks of local and national patronage. But economic liberalization was the mantra of the 1970s, and Sadat dreamt of a fully-fledged alliance with America.

There was however an obvious continuity between Nasser and Sadat in the pre-eminence of the intelligence barons. As the historian Amira el-Azhary Sonbol described: 'It is not an exaggeration to say that many of those who managed to win the most-sought after positions in the export and import organisations and in the foreign service during both the Nasser and Sadat regimes belonged to Egypt's *mukhâbarât*. Members stood together and assisted each other to create "truths" that would allow them to benefit by virtue of their role.'[14]

In January 1977, a callous slashing of government subsidies for basic commodities triggered countrywide 'bread riots'. Those were the wildest popular troubles since the infamous 'Cairo burning' of January 1952, a violent outburst of anti-British and anti-monarchy rage that paved the way for the Free Officers' coup. Sadat had to escape the crowd in Aswan and return to Cairo by helicopter, while Mubarak's residence near Alexandria was torched.

The president sent in the army to restore order. Though 160 demonstrators were killed in two days, only the reinstatement of the subsidies restored peace on the Egyptian street. Sadat, determined no longer to depend on the military for his regime's survival, decided to beef up the paramilitary units of the Ministry of the Interior, the Central Security Forces (CSF), whose ranks grew from 100 to 300,000 members.[15]

Sadat then passed a law on political parties that led to the division of the ASU into three platforms (*manâbir*), deemed to fit the right wing, the centre and the left wing of the political spectrum. The centrist platform was the most powerful and inherited most of the clout of the ASU. It was eventually named the National Democratic Party (NDP), in a smooth transition from one-party rule to a system dominated by a hegemonic party. Most of the VO cadres migrated from ASU to NDP, bringing along with them a sizeable intelligence capacity.[16]

Reassured on the domestic front, Sadat performed his bold move towards a US-sponsored peace with Israel. He started with a surprise visit to Jerusalem in November 1977, before the tripartite summit with Israeli PM Menachem Begin, hosted by Jimmy Carter at Camp David in September 1978. An Egyptian–Israeli peace treaty was eventually signed in March 1979. To reward the armed forces for their continued loyalty, the USA agreed to earmark a yearly transfer of $1.3 billion in military aid to Egypt.

Sadat could sincerely believe he had it made, but on 6 October 1981, during the celebration of the eighth anniversary of the military's advance across the Suez Canal, the Egyptian president was shot dead by a jihadi commando who had infiltrated the military parade. One week later, Mubarak, the heir designate as vice president, was voted in as the new head of state after a referendum which approved his nomination for president with 98.4 per cent of the ballot. In the interim period, an Islamist uprising focused on the Upper Egypt city of Asyut was crushed by the military.

Mubarak's minister of defence was field marshal Abdel Halim Abu Ghazala, who had commanded the artillery during the October 1973 War. Like Shazly before him, Abu Ghazala nurtured no Amer-like ambition to political power. When the CSF conscripts, fearing an additional year of compulsory service, rebelled in February 1986, Abu Ghazala sent the army in to quell the revolt in a matter of days (with 107 policemen killed). But once the mission was accomplished, the military loyally withdrew to their barracks.

This respectful stance did not save the minister of defence when, two years later, he was accused of smuggling illegal material to Saddam Hussein's Iraq.[17] Abu Ghazala was ultimately forced to resign in April 1989. His demise smoothed the transition of Mubarak's Egypt from its crucial part in supporting Iraq during its war against Iran (1980–88) to its key role in the anti-Saddam coalition in 1990–91 (Egyptian forces were among the first to enter 'liberated' Kuwait).

Amer died from poison, Shazly was exiled, but Abu Ghazala stayed quietly home after his retirement. He enjoyed a widespread popularity in Egypt and was even tempted, in June 2005, to compete in the first multi-candidate presidential election. But Mubarak's visit to his house was enough for the former marshal to forsake any political ambition.[18] Compared with Sadat's era, and of course Nasser's, Mamluks had become unprecedentedly tamed during Mubarak's presidency.

Syrian Intrigue

We saw how the traumatic experiment of the Egyptian-led United Arab Republic (UAR) dealt a terrible blow to the Syrian polity and its pluralistic nature from 1958 to 1961. Egyptian Mamluks imported their security apparatus and its aggressive repression into Syria. Thereafter, the polarization of Arab nationalism between Nasserism and Baathism led logically to the militarization of the Baathist structure, basically to survive the assaults of their (pro-) Egyptian rivals.

A secret cell of Baathist officers blamed the civilian leadership of their party for having sold Syrian independence to Nasser. They organized an underground 'military committee' in 1960, to prepare the downfall of the UAR and, eventually, their own takeover. Their leader was lieutenant colonel Mohammad Umran, the son of an Alawi sheikh from Homs.

The five other members of this clandestine committee were Salah Jadid and Hafez al-Assad, both Alawis; Abdelkarim Jundi and Ahmad al-Mir, both Ismailis; and Usman Kanaan, a Sunni from Iskenderun.[19] This over-representation of Muslim minorities in such a group was the unexpected result of the viciousness of Egyptian repression: the Baathist plotters trusted only their closest comrades, and therefore put a strong emphasis on social proximity.

It was a Saudi-backed right-wing coup that restored Syrian independence in September 1961. But the 'military committee' waited only eighteen months before seizing the prize. In March 1963, Umran and Jadid deployed their tanks in Damascus, while Assad occupied the nearest airbase. One fellow plotter, the Druze captain Salim Hatum, moved into the radio station where the traditional 'communiqué number one' was broadcast.

Jadid controlled the Bureau of Officers' Affairs where he promoted Baathist conspirators (lieutenant-colonel Assad soon became general) and purged rival activists from the armed forces. The 'military committee' operated as a 'junta within the junta'[20] and left the front row to a non-Baathist Sunni general, Amin al-Hafiz, who combined the portfolios of defence and interior. Meanwhile, the Baath established its own paramilitary 'National Guard'.

The founding fathers of the Baath party tried to regain power by gambling on ambitious Umran against his former partners. But Jadid and Assad anticipated the move and, in February 1966, Hatum led a bloody assault on Amine al-Hafiz's palace. The party militia, commanded by Rifaat, Hafez al-Assad's younger brother, joined the fray. Hafiz and Umran were jailed in the Mezze prison, on the outskirts of Damascus. The civilian leadership of the Baath was thoroughly dismantled.

Jadid now ran the country, but the over-cautious plotter led Noureddine Atassi as a civilian front at the presidency of the Republic. Assad was appointed minister of defence, while Hatum, who coveted this portfolio, in September 1966 mounted a retaliatory ambush against Jadid. Assad's air force thwarted this attempted coup; Hatum fled to Jordan, before Jadid and Assad purged the armed forces for the fifth time in three years.

Instead of adopting a low profile towards Israel, Syrian Mamluks, echoing their Egyptian counterparts, indulged in verbal escalation against 'Zionism' and 'imperialism'. They saw it as a paradoxical way to defuse the tension inside the armed forces, now that the 'military committee' had split twice in 1966. Jadid was also committed to protect the Palestinian Fatah guerrillas, whose infiltrations into Israel triggered reprisals against Syria.

As the Middle East historian David Lesch put it, 'Syria was severely unprepared for war: despite the bombastic and jingoistic rhetoric, the Baathist regime viewed its actions against Israel as low-level warfare that was not meant to lead to an all-out war.'[21] The Syrian challenge to Egypt for the regional leadership aggravated the power struggle inside Egypt between Nasser and Amer. So the egocentric Mamluks in Cairo and Damascus fuelled the flames of the disastrous 'Six Day War' in June 1967.

The Syrian Baathists stood paralysed during the first four days of the conflict. They let Egypt and then Jordan be crushed, without offering any 'Arab solidarity'. Then the Israeli military turned against the Golan Heights on 9 June. The Syrian army fought bravely, but it lost 600 soldiers and 86 tanks. The remaining units withdrew into the city of Quneytra, where they consolidated their positions and secured the strategic road to Damascus.

On the following morning, 10 June, Assad broadcast on Damascus radio the now infamous 'communiqué 66', announcing the fall of Quneytra. This statement, though inaccurate, sent panic waves through the Syrian defence lines, accelerating the effective capture of Quneytra by the Israelis and generating a disorderly retreat towards Damascus. Such a communiqué has been interpreted either as a blackmail trick to drag USSR into direct intervention, or as a sinister manoeuvre to protect the Baath leadership in Damascus at the cost of Quneytra.[22]

Syria had lost the Golan, half of its air force and half of its tanks, along with probably 2,500 soldiers.[23] But the regime was safe and it even found a convenient scapegoat: Hatum had volunteered to fight Israel and he had then been amnestied back from Jordan; but he was soon tried for treason, allegedly for betraying Syria to the Americans and British. A few days after the end of the war, Hatum was shot by firing squad.

Assad also blamed the June 1967 disaster on Jadid and Atassi's radical adventurism. The minister tightened his control on the officer corps through Mustafa Tlass, his protégé as chief of staff. He forced Ahmed al-Mir to retire and 'promoted' him to ambassador in Madrid. But Abelkarim Jundi, another of the founding members of the 'military committee', and now military intelligence czar, remained loyal to Jadid.

Assad therefore engineered a showdown, in February 1969, between his brother Rifaat, commander of the party militias, and Jundi who, humiliated and cornered, committed suicide. Jundi's fall triggered a new purge in the security apparatus, this time

against Ismaili officers. After the 1966 purge against Druze followers of Hatum, this elimination of undesirables set the stage for
the final battle between Jadid and Assad, both relying on their
hard-core Alawi networks, in alliance with key Sunni players
(president Atassi for Jadid and chief of staff Tlass for Assad).

Assad bitterly criticized Jadid's support for Fatah, who had
taken control of the Palestinian Liberation Organization (PLO)
and established a 'state within the state' in neighbouring Jordan.
During the Black September 1970 crisis, Jadid decided to send
Syrian tanks to assist the Palestinian guerrillas against the Jordanian army. But Assad ordered his air force to hold back and the
Syrian units were annihilated by Jordanian warplanes.

Echoing the loss of the Golan Heights in 1967, what was a
disaster for Syria turned out to play into the hands of Assad's
obsessive quest for absolute power. In November 1970, the conference of the Baath party seemed a victory for Jadid and Atassi,
but both of them were soon jailed, along with thousands of their
supporters. Assad proclaimed the 'corrective movement' and,
three months later, was the only candidate in a presidential plebiscite where he reaped 99.2 per cent of the votes.

The parallel is obvious between Assad and Sadat, although
the former had to fight for power whereas the latter inherited
and was forced to defend it. They both eventually defeated their
rivals, whose errors had to be 'corrected'. This is also why they
both had to compensate for the 1967 disaster, at least to erase
their personal responsibilities in the historical defeat of the
Arabs. But we saw that the October 1973 war was for Sadat a
military gamble to reach an American-sponsored agreement, an
option that Assad was therefore compelled to endorse.

Henry Kissinger's 'shuttle diplomacy' brokered separate disengagement accords, first between Israel and Egypt, then
between Israel and Syria. Assad and Sadat, now safe on the
Israeli front, could benefit from the post-oil-shock largesse of
the Gulf monarchies, generous sponsors of the 'front-line states'

(with Israel). But while Sadat had chosen a *Pax Americana* that would lead him to the treaty with Israel, Assad kept the 'anti-imperialist' rhetoric alive, with the attached and substantial Soviet support.

In June 1976, the Syrian army invaded Lebanon at the request of the Christian president of the Republic, and in order to counter the revolutionary coalition of the PLO guerrillas and the Lebanese left. This military intervention echoed Assad's anti-PLO stand during the Black September crisis in Jordan. The Syrian dictator was shrewd enough to garner the public endorsement of Saudi Arabia and the tacit agreement of Israel (and America) for an occupation that would last nearly three decades.

Assad had now made his armed forces a pillar of 'regional stability', through the durable ceasefire on the Golan and the control he exerted over the various militias in Lebanon. But the militant faction of the Syrian Muslim Brotherhood launched a terror campaign against the regime and the Alawi community in 1979. The battle in Aleppo went on through most of 1980 and left some 2,000 dead. The jihadi uprising in Hama was quelled in March 1982 in an unprecedented bloodbath (estimates of the toll ranged from 8,000 to 20,000 dead).[24]

The Israeli invasion of Lebanon in June 1982, far from weakening Assad, helped him to erase the memory of the Islamist insurgency and to regain his position as a great Arab champion. The fact that his army refused to fight Israel until it was forced to do so (and to concede defeat) was quickly forgotten. The USSR opened its arsenals to boost the Syria's defences in what increasingly resembled a new Cold War. Never had Assad appeared so powerful, internationally and domestically.

But the president's health problems, during autumn 1983, convinced the hot-headed Rifaat al-Assad that he could replace his older brother. Rifaat had led the Defence Brigades, the armoured units of the former party militia, during the civil war of 1979–82 and he believed that such a mass killing justified his aspiration for power. In an Alawi community once targeted by jihadi terrorism, this discourse struck a chord. The Alawi generals nevertheless stood by Hafez al-Assad in March 1984 when rival tanks, each column bearing the portrait of one of the competing brothers, moved into downtown Damascus.

Rifaat al-Assad, appointed as one of the three 'vice presidents', was soon exiled to USSR, after which he chose to settle ultimately in France. The final crisis of the Syrian Mamluk system was over: the despot was re-elected in February 1985 with 99.6 per cent of the vote (compared to 99.2 per cent seven years before) and the slogan 'Assad for ever' became the predictable theme tune at party rallies. The Syrian dictator was there to stay, and we shall see in the next chapter how the Iraqi invasion of Kuwait would rejuvenate and reinforce Assad's regime.

The Never-Ending Liberation Struggle of Algeria

When Algeria gained its independence in the summer of 1962, we saw how Boumediene's military apparatus eliminated any domestic resistance to install Ben Bella as president of the new Republic. This dictatorial takeover was facilitated by the devastating impact of French colonial repression on nationalist networks in Algeria. Nearly 1.7 million French soldiers fought in Algeria between 1954 and 1962,[25] while the FLN guerrillas, even at the apex of their power in 1958, never exceeded 25,000 combatants.[26] The French offensives under Charles de Gaulle's presidency (1958–62) destroyed the core of the FLN fighting force, paving the way for the takeover by the 'army of the frontiers', based in Morocco and Tunisia.

In fact, de Gaulle had won the military war against the FLN, but he knew from his own history, as the leader of the 'Free French' during WWII, that such a victory was meaningless so long as an overwhelming majority of the Algerian people was in favour of FLN-led independence. Eventually de Gaulle had to sever ties with Algeria to save the French Republic from the militarized extreme-right (the 'French Algeria' fanatics nearly assassinated the French president in August 1962).

President Ben Bella and Boumediene, his minister of defence, wrested power from the activists who had made Algerian independence possible and from the political leadership who had negotiated this independence with the French authorities. The losers of summer 1962 were erased from the official narrative, where 'revolution' was equated to 'jihad' and 'liberation struggle', and therefore stripped of any other possible revolutionary dimension. Might was right, since it had created the basic legitimacy of the new rulers.

The historical roots of this forced militarization could be traced back to the Special Organization (OS), created in 1947 by the nationalist Movement for the Triumph of the Democratic Liberties (MTLD) in order to prepare an armed uprising. Ben Bella had been the leader of the OS, before joining the 'founding nine' nucleus of the FLN in 1954. The celebration of the military struggle in contrast to the illusions of the political game lay at the core of the anti-French liberation campaign.

Algerian independence could have taken a wholly different turn if the decisions adopted by the FLN in its Soummam conference, held clandestinely in August 1956, had been implemented. The charismatic leader Abbane Ramdane, nicknamed 'the architect of the revolution', had convinced the FLN congressmen that national unity and popular support were key to achieving independence. He had therefore secured the subordination of the military to the political wing, as well as the primacy of the domestic leadership over the exiled one.

Ben Bella, at that time exiled in Cairo, had failed to defeat this line. The Soummam conference had also divided Algeria into six *wilayas* (governorates), each with a 'people's assembly' and a military structure. The fifth *wilaya*, covering the west of the country, was officially based in Oran, but practically in the

Moroccan city of Oujda. It was run by Abdelhafid Boussouf, aka 'Si Mabrouk', a veteran from the OS, who had reached the rank of colonel (the highest in the Algerian liberation army). In December 1957 Ramdane was lured into Morocco, where Boussouf had him strangled[27] (the FLN announced later that Ramdane had been killed in combat).

Ramdane's assassination dealt a fatal blow to the Soummam vision and platform. People's assemblies soon disappeared in insurgent Algeria. Ten years after the launching of the OS, its anti-civilian ethos had eventually prevailed. As the Algerian political sociologist Lahouari Addi described it, 'the OS-driven dynamics imposed the army as the embodiment of the nation and the source of political power. This is why the army chief is potentially the political leader'.[28]

Boussouf, unchallenged after Ramdane's murder, consolidated his brutal grip over the fifth *wilaya*. His security obsession in an ever more militarized FLN led him to establish the Algerian government-in-exile (GPRA) intelligence services, known as MLGC, then MALG (Ministry of Armament and General Liaisons). This promotion compelled him in 1958 to transfer the leadership of the fifth *wilaya* to his deputy, Colonel Houari Boumediene.

The fifth *wilaya* remained a strong power centre, designated as the 'Oujda group' (or 'clan'), where Boussouf and Boumediene could rely on the factional loyalty of ambitious militants like Abdelaziz Bouteflika (Boumediene's private secretary) or Ahmed Medeghri. The promotion of Boussouf to Algerian intelligence czar preceded Boumediene's taking control of the whole 'army of the frontiers': the Oujda command structure in Morocco had a counterpart in the parallel Ghardimaou outfit based in Tunisia.

Boussouf and Boumediene's clout reinforced each other and attracted new allegiances. Boussouf sent a 'Red Carpet' class of elite intelligence operatives for training with the KGB[29] and decided to place Kasdi Merbah, one of his most talented recruits, under Boumediene's command. Chadli Bendjedid became Bou mediene's deputy in Ghardimaou. A few dozen Algerian NCOs then defected from the colonial forces, often to join Boumediene's staff, like Khaled Nezzar. They were called the DAF, the French acronym for 'Defectors from the French Army'.

This flashback to some of the murkier episodes of the anti-French liberation struggle is essential to understanding the dynamics of the Algerian Mamluks and the resilience of their power networks: just as the Egyptian 'Free Officers' abolished parliamentary pluralism with their monarchy, the Algerian masters would, a decade later, liquidate the liberal legacy of the domestic resistance with the end of French domination.

This 'new Algeria' became literally 'theirs', since they would deny any rival's nationalist credentials. The mythical 'French party' (*hizb Fransa*) acquired ubiquitous attributes in official propaganda, with every opponent being accused of membership of this anti-FLN Fifth Column. The militarization of the liberation struggle (with the subsequent elimination of any dissent) led to a militarization of independent Algeria, under the one-party rule of the FLN.

Boussouf rapidly understood that he had been outflanked by his disciple, Boumediene: he wisely decided to quit politics and move to the business sector, with a very profitable outcome.[30] More generally, a new bourgeoisie embedded in military and intelligence circles could benefit from properties that had been abandoned by the Europeans (90 per cent of the French Algerians fled in 1962). The best real estate and the richest agricultural land ended up in the hands of Boumediene's protégés and clients.[31]

The minister of defence was patiently waiting patiently in the shadows for President Ben Bella to antagonize wider segments of the population through his autocratic and erratic style of governance. The sole candidate for the presidency, Ben Bella had been elected with 99.6 per cent of the official vote in September 1963. He was at the same time leading the FLN party and the government (staffed with 'Oujda clan' pillars like Bouteflika in foreign affairs and Medeghri at the interior).

Soon after the presidential plebiscite, Ben Bella launched the 'Sands War' against Morocco. Mohammad V had agreed with the GPRA to renegotiate the Saharan borders between Algeria and Morocco, but Ben Bella had denounced the very idea of such a discussion. Algeria now stood by the inviolability of the post-colonial boundaries, which led to an armed conflict in October 1963 over Tindouf (in Algeria) and Figuig (in Morocco). Algeria was backed by the Egyptian and Cuban militaries, but the Moroccan army fared much better in desert combat.

A ceasefire was signed in February 1964, under the auspices of the Organization for African Unity (OAU), which endorsed the principle of the inviolability of post-colonial borders. This symbolic victory cheered Ben Bella, who did not grasp how much the military blamed him for the misconduct of the war with Morocco. The FLN congress, held in Algiers in April 1964, became a showcase for Ben Bella's hubris.

The president/PM/party chief started to demote senior ministers from the 'Oujda clan' and take up their portfolios. After sacking Medeghri from his interior post, he turned against Bouteflika at foreign affairs, a move that would trigger Boumediene's coup in June 1965. Chief of staff Colonel Tahar Zbiri arrested the president at his residence. The deployment of tanks in the capital was ironically thought by local residents to be connected to the filming, on that very day, of *The Battle of Algiers*, a movie directed by Gillo Pontecorvo and dedicated to the 1957 confrontation between the French army and the Algerian resistance.

Boumediene went on TV to proclaim the 'revolutionary rectification' (*redressement*). Even though the coup was presented as bloodless, scores of Ben Bella's supporters were liquidated in the following weeks, especially in Annaba. Boumediene established a 26-member Revolutionary Council, whose presidency he combined with the party leadership and the defence portfolio. The 'Oujda clan' controlled the party, while Medeghri recovered full control of the interior ministry (Bouteflika naturally remained at foreign affairs).

The exclusive hold on power of the 'Oujda group' eventually embittered the main ouster of Ben Bella. The Chief of Staff Zbiri staged his own coup in December 1967, but he was quickly neutralized and had to flee. Boumediene, who a few weeks later escaped an attempt on his life, absorbed the position of his chief of staff into his own defence portfolio, coupled with the presidency and the party leadership. He also decided to give even more powers to the military intelligence, the former MALG, and now *Sécurité militaire* (SM), run by the KGB-trained Kasdi Merbah, one of the historical 'Boussouf boys'.

The SM extended its tentacles all over the country, infiltrating the various associations, recruiting potential or active opponents, and even mounting provocative actions to discredit their targets. The Offices for Security and Prevention (BSP, in their French acronym) became the local arms of the SM, spying on everybody, informing on any activity. Boumediene's Algeria became a SM-monitored world, where every citizen knew the cost of criticism.

The SM was also believed to have carried out the 'dirty work' of liquidating dissidents abroad, including some of the FLN 'founding nine': Mohammad Khider was gunned down in Madrid, in January 1967; Krim Belkacem, sentenced to death in absentia, was strangled with his own tie in Frankfurt, in October 1970. The power of the SM was feared even within the army, and in the now rival Ministry of the Interior. When Medeghri, who had run it practically since 1962, was found dead at his home in December 1974, the official version, 'suicide', was widely disputed.[32]

Boumediene had relied on the SM to get rid of the FLN founding nucleus, and then to dispose of the 'Oujda clan' (with the notable exception of Bouteflika, whose foreign affairs portfolio kept him away from domestic intrigue). Boumediene was now the sole and absolute master, a position Nasser achieved only from 1967 to 1970, and as an unexpected consequence of a disastrous war with Israel. Boumediene could bank on seemingly un-extinguishable hydrocarbon resources that generated colossal revenues after the 1973 oil shock. Agrarian reform and the industrialization-first strategy were financed by the oil boom in a Soviet-style planned economy. The political scientist Miriam Lowi aptly described this process:

> This institutional arrangement did away with pluralism, while providing the illusion of popular incorporation. By controlling the extension of participation in this way, it protected elite privileges and Boumediene's agenda. This was, indeed, an authoritarian regime aimed at radically reshaping Algerian society and economy in the absence of political participation.[33]

This institutional reshaping from above was completed in the second half of 1976: in June, the 'National Charter' enshrined the monolithic role of the FLN; in November, a referendum approved a new constitution and the reactivation of the assembly, suspended since the 1965 coup; the following month, Boumediene was voted in as sole candidate for the presidency of the Republic with the by now mandatory 99.5 per cent of the ballot.

This constitutional whitewashing, far from reducing Boumediene's powers, consolidated them: the president was also prime minister, commander in chief of the armed forces and nominal head of the FLN. Even Assad in Syria had always kept a front man at the head of government. But then during an official visit to Damascus Boumediene was diagnosed with a rare blood disease that caused his death in December 1978.

A forty-day period official mourning was proclaimed in Algeria, and Rabah Bitat, the only remaining member of the FLN 'founding nine', became the interim head of state as president of the National Assembly. As with Nasser's sudden death in 1970, the putative heirs were caught unprepared, with party boss Salah Yahyaoui and MFA Bouteflika topping the list.

The military leaders settled for a local version of Sadat, Chadli Bendjedid, whose absence of personal ambition reassured all the 'decision-makers' (*décideurs*), an expression that would flourish later in Algeria. Bendjedid deputised for Boumediene in the 'army of the frontiers', took over Constantine from the GPRA in 1962 and became the docile commander of the Oran military region from 1964 to 1978.

A colonel, like his departed mentor, Bendjedid was nominated by the FLN as sole candidate for the presidency. In February 1979, he was voted in but with only 99.4 per cent of the ballots cast. That he secured 0.1 per cent fewer votes compared to Boumediene's plebiscite in 1976 might have been intended as a mark of respect towards the deceased president. Bendjedid kept the ministry of defence, but appointed a civilian prime minister. Continuity was the motto but, as happened with Sadat after Nasser, the new leader would soon strike out in his own direction.

In July 1979, Bendjedid released Ben Bella from jail where he had been detained since the 1965 coup. The first Algerian president was placed under house arrest for one year, before being allowed to settle in Switzerland. Bouteflika lost his foreign affairs portfolio to be appointed 'counsellor' to the president. In July 1980, he had to flee the country to avoid a trial for embezzlement. The same month, Yahyaoui was ousted from his key position in the FLN party.

Bendjedid knew that he also had to rein in the SM. The military top brass actively supported him in this neutralization campaign. First, Merbah was replaced by one of his aides, Noureddine Zerhouni, aka 'Yazid', who ran the intelligence service until 1982. Then came the era of the generals, since Bendjedid had decided to upgrade the Boumediene-style 'colonel' glass ceiling. The president soon named General Lakehal Ayat as chief of the SM.

While the FLN had held no conference during Boumediene's presidency, it was now expected that the ruling party would convene every five years to confirm Bendjedid as its candidate (and therefore the sole one) for the next poll. This was done in 1984, with Bendjedid being voted back the following month by the same 99.4 per cent of the ballot, just as in 1979. The president felt strong enough to pursue his Sadat-like 'opening' policy, undermining state monopolies in industry and mass distribution.

Such a campaign against the hard core of Boumediene's profiteering networks was much more demanding for Bendjedid than the political challenges of his previous mandate. He could no longer tolerate a unified SM and so dismantled it in 1987: army security was given to General Mohammad Betchine and stayed in the broader defence organization scheme; while Ayat remained chief of an emasculated General Directorate for Prevention and Security (DGSP),[34] under the direct authority of the president.

By uncoupling the presidency and the prime ministry, Bendjedid had managed to transform Boumediene's legacy of a security state into a less Sovietized monitoring structure. But he was wary of the intrigues of his subordinate Mamelouks. A military man by profession, he could trust only a fellow general to handle such a sensitive job. That was the mission assigned in 1986 to Larbi Belkheir, first as secretary general of the presidency, then as director of the president's cabinet. The next chapter will explore how Belkheir eventually sided with the other Mamluk leaders against his constitutional master.

Yemeni Bipolarity

Imam Yahya had secured the independence of the main part of Yemen in 1918, while Aden and its hinterland remained a British colony. Sixteen years later, two treaties settled the borders of the Yemeni kingdom with 'Occupied Southern Yemen' and Saudi Arabia. Fiercely isolationist, adamantly reactionary, Imam Yahya relied on his genealogical prestige as a religious leader (he was 65th in a thousand-year line of imams). Half of his 5 million subjects shared his Zaydi creed, a local offshoot of Shiism, but only 100,000 aristocrats (*sayyid*, plural *sada*) could access economic or political power. The other half, consisting of Sunni Yemenis, were thoroughly marginalized.

Imam Yahya nominated his eldest son Ahmad as crown prince. This move infuriated Prince Ibrahim, another of his fourteen sons, and led him to join the Free Yemeni movement in Aden, now calling for constitutional monarchy. In February 1948, Imam Yahya was ambushed near Sanaa along with his prime minister. The Yemeni king died gallantly at the age of 79, his body ridden with machine-gun bullets, trying to protect one of his grandsons.

Crown Prince Ahmad gathered a crowd of tribesmen in Taez, outraged by the assassination of the Imam. They moved to Sanaa to besiege and plunder the city associated with such a sacrilege. The main plotters were soon executed, while Prince Ibrahim died in jail of a 'heart attack'.[35] The new Imam Ahmad chose Taez as his capital. In April 1955 the king suppressed an attempted coup by one of his brothers, Prince Abdullah, whom he ordered to be beheaded.

The 1948 and 1955 failed plots were not aiming at toppling the Imamate, but at reforming it. Things changed dramatically when the Egyptian Mamluks vowed to fight both 'colonialism' in South Yemen and 'reaction' in the North. In March 1961, Imam Ahmad was seriously wounded when trapped in the Hodeida hospital. Colonel Abdullah Sallal, the Hodeida commander (and an Egyptian agent) was organising the plot, but escaped the subsequent crackdown.

The Syrian secession from Egypt-led UAR emboldened Imam Ahmad publicly to defy Nasser. In December 1961, he used a radio-broadcast poem to vilify those who 'shout over the microphone with every incongruous voice'.[36] The Egyptian propaganda retaliated by calling for revolution in Yemen. When Imam Ahmad died peacefully in September 1962, the designated heir and new king, Mohammad al-Badr, was a pro-Egyptian reformist: his reign started with a general amnesty and the nomination of Abdullah Sallal as chief of staff.

Imam Badr ruled for only eight days before Sallal toppled him. Badr was declared dead by the revolutionary propaganda, but the deposed king, though wounded, had managed to escape to Saudi Arabia. Sallal soon promoted himself to general, then field marshal, a meteoric ascension reminiscent of Amer's 'career'. Field Marshal Amer indeed visited Sanaa just after the coup, leaving an Egyptian imprimateur all over the new leadership. A Republic was proclaimed by the Yemeni 'Free Officers' who, like their Egyptian mentors a decade earlier, constituted a Revolutionary Command Council (RCC).

Nasser and his allies had needed many years to achieve, in a far more advanced Egyptian society, what their Yemeni disciples vowed to complete in just a few weeks. But the Yemeni army was no match for the wide tribal coalition that soon rose in defence of the Imamate. So the Egyptian Mamluks had to step in to prevent their protégés' collapse. The leadership struggle in Cairo also favoured the intervention: Amer, challenged by Nasser as commander-in chief, bet on a quick war to consolidate his position, but once the invasion had started, defeat was the unthinkable option, which led to a rapid escalation in hostilities.

Sadat, one of Nasser's closest supporters, was also pushing for an all-out war, basically to punish Saudi Arabia for supporting the break-up of the union with Syria.[37] Yemen would then become the main battlefield for the 'war by proxy' waged between Cairo and Riyadh, a fight that Nasser was confident of winning. By the end of 1962, the Egyptian expeditionary force numbered 13,000 soldiers but this eventually increased to 70,000 Egyptian military personnel in Yemen.[38] Egyptian 'counsellors' were now shadowing every Republican official.

The Yemeni Republic was officially recognized by both USSR and USA. But it controlled only half the country, including Sanaa, Taez and Hodeida (the main entry port of entry for Egyptian supplies and reinforcements), while the royalists, strongly backed by Saudi Arabia, held fast in the northern and eastern highlands. Despite its overwhelming superiority in tanks, artillery and its monopoly over the air force, the Egyptian–Republican camp was not able to win a significant victory. Nor did air raids on Saudi border towns succeed in dismantling the rear bases of the royalist insurgency.

Nasser's visit to Yemen, in April 1964, precipitated the adoption of a new constitution, with a Yemeni Popular Union mimicking the Egyptian ASU. Republican dissidents became increasingly uneasy with the constant Egyptian interference. Marshal Sallal had concentrated the presidency, the prime ministership and the party leadership in his own hands, along with the supreme command of the armed forces. Beheading was no longer implemented, but firing squads were kept quite active against various forms of dissent.

In September 1966, a prominent Republican delegation travelled to Cairo to protest against Sallal's dictatorship. They were detained by their Egyptian hosts, since the Mamluk ruling tandem was gambling on the total victory of his Yemeni protégé: Nasser dreamed of extending his protectorate over a British-free South Yemen, while Amer intensified his offensives in order to quell the royalist guerrillas.

Poison gas had previously been tested on a small and limited scale by the Egyptian forces in Yemen, despite their claim to be using only napalm. But the late 1966 escalation led to several air raids in which chemical weapons were used, the targets being royalist strongholds that had to be annihilated. The worst poison gas attack occurred in January 1967, when hundreds were killed in the Egyptian bombing of Kitaf,[39] some 300 km north of Sanaa.

Nasser and Amer were both anxious not to leave the Yemeni prize to be seized by the other. As we saw above, this power struggle, and Yemeni shortsightedness, contributed to the disaster of the 'Six Day War'. Nasser could then get rid of Amer, but to do so he had to settle the Yemeni dispute with King Faisal of Saudi Arabia. An agreement was reached on the withdrawal of

Egyptian forces from Yemen. The abandoned Sallal turned angrily against Nasser, but was deposed in a bloodless coup (a rare occurrence in Yemen) while visiting Baghdad in November 1967.

The Egyptian retreat played into the hands of the royalist forces who closed in on Sanaa in the final days of late 1967. The besieged Republicans, led by Abdurahman al-Iryani, a religious judge, were now directly supported by the Soviet Union and adamantly rejected any form of monarchy, even a constitutional one. Their heroic resistance, celebrated as the 'Seventy Days Battle', succeeded in breaking the siege of the capital city and later in reopening the vital route to Hodeida. Meanwhile the National Liberation Front (NFL) had taken over from the British after the latter's withdrawal from Aden and 'South Arabia'.

The Marxist wing of the NFL eliminated its rivals in Aden in June 1969. This communist breakthrough forced Riyadh to reassess its Yemeni policy: striking a deal with pro-Western Republicans in the north appeared now more important than pushing for an elusive royalist victory. In July 1970, King Faysal recognized 'Sheikh' Iriyani as president of the Yemen Arab Republic (YAR). The disgruntled Imam Badr left Saudi Arabia for permanent exile in the United Kingdom. A few months later, South Yemen became officially a People's Democratic Republic (PDRY), the only such affiliate of the Soviet bloc in the Arab world.

For nearly a decade, YAR and PDRY would live their parallel and troubled political existences, with occasional clashes (in 1972 and 1974) and frequent trading of accusations. The two independent state systems functioned in a disconnected way, echoing the lack of impact of the North Yemeni civil war on the decolonization process of South Yemen

In July 1974, Iryani was exiled to Syria after a 'corrective movement', led by Colonel Ibrahim al-Hamdi.[40] Iryani would remain the only civilian president of the YAR. The army coup that ousted him was therefore, despite its 'corrective' ambition, different from the takeovers engineered by Assad and Sadat under the same name, since the Syrian and Egyptian 'corrections' were basically targeted at military rivals and/or threats.

Prior to 1974, Colonel Hamdi had been deputy to Iryani as president and commander of the armed forces. He then concentrated both civilian and military powers in his own hands. Hamdi inaugurated the era of the indigenous Mamluks and was, not unexpectedly, betrayed by his own chief of staff, Ahmad al-Ghashmi. Since Hamdi was largely popular, his assassination in October 1977 was never claimed by anyone or by any organisation. Various versions circulated, involving Saudi agents, or an ambitious young officer, one Ali Abdullah Saleh, whom Ghashmi appointed military governor of Taez after the killing.

What Hamdi's murder did unleash was bloody retribution. President Ghashmi was killed after only seven months in power, when a bomb, supposedly carried by a South Yemeni envoy, exploded in his office. This assassination triggered a coup in Aden, where Prime Minister Ali Nasir Mohammad toppled and executed President Salim Rubaï Ali (aka 'Salmin'). The new South Yemeni ruler replaced the NLF with a Soviet-style Yemeni Socialist Party (YSP).

In Sanaa, a four-member presidential council was formed, including the zealous Major Saleh, and in July 1978, the YAR parliament elected the 32-year-old as president. Now chief of staff, the new commander of the armed forces set in motion a brutal purge of the officer corps. Saleh appointed his own brother to the top job in the Central Security, the main police force. He designated the powerful General Ali Mohsen al-Ahmar from his own Sanhan tribe as commander of the first artillery brigade, positioned in the northern part of Sanaa.

The Sanhan tribe was a minor component of the highland confederation of Hashid, while the assassinated presidents Hamdi and Ghashmi belonged to a larger Hashid tribe, the Hamdan. The Hashid, along with their historic contenders/partners from the Bakil confederation, represented the main powers in the Zaydi tribal structure. But Saleh had also developed enduring connections with the Sunni business class of Taez, first as key officer on the 'whisky road' from Mocha (the main centre for smuggled alcohol), then as governor of Taez. Local merchants even chartered a plane to fly him to the presidential palace in 1978.[41]

So Saleh could bridge the regional and sectarian gap between the Zaydi highlands and the Sunni midlands. But his main challenge was to escape the brutal end meted out to his sundry predecessors. The security apparatus was therefore staffed with relatives, cronies and supporters. And that protection in the military hierarchy meant a blank cheque on tax exemption. As Stephen Day, a scholar of Yemeni politics, described it: 'like the Zaydi imams of old, president Saleh operated from his base in Sanaa, while drawing revenues from the high production regions to the south and west'.[42]

The echoing coups in Sanaa and Aden in 1978 boded ill for the destiny of the two parts of Yemen and their leaders. A border war flared up in 1979, with Marxist guerrilla groups operating in North Yemen over the next three years. Ali Nasir Mohammad soon wanted to settle this conflict with Saleh, but he met strong opposition within the Yemeni Socialist Party (YSP), led by the ultra-leftist Abdelfattah Ismaïl. The ceasefire option prevailed only in 1982. Ali Abdullah Saleh, then reassured on his southern flank, organized his own presidential party, the General Congress of the People (GCP).

Now at peace with its northern half, South Yemen became increasingly at war with its own self. In January 1986, the presidential security shot dead Abdelfattah Ismaïl and his main allies inside the very Political Bureau of the ruling YSP. The party and the military were split between warring factions that left thousands dead in a devastated Aden. Ali Nasir Mohammad had to flee to North Yemen with his supporters, while his enemies nominated Ali Salem al-Bid as head of state.

The People's Democratic Republic of Yemen (PDRY) was in a shambles. Its two central provinces of Abyan and Shabwa were now marginalised for appearing too favourable to the exiled president. The collapse of the Soviet bloc aggravated the crisis even further within its only Arab satellite state. Ali Abdullah Saleh knew how to use the South Yemeni dissidents he was protecting and hosting to ratchet up the pressure on Ali Salem al-Bid.

The North Yemeni president had become an expert at the game of checks and balances in order to weaken the various contending centres of power. He had appeased the paramount sheikh of the Hashid confederation, Abdullah bin Hussein al-Ahmar (who had dramatically left Sanaa in protest against Hamdi's presidency), he had maintained the 'tribal affairs' administration (when leftist South Yemen had vowed to erase tribal identity once and for all), but he had relied on his own patronage network to guarantee the loyalty of the security apparatus.

Saleh was also the beneficiary of the Marxist subversion campaign, which led to strong US and Saudi support for him in response, in line with the anti-Soviet and pro-Islamist covert action they undertook in Afghanistan. But the North Yemeni president shrewdly played on the competition between the Muslim Brotherhood in the Sunni midlands and Saudi-inspired Salafism in the tribal highlands, thereby preventing the dominance of one specific Islamist trend over the other. He also courted Saddam Hussein's favour to avoid being too dependent on Saudi Arabia.

The discovery of oil in Marib province, in 1984, reinforced Saleh's power in the years that followed. The North Yemeni president was clearly in a position of strength when he visited Aden, in November 1989, and signed an agreement on the unification of the country with Ali Salem al-Bid. He made sure he had the final say in the composition of the five-member presidential council (with three members from the North and two from the South). Saleh also wanted to merge his ruling GCP with the Yemeni Socialist Party, a revealing sign of his authoritarian vision of politics, though ultimately he had to concede the principle of party pluralism.

In May 1990, Saleh became the first president of the united Republic of Yemen, at the age of forty-four, with Ali Salem al-Bid as his deputy (the prime minister was a Southerner and his deputy a Northerner). His record in the Yemeni revolution had been pretty thin, even though he boasted of his participation in the 1967 'Seventy Days' battle in Sanaa. He had consolidated his one-man rule through a creative mix of tribal intrigue, military gambles and international manoeuvres. Unlike his fellow Mamluks in Egypt, Syria and Algeria, Saleh had not hijacked the independence of Yemen, but he had controlled for his sole benefit the unification between North and South.

*

Nasser might have easily passed as a contemporary Baybars. As always with such celebrated heroes, their alleged achievements are best assessed from a safe distance. A closer look quickly reveals how petty and vengeful those brave war commanders could become during domestic power struggles. Nasser had his Ayn Jalut moment in 1956, even though it was American power, and not the Egyptian military, that forced the complete withdrawal of the Israeli, British and French aggressors. But the myth of the twentieth-century Baybars, tarnished through the Syrian secession and the Yemeni quicksands, collapsed after the rout of the 'Six Day War'.

There is however one legacy of Baybars that remained a trademark of the modern Mamluks. Routine allegiance to the caliph, the paying of mere lip service to justify absolute power, was transformed into the phenomenon of unanimous plebiscites. The people had no more leverage on the 'elected' presidential Mamluk than the Abbassid caliph had over his 'subordinate' Mamluk sultan. The caliph lived, heavily guarded, under an unofficial form of house arrest, a situation comparable to that of the populations of the newly independent Arab states, who fell under the intimidating control of the security apparatus.

Modern Mamluk leaders needed the cyclical rite of mass plebiscites to rejuvenate their authority, as an echo of the loyalty pledged by the sultans of Cairo to the caliph of the day. Prayers and decisions were pronounced in the name of the powerless caliph, while contemporary constitutions and parties would extol the people as the only source of a power in fact monopolized by the Mamluk clique. Even Boumediene, after eleven years as Algerian president, and Saleh, nine years after the reunification of Yemen, felt the need to poll more than 96 per cent of the vote in carefully staged presidential elections.

Those electoral celebrations were farcical by democratic standards, but they were crucial for the smooth transition from one presidential sultan to the other, or to reinvigorate the populist capital of the ruling Mamluk. This is a fundamental difference between those Mamluk authoritarian regimes and the aspiring totalitarian systems established by Moammar Qaddafi in Libya and Saddam Hussein in Iraq.

After his anti-monarchy coup in 1969, Qaddafi had to heed the views of his fellow Free Officers, gathered in a Nasser-style Revolutionary Command Council (RCC). But a failed coup emanating from the very RCC, in 1975, led Qaddafi, two years later, to change the Libyan Arab Republic into a 'Jamahiriyya', literally a 'mass-ocracy'. Under the disguise of 'direct democracy', parties were abolished, revolutionary committees became ubiquitous and elections were vilified as an obsolete legacy of a 'reactionary past'.

Contrary to the Syrian Mamluks, it was as a civilian that Saddam Hussein rose steadily through the hierarchy of the Iraqi Baath. This party, already a leading force behind the 1963 coup, assumed a dominant position only five years later. Saddam was then appointed vice president of Iraq by his distant relative, Ahmad Hassan al-Bakr, head of state as well as of the party, and the former leader of the Baath military branch.

In 1979, Saddam forced Bakr to resign from all public posts because of his 'poor health' and concentrated unprecedented powers in his own hands. But the Iraqi despot was not interested in staging Mamluk-style electoral celebrations. He waited until 1995 to organize a referendum to endorse his presidency, a rite echoed in 2002. The 100 per cent positive 'result' disclosed a rationale designed mainly to defy the outside world, since Iraq was under tight UN sanctions.

In Egypt, in Syria, in Algeria and in Yemen, the disciples of Baybars had managed to control power and to retain it for decades, despite recurrent conflicts, intrigues and tensions. The following chapters will explore how their monopolistic streams of revenue and their redistribution contributed significantly to sustaining their regimes. It is however easier to maintain a caliph under eternal lock and key than perennially to suppress a population demanding liberty. The Algerian military would be the first to be hit by such popular protest and it was they who offer a way out of this dilemma to their fellow Mamluks: let the people or the caliph rot in their not so gilded cages; and never for one moment fail to fight ballots with bullets.

4

THE ALGERIAN MATRIX

The democratic uprising that shook the Arab world in early 2011 might have happened two decades earlier. This aborted 'first wave' went largely unnoticed as a regional phenomenon in a world obsessed, at the time, by the collapse of the Soviet bloc. But the end of the USSR and its empire sent shockwaves through the Arab regimes: they had often adopted the coercive techniques of the KGB and the political strategies of a one-party repressive system, no matter how close they were (or were moving) to the West. (Sadat's Egypt was the best illustration of this hysteresis of Soviet-like control, even after the peace was secured with Israel.)

There was also an onset of biological fatigue in regimes increasingly paralysed by an ageing leadership. 'President for Life' Bourguiba had become a caricature of his former self, enjoying only a few hours of lucidity every day. After crushing riots in 1978 and 1984, in which hundreds of protestors were killed, the Tunisian dictator sought to liquidate the Islamist opposition by sending to the gallows its most prominent activists.

Prime Minister Zine al-Abidine Ben Ali, a police general and former minister of the interior, staged a 'medical coup' on 7 November 1987. The 84-year-old despot was deemed senile and placed under house arrest. The Tunisian public welcomed with palpable relief this 'Jasmine Revolution'; the founding date of the new regime, 7 November, was celebrated from that moment on as the symbol of 'change' (echoing Boumediene's 'rectification' of 1965, or Assad's and Sadat's 'corrective' coups in 1970–71).

Bourguiba had nipped in the bud other potential Mamluks by emasculating the army, so the new uniformed ruler came from the police, rather than from the military. The single party changed its name (from Socialist Destourian Party/PSD to Constitutional Democratic Rally/RCD), albeit while pursuing its incestuous relationship with the security apparatus. After a year and a half of the 'Tunisian spring', the opposition in general, and the Islamists in particular, fell victim to the same vote-rigging and police repression. But Ben Ali had fulfilled the dream of any dictator: first, absolute power; then visible 'change' to avoid making any substantial concessions.

We saw how King Hussein of Jordan, after thirty-five years on the throne, had been forced in 1988 to sever his formal ties with the Palestinian West Bank, annexed to his Kingdom till its occupation by Israel in 1967. This dramatic decision was precipitated by pressure from the intifada that sought the establishment of an independent Palestinian state in the West Bank and Gaza. The monarch succeeded in defusing the Palestinian threat, but the recognition that Jordan was in fact only Transjordan was a startling reminder to the Hashemites of what their national project really amounted to.

In April 1989, riots erupted in and spread throughout the historically Bedouin parts of Jordan, from Maan to Tafileh, Kerak and Salt. Triggered by offcuts in government subsidies for basic commodities, the protest quickly escalated into demands for official accountability and condemnation of the state corruption. Instead of sending in the army, King Hussein agreed to hold the first parliamentary elections since 1967. The vote took place in

November 1989 and the Muslim Brotherhood gained twenty-two out of eighty seats (with twelve 'independent Islamists' being also elected as MPs).

The Islamist party was thus empowered to select the Speaker of the House, and a year later the Muslim Brotherhood entered government with five ministerial posts (and two more for 'independent Islamists'), including education, justice and agriculture. This engagement with the main opposition party ultimately proved beneficial to King Hussein and the stability of his regime. But the Jordanian monarch was no Mamluk, so he could afford to usher in domestic reforms without jeopardizing his legitimacy.

The republican dictatorships had no such room for manoeuvre. According to their worldview, democratization, even on a limited scale, could only ever be a zero-sum game, and they were far too well aware of their own unpopularity to relish the prospect on winning a free vote. They had escaped political concessions thanks to economic liberalization (Bendjedid in Algeria, Sadat and Mubarak in Egypt) or through territorial expansionism (via intervention in Lebanon for Assad and unification of the two Yemens for Saleh). Liberalization and expansion offered renewed opportunities for redistribution among the ruling elites and their protégés.

The crumbling of the Soviet system was a terrible blow for the modern Mamluks. But the main trigger for the aborted 'first wave' of Arab democratization was the 1986 oil counter-shock. Oil prices fell by half during that year and Algeria—much more vulnerable than Egypt, Syria or Yemen—was hit the hardest. Bendjedid, whose initial largesse had been financed on the back of the 1979 oil shock, was caught offguard, and defenceless. Algerian GDP growth slowed sharply, before turning negative in 1987 (-1.4 per cent) and 1988 (-2.7 per cent). The informal economy flourished, especially *trabendo*, as smuggling is called in Algeria, while popular protests against state institutions became increasingly common.

From Riots to Ballots

From 5 to 10 October 1988, rioting broke out in the Algeria's major cities, and hundreds of protesters were killed, most of them in Algiers itself. In the deceptive environment of Mamluk intrigues, each Algerian clan accused its rival of manipulating the crisis. Irrespective of who fuelled the flames, the situation quickly careered out of control. President Bendjedid proclaimed a state of emergency and General Khaled Nezzar, commander of the land forces, crushed the uprising with extreme brutality.

The Algerian military treated its fellow citizens with a ferocity akin to that deployed by a force of occupation. Tanks roamed urban centres, heavy machine-guns were fired at protest marchers and torture was widespread. Islamist leaders were called in to appease the demonstrators, yet crowds who gathered near militant mosques were harassed by the military. The immediate effect of these planned or unintended provocations was to enhance the political aura of Islamist dissent.

Bendjedid placed the blame on the political branch (DGPS) of the former Military Security (SM) and sacked its chief, General Ayat. Meanwhile Nezzar, the main architect of the 'iron fist' crackdown, was promoted to the resurrected position of Chief of Staff of the armed forces, a position that Boumediene had abolished in 1967 after an attempted coup. This restructuring of the top military hierarchy led to the retirement of most of the generals from the '1954 generation' who were associated with the anti-colonial liberation struggle against France. Bendjedid felt protected by 'his' two loyal generals, Belkheir (his right hand man at the presidency, who sat at the hub of political intrigue) and Nezzar (head of the armed forces), and he moved forcefully towards democratizing political détente.

Following the rites of the two previous presidential elections, a conference of the ruling FLN party endorsed Bendjedid as its sole candidate in December 1988, before the president was re-elected with 93.3 per cent of the vote (a marginal, but significant dip compared with the previous 99.4 per cent). Far more important was the constitutional referendum of February 1989: the 1976 reference to the 'socialist' state and to the FLN one-party system was abolished, while the independence of the judiciary was guaranteed. In the following months, clandestine parties were authorized (like Hocine Aït Ahmed's FFS 'front' or Ben Bella's MDA 'movement') and an Islamist party, the Front for Islamic Salvation (FIS in its French acronym), was legalized.

The vibrant populism of the 'old' FLN was reinvigorated in the 'new' FIS, with the same emphasis on an ideally monolithic Algerian community, cemented now by Islam more than by nationalism.[1] The FIS's celebration of private business struck deeper chords with the Algerian public than the obsolete 'industrialization first' slogans of the FLN. The popular rejection of bureaucratic corruption was such that the FIS emerged as a clear winner from the local elections of June 1990, with twice as many votes as the FLN (54 per cent against 28 per cent).

This landslide victory convinced Bendjedid that the reformist option was the only route out of confrontation. In July 1990 he became the first Algerian president in twenty-five years to relinquish the defence portfolio, assigned to General Nezzar, while General Abdelmalek Guenaizia, chief of the air force, was promoted to chief of staff.

However, the desire to 'civilize' the top state hierarchy was tarnished with the promotion of Nezzar, the main executioner of 'Black October' 1988. In the same ambiguous spirit, the dissolution of the DGPS was supposed to close the story of the ubiquitous SM, but the military soon reconstituted a DRS[2] (Department of Intelligence and Security), under Colonel Mohammad Mediene (aka Tewfik).

Parliamentary elections were scheduled for 27 June 1991, but the FLN-staffed National Assembly passed a gerrymandering law, with up to ten times fewer votes needed to elect an MP in a pro-FLN constituency than in a pro-FIS one. The Islamist party retaliated by launching a national strike on 25 May until the electoral law was repealed. Four days later, the government agreed to allow FIS militants to occupy peacefully designated public squares. Yet incidents and provocations escalated: Nezzar moved 10,000 soldiers and 200 tanks into Algiers, with Bendjedid proclaiming a state of siege.

As in October 1988, the army was once again in charge of internal security. The government promised 'free and fair' elections, but postponed them to December 1991. General Belkheir exited the presidency, where he was Bendjedid's director of the cabinet, to become minister of the interior. He was too intimate with Nezzar to even try to counterbalance the swing of the pendulum towards military repression. The newly promoted General Mediene fully restored the aggressiveness of the Military Security (SM) into his revamped Department of Intelligence and Security (DRS).

In July 1991, the top leadership of the FIS was arrested for having planned an 'insurrectionary strike'. When the state of siege was lifted, in September, hundreds of Islamist militants had been detained, with special camps to hold them set up in the Sahara. This intense repression triggered a fierce internal debate within the FIS, but the supporters of the political boycott lost the battle and their party agreed to run in the parliamentary elections.

The first round was held on 26 December 1991 and FIS reaped 47.5 per cent of the votes. There would be no second round: outraged by Bendjedid's readiness to share power with an Islamist-led government, Nezzar led a group of generals into the president's office and forced him to resign. A civilian front, a five-member 'Higher State Council', was established as cover for the military coup. A State of Emergency would become the norm over the next two decades.

The parallel with Ben Bella's 'rectification' and with the collapse of the Soviet Union is enlightening. As in 1965, the Algerian president was toppled by a minister of defence he trusted enough to appoint as his senior ally. But Boumediene's coup was a personal venture in pursuit of personal glory, while Nezzar moved as the senior leader of a collective 'decision-making' body. Ben Bella's ousting was a sequel to the power struggle of summer 1962 and completed the elimination of the FLN's founders, while Bendjedid's overthrow aborted the multi-party transition and signalled a return to the previous rules of the game.

Nezzar and his associates scorned Bendjedid as a dangerous Algerian version of Gorbachev, an elite member of a system who was bound to destroy it while pretending to 'reform' it. The Algerian top brass, convinced they were the guardians of the supreme interests of the nation, considered Bendjedid as a mere traitor and congratulated themselves on their clemency in sparing his life. No significant voice to defend Bendjedid emerged from within the military apparatus. Three decades after Algerian independence (won by FLN politicians, despite the defeat of the 'liberation army'), the Algerian Mamluks were now bracing themselves for a fully-fledged war. And this is exactly what they got.

The New World Order

The Algerian crisis was closely monitored by the Arab autocrats, more anxiously in Syria than in Egypt. Mubarak, the sole candidate, had been re-elected in 1987 for a second six-year mandate with 97 per cent of the vote. And in 1989, the Egyptian president had dismissed his far too popular minister of defence, Field Marshal Abu Ghazala, who quietly accepted his marginalization. More than a billion dollars of American military aid was allocated each year to the Egyptian armed forces, with a wide range of business investments now open to any member of the officer corps.

Hafez al-Assad was not worried by the loyalty of his military, but rather by the crumbling of the Soviet empire, which was eroding his international position, only years after he had boasted of soon attaining 'strategic parity' with Israel.[3] His hatred of the Muslim Brotherhood remained profound and he forced King Hussein to apologize publicly, in 1985, for Jordanian support of the Islamist uprising in Syria. Now Assad had to endure the Brotherhood's electoral victory in Jordan, where Prime Minister Mudar Badran was ready to include Islamist ministers in key positions. (In 1981, Syrian intelligence had tried to assassinate him.)[4]

However, Assad could enjoy the fulfilment of his Lebanese dream with the signing of the Taif Agreement in Saudi Arabia, in October 1989, and its endorsement by the Lebanese parliament the following month. Lakhdar Brahimi, the Algerian mediator who had conceived 'Taif', had enshrined Syrian guardianship over Lebanon. The Saudi kingdom blessed this formula because it enhanced the position of the Sunni prime minister, now responsible to parliament, while he used formerly to be accountable only to the Christian Maronite president of the Republic.

The first Christian president elected under the Taif formula, René Moawad, was killed in a bomb attack after only seventeen days in office. His successor, Elias Hrawi, was far more docile towards Syria (the parliamentary session that elected him was held in the Lebanese city of Chtaura, only a few km from the Syrian border). The same MPs approved the appointment of Selim Hoss, a Sunni veteran politician, as the new prime minister. But the Maronite General Michel Aoun, who had declared the 'war of liberation' against Syria in March 1989, continued to cling on as prime minister.

Assad waited for the most opportune moment to strike a fatal blow at Lebanese resistance to Syria. His arch-enemy Saddam Hussein facilitated such a move when Iraq invaded Kuwait and annexed it in August 1990. The panicked Saud family turned to George H. W. Bush for immediate assistance and demanded the deployment of American troops, soon to reach a six-figure number in the Arabian Peninsula. Nonetheless, Washington needed credible Arab partners to join the anti-Saddam coalition. Egypt and Syria topped the US wish list and Mubarak joined the fray with something approaching alacrity: his armed forces had not fought a foreign enemy since 1973 and a new generation of officers craved for combat experience in order to burnish their prestige. The Egyptian president also hoped to become the benevolent patron of Gulf security, finally erasing the disastrous legacy of Nasser's Yemen war.

Assad had much more to gain in terms of Saudi largesse and post-Soviet realignment. But, always shrewd and patient, he let the Bush administration up the ante. In October 1990, Washington tacitly approved Syrian intervention in Christian Beirut, where the Maronite stronghold of Aoun's followers was overrun (the defeated general took refuge in the French embassy, the only Western country to condemn the Syrian invasion).

Both Mubarak and Assad knew full well that their population, as in every Arab country beyond the Gulf, was supporting Saddam's vibrant attacks against Israel, America and its royal protégés. The Egyptian and Syrian despots could afford blatantly to ignore public opinion. But their fellow Mamluk, Ali Abdullah Saleh, was too new at the command of a unified Yemen to swim against the popular wave of pro-Iraqi solidarity.

The same happened with King Hussein of Jordan: East Bankers had prospered from the trade and smuggling with Iraq during its war against Iran (1980–88) and Palestinians were fascinated by the 'new Saladin' who dared to strike Israel with SCUD missiles. 'No East, no West, Iraq is best', 'Israel is a cancer, SCUD is the answer' were some of the slogans painted in downtown Amman in support of Saddam (in English, so the Western press would get the message).

The Muslim Brotherhood was also swept away by this powerful undercurrent. The Islamist leadership had to choose between its financial backers (in the Gulf) and its popular supporters (on the Arab street). The Brotherhood opted for the latter (and condemned the US deployment in Saudi Arabia), while trying to appease the former (opposing the annexation of Kuwait). This position infuriated the Saudis, who felt betrayed after so many decades of generous support for the Muslim Brothers.

Saudi Arabia was not slow in retaliating against the Brotherhood, cutting its stipends, expelling its cadres from their official positions, and even from the Kingdom. The downgraded Brothers were replaced by loyalist Salafis, also described as 'quietist' or 'scientific', who preached allegiance to the Saudi throne. A radical minority condemned both Salafi blind conformity and the Brotherhood's populist tendencies. This minority called for jihad against Saddam and America, until its most vocal leader, Usama Bin Laden, had to leave Saudi Arabia.

The closing months of 1990 saw a clear differentiation, throughout the Saudi–Iraqi crisis, between the three trends of 'Islamist' Brotherhood, 'Salafi' conservatism and 'jihadi' extremism. In January 1991, the US-led coalition launched a devastating air campaign against Iraq and in the final days of the following month a mass land offensive wiped out the Iraqi defences and liberated Kuwait.

The Iraqi opposition believed the moment was ripe to rise against Saddam's regime. In March 1991, most of the Kurdish north and the nine Shia-majority governorates, south of Baghdad, fell to armed insurgents. Entire military units defected in defiance of the defeated autocrat.[5] But the Bush administration did not want revolutionary change in the Middle East, so the US army stood aside while the remnants of Saddam's forces quelled the Iraqi resistance. The 'new Saladin' killed tens of thousands of Iraqis to restore its absolute power, and the aborted uprising was officially called 'the page of betrayal and treason'.[6]

Washington abandoned the Iraqi rebels, even though it would have supported an anti-Saddam coup.[7] Strict UN sanctions were imposed on Iraq, leaving Saddam a free hand on his domestic front, but boxing him in within his country's borders. Saudi Arabia was perfectly happy with the liberation of Kuwait, since it feared Iranian influence in post-Saddam Iraq. The Egyptian and Syrian Mamluks had been lavishly rewarded for their contribution to the US-led Coalition, and they could use Saddam as an ideal bogeyman to keep pumping financial support from the Gulf.

The Iraqi dictator was therefore spared, but his Arab allies were severely punished by the Gulf countries. Hundreds of thousands of Yemeni and Jordanian nationals were expelled from Saudi Arabia, Kuwait and the United Arab Emirates. The combined effect of this mass repatriation and the loss of remittances was serious for the already fragile economies of Jordan and Yemen. This compelled King Hussein and Ali Abdullah Saleh to foster consensus amid such a volatile political and economic environment (the Yemeni constitution of May 1991 guaranteed free elections and a multi-party system, even though the first pluralistic elections would be held only two years later).

Meanwhile America's leaders felt the clock was ticking for the USSR and therefore worked to establish a post-Soviet 'new world order'. The Middle East seemed, after the forceful liberation of Kuwait, the best region to promote such a US-inspired 'order'. This paved the way for the October 1991 Madrid Peace Conference involving Israel, Syria, Lebanon and Jordan (along with a Palestinian delegation under the Jordanian flag). George H. W. Bush courteously invited Mikhail Gorbachev to join him as a co-sponsor of the event, even though the Soviet Union would disintegrate soon afterwards.

Madrid was a failure in terms of the 'peace process' and there was no breakthrough in the parallel talks that were held. Still, it consolidated US leadership in the Middle East. Jordan was then absolved from its pro-Saddam transgressions, thanks to its peace option with Israel and its containment of Palestinian nationalism. And Syria was strongly committed to a *Pax Americana* that would jeopardize neither its alliance with Moscow or with Tehran.

Ali Abdullah Saleh's rehabilitation took much longer and he had to endure the lasting resentment of the Saudi royal family. On top of that, a unified Yemen presented a strategic threat as far as Saudi officials were concerned, which is why they discreetly assisted the Southern secessionist movement that proclaimed a Democratic Republic of Yemen (DRY) in Aden, in May 1994. Washington condemned the split, so Riyadh had to keep a low profile, letting the DRY collapse after a few weeks. In October, Saleh was elected president through a parliamentary vote in a still deeply divided country.

The 'first wave' of the Arab quest for democracy struck the Algerian regime at its very core, but it had been absorbed within the broader Middle East by the Kuwait crisis and its aftermath. Egyptian Mamluks, and their Syrian equivalents even more so, had benefited from the confrontation where they served as mercenaries of the Gulf countries, under US leadership. This episode proved how the classical oil dividend could be multiplied by the geopolitical bounty attached to the 'new world order'. It would take ten more years for the Algerian and Yemeni Mamluks to find their own way to plug directly into those resources.

The Generals' War

The Algerian top brass closely scrutinized Washington's passivity as Saddam Hussein quelled the March 1991 Iraqi uprising by means of a terrible bloodbath. They became convinced that the now sole superpower was far more interested in stability, even in its 'iron fist' version, than in democracy, especially if this opened the gates to Islamist unpredictability. It was crucial for the Algerian military to rely on, at least, the benign neglect of America, now that USSR was disappearing from the scene.

The generals who toppled Bendjedid in January 1992 also paid close attention to the French reaction. Some key actors in the coup, like Nezzar or Belkheir, had started their careers as

NCOs in the colonial forces before defecting to the FLN, where they were known as DAF ('Defectors from the French Army'). During the power struggles of the 1960s and 1970s, they had to claim and reclaim their nationalist credentials and to join the fray against the mythical 'French party' (*hizb Fransa*).

On the opposite shore of the Mediterranean, French politicians laboured under a severe guilt complex towards Algeria for decades, given the horrendous toll of its 'liberation war'. François Mitterrand, elected President in 1981, struck a major gas deal with Chadli Bendjedid the following year: the French government would pay an additional 14 per cent on top of the going market price as a substantial contribution to Algerian development.[8] But the French negotiating team discovered that their Algerian counterparts were less interested in development issues than in securing the rulers' grasp over this new income stream.[9]

The aura of 'socialist Algeria' therefore faded in the eyes of the socialist French president. He knew too well how any clear-cut statement about the post-1988 crisis would be rejected as intolerable interference from the former colonial power. So, when asked in a press conference about Bendjedid's overthrow, Mitterrand was careful to describe such a 'resignation' as a 'rather unusual act'. After having solemnly recalled his respect for Algerian sovereignty, he advised 'the Algerian leaders' to 'resume the necessary democratization, for which free elections are a prerequisite'.[10]

This comment, no matter how cautiously expressed, was received by the Algerian military with self-righteous fury. The official propaganda machine turned this isolated quote from Mitterrand into a whole volume of arguments depicting the FIS as the sinister creation of French neo-colonialism with, of course, the army as the brave defender of Algerian independence. This revamping of the 'liberation struggle' narrative might have appeared far-fetched, but it was soon echoed throughout the government-controlled media.

Nezzar was no Boumediene. In true Mamluk style, he believed the supreme interests of the Algerian state were best served when equated with the vision of the top brass and the preservation of its corporative interests. Bendjedid's sacking was not the opening act of a personal dictatorship, but the result of a collective initiative endorsed by the decision-makers, the ominous *décideurs* whose shadow loomed over Algeria as it bled throughout its new civil war.

Many lists of the so-called decision-makers circulated and they were all probably accurate, since this amorphous entity was not a structured body, but rather a coalition of major power-brokers (and warlords fighting against a significant proportion of their fellow citizens, whom they branded as 'terrorists'). But it is fair to assume that the January 1992 nucleus comprised the following generals: ministers Nezzar (defence) and Belkheir (interior), chief of staff Guenaizia, DRS chief Mediene, land forces chief Mohammad Lamari, and gendarmerie chief Ben Abbès Ghezaiel.

We have seen that these discreet 'decision-makers' had chosen a collective front leadership, the Higher State Council (HCE), to be publicly charged with executive power in the coming two years. In order to buttress the nationalist legitimacy of this HCE, the military 'decision-makers' brought back Mohammad Boudiaf (one of the FLN 'founding nine') from his twenty-eight-year exile. Boudiaf, as chair of the HCE, was officially the Algerian head of state, but he had absolutely no leverage over the real power centres.

In February 1992, the State of Emergency was reinforced, soon leading to the dissolution of the FIS (as a party) and of the Islamist-led municipalities. Dozens of protesters were killed after Friday prayers. Thousands of opponents were detained, sometimes transferred to the Sahara relegation camps, while an increasing number of 'suspects' went missing. Boudiaf might have believed (rightly) that this devastating repression was only fuelling the radical insurgency. Anyway, he was killed in June by one of his bodyguards, during a political rally at Annaba.

Boudiaf's assassin, a junior officer with controversial links to the DRS, was first portrayed as an Islamist 'lone wolf', before the investigation revealed major breaches in presidential security. The real mastermind behind the Annaba murder was never uncovered, but this drama proved how Mamluk-fuelled violence would not spare any quarter. Boudiaf's successor as HCE chair was the innocuous Ali Kafi, a former colonel in the anti-French guerrilla forces, turned ambassador after 1962, and now secretary general of the veterans' organization, a stronghold of FLN orthodoxy and patronage.

During spring 1992, the military announced 'the dismantling of two-thirds of the subversive groups'.[11] The FIS had indeed suffered terrible blows (its two leaders, Abassi Madani and Ali Benhadj, received twelve-year sentences from a military tribunal). But the FIS was vulnerable because of its legalist approach, while close-knit jihadi groups, each with its own commander/ *émir*, had prepared for a confrontation that they deemed inevitable. Those jihadi organizations eventually formed the loose coalition of the Islamic Armed Group (GIA).[12]

An unprecedented escalation of violence occurred in 1993 and 1994, with up to 500 people killed each week. A special anti-guerrilla corps was set up based on elite units drawn from the army, gendarmerie and police, with an initial force of 15,000 members, soon to be quadrupled.[13] The shadow of the hooded 'Ninjas', as the police commandos were nicknamed, loomed over the country. Militias were formed initially for self-defence, then to assist the military against the insurgency, in an ominous re-enactment of the French-led *harkis* (auxiliaries) against the FLN. Communal guards were recruited en masse to patrol and safeguard urban centres, once the military had 'cleared' them of 'terrorists'.

The Algerian Mamluks wanted nothing less than the 'eradication', as they declared, of the so-called 'terrorists', a catch-all category that amalgamated Islamist and jihadi activists, but also secular opponents of the military junta. Diplomatic relations were severed with Iran, and with Sudan, accused of supporting terrorism in Algeria. But the expectations of a quick and definitive victory in spring 1992 had faded away. The need to adapt to a sustained war forced the 'decision-makers' to a major reshuffle of their power structure in July 1993.

Nezzar left the defence portfolio to a fellow general, Lamine Zeroual, who had been marginalized since 1990. Since Zeroual had no personal constituency within the armed forces, Nezzar retained substantial power from behind the scenes even though he was 'off duty'. Mohammad Lamari became chief of staff, while Guenaizia was exiled to the Algerian embassy in Switzerland. Mediene's deputy at the DRS, Colonel Smaïn Lamari, was promoted to general as a sign of the major role played by military intelligence in the conflict.

Kasdi Merbah, who had run the Military Security (SM, now DRS) under Boumediene, had acquired the status of 'godfather' in the intelligence underworld. His killing in an eastern suburb of Algiers, in August 1993, left Algerians stricken, no matter how prepared for the worst they were since Boudiaf's assassination. Merbah's son, brother and driver were shot dead in the same ambush, which the authorities blamed on the GIA. The FIS, on the contrary, accused the regime itself of this murder.

In January 1994, Zeroual succeeded Kafi as HCE chair. His conciliatory tone appeased the outside world, while the violence in Algeria continued unabated. This time, Belkheir opted for a golden exile in Switzerland, where his friend Guenaizia was already ambassador. The new minister of the interior, Meziane Cherif, was a civilian, but a fanatical 'eradicator'. Nezzar kept pulling many of the strings from the wings.

The GIA had five successive commanders during those two years. Some *émirs* were killed in combat, others were purged or disappeared in murky circumstances. Rival Islamist groups accused the military, and especially the DRS, of manipulating and infiltrating the GIA in order to divide, radicalize and isolate the insurgency.[14] French-speaking professionals and intellectuals became routine targets for GIA killings, before the jihadi commandos started attacking foreigners as well.

By the end of 1994, estimates circulated that about 40,000 people had been killed in nearly three years of civil war. The military repression, far from containing the guerrilla forces, had boosted them from 2,000 fighters in 1992 to 22,000 in 1993 and 40,000 in 1994, when the FIS, tired of waiting for a political breakthrough, launched its own armed wing, the Islamic Salvation Army (AIS). Such human devastation led the main political parties to gather on neutral territory in Rome to discuss a way out of the crisis.

The talks, held under the auspices of the Sant'Egidio Catholic community, prepared the adoption, in January 1995, of a 'platform for a political and peaceful solution'. The FLN had, significantly, joined forces with the FFS and the FIS (along with Ben Bella's MDA and other smaller groups) on that occasion. But the Algerian Mamluks, now fully dissociated from the FLN, refused any 'political solution' that would turn back the clock to the 1991 electoral logic.

The military junta set the stage for a radical revamping of the political scene. First, an alleged attempted breakout from the Serkadji prison, in February 1995, was treated as a 'mutiny' and savagely dealt with by the authorities: more than a hundred detainees were killed, including many FIS officials. Second, Mahfoudh Nahnah, a reformed Muslim Brother who had always distanced himself from the FIS, launched his Movement of Society for Peace (MSP, or Hamas in its Arab acronym).

Finally, presidential elections were scheduled for November 1995. The FLN, FIS and FFS, in line with their Sant'Egidio platform, called for a boycott. But the turnout was impressive, even if it was far below the official 71 per cent: war fatigue had driven the population to the polls, in the hope of halting the disaster. On election day, some 350,000 military personnel were deployed[15] (to control slightly fewer than 30 million Algerians). Zeroual won with 61 per cent of the vote, against 25 per cent for Nahnah, who had attracted a significant chunk of the former FIS's electoral support.

The new president could now impose a 'national dialogue' on his own terms. The FIS, still illegal, remained excluded, but the FLN and the FFS were invited in to the political fold. Zeroual's political adviser, Ahmed Ouyahia, became his first prime minister of the new era. In November 1996, amendments to the seven-year-old constitution were approved by referendum: the Berber identity of Algeria was enshrined alongside to the Arab and Islamic one; any religion-based party was banned; and the president could run for only two terms of office.

Parliamentary elections were held in June 1997 and a new presidential party, the National Democratic Rally (RND), was established a few months before the vote. The state machine fully backed the RND, which won 156 of the 380 seats (69 for the MSP, 62 for the FLN and 20 for the FFS). Pro-regime analysts hailed the fact that the system was so pluralistic that the ruling party had not reached a clear-cut majority. But others underlined the de-legitimization of those parties that had dominated the 1991 elections, and were now banned (FIS) or marginalized (FLN and FFS).

From that moment on, official figures about electoral turnout had very little to do with the actual reality, but became milestones to calibrate the relative importance of the various elections. Since the official turnout for the presidential vote in 1995 was 71 per cent, the one set for the 1997 parliamentary contest was 65 per cent (with unofficial estimates around 45 per cent, and only 36 per cent in Algiers). European observers denounced various irregularities, even though the Arab League team complimented the Algerian authorities.

This institutional updating took place against the background of a horrendous wave of mass killings (punctuated by bomb explosions in urban centres). Some 4,000 civilians were killed in 1997 in a series of attacks against defenceless localities where many were mercilessly butchered. The climax of horror was reached at Bentalha, in late September, and at Relizane, at the end of December, with hundreds of innocent people massacred in each place. These crimes were mainly attributed to the GIA, its internal purges, the all-out war declared against the rival AIS, and the terror spiral unleashed against any kind of dissent.[16]

Others accused the military of passive complicity (especially in greater Algiers) at the least, and at the worst of waging a 'dirty war' against the population itself,[17] in order to 'eradicate' not only the Islamist networks, but also their political base. Foreign human rights NGOs called for an international investigation into the massacres. Amnesty International estimated that around 80,000 people had been killed during the six years of the crisis, accusing security forces and pro-government militias as well as 'Islamic groups'.[18]

This descent into hell certainly broke the backbone of the insurgency. In September 1997, the AIS accepted a ceasefire. One year later, the Salafist Group for Preaching and Combat (GSPC) pledged to fight only the security forces and seceded from the GIA, then downsized to only a shadow of its former self. Massacres were still frequent, but their scale was smaller in 1998 than in 1997. The military had seemingly abandoned the folly of 'eradication' and seemed ready to tolerate a measure of 'residual terrorism' (after General Smaïn Lamari, the DRS deputy chief, had conducted secret talks with the AIS).[19]

This reality check dealt a fatal blow to Zeroual's power. An unprecedented press campaign targeted the president's military adviser, Mohammad Betchine, a former intelligence general, forcing him to resign. The head of state, whose mandate ended only in late 2000, had to concede defeat: Zeroual announced his withdrawal and set anticipated elections for early 1999. Such an aborted experience reopened old wounds inside the Mamluk camp. After years of dealing in a consensual way with the worst crisis of independent Algeria, the top brass appeared more confused than divided.

The three pillars of the system (Mohammad Lamari as chief of staff, 'Tewfik' Mediene as DRS chief and Ghezaiel as gendarmerie chief until 1997) agreed to let one of their fellow plotters, the Swiss-based Belkheir, design an exit formula. With Zeroual now out of the game, the option of a retired general was no longer valid. But Belkheir, unable to think outside the Mamluk frame, rewound the tape of the power struggles of the previous decades. He stopped at year 1980, when Bendjedid had pushed Bouteflika into exile.

Boumediene's minister of foreign affairs had been living in Abu Dhabi for most of those eighteen years. Belkheir convinced the military 'decision-makers' that Bouteflika was the best choice, at least by default: he would let them run the country while rejuvenating some of the international prestige of 1970s Algeria. The fact that Bouteflika could be considered a 'new' man was a startling indication of how fossilized the Mamluk vision had become through years of security intrigue and counter-insurgency planning.

But the main actor of the 1992 coup, retired General Nezzar, remained strongly prejudiced against Bouteflika. He accused him of opportunism and cowardice, calling him a nag (*canasson*).[20] Nezzar claimed that Bouteflika had coveted the presidency in 1994 throughout his private meetings with the military 'decision-makers', but that he had finally dropped out for fear of an Islamist victory in the civil war.[21] Belkheir tried to appease Nezzar, to no avail. The Bouteflika operation went ahead as planned and the side-lined Nezzar continued to vent his frustration to the media.

In December 1998, Bouteflika declared he was running as an 'independent' candidate for the presidential race. The state mobilization on his behalf was so blatant that the six other candidates withdrew before the April 1999 vote. But the regime insisted on still submitting their ballots, along with Bouteflika's, to the Algerian electorate. In this unique situation, Bouteflika romped home with 73 per cent of the votes cast against six challengers who refused to have their votes counted.

The most revealing dimension in such a bizarre contest was the 12.5 per cent votes that went in favour of Ahmed Taleb Ibrahimi. Not only had this veteran minister of Boumediene and Bendjedid refused to run, like the other five opponents; but he had kept accusing the military intelligence (DRS, former SM) of various crimes, while reaching out to the militants of the banned FIS. Thus a highly symbolic vote had been cast in defiance of the military's 'Islamist terrorism' narrative.

Official participation was set at 60 per cent, but the real turnout was closer to the disturbing figure of 23 per cent.[22] This was not the most promising début for the 'independent' head of state. Bouteflika therefore decided to play it safe and appointed as his cabinet head the very same Belkheir who had occupied that position under Bendjedid. A civilian outsider in this Mamluk world, the Algerian president now had to bring the war to a close without upsetting his military kingmakers.

Bouteflika's Reconciliation

The new president enjoyed a very personal revenge when he was sworn in just after his frustrating plebiscite. Amar Benaouna, the chief of protocol who bestowed upon him the insignia of the supreme rank of the Algerian Republic, had chaired in 1980 the FLN investigation committee that had charged Bouteflika with embezzlement and subsequently expelled him from the party. Benaouna could only now cry publicly when honouring the new head of state. But while the regime old guard was settling its accounts, Algeria remained engulfed in violence and despair.

In June 1999 Bouteflika mentioned in a press conference a death toll of more than 100,000 in the course of the civil war.[23] Not a day passed without fresh casualties. Relatives of the 'missing', the colloquial designation for those citizens abducted by the security apparatus, kept demanding even a modicum of truth (5,000 missing citizens was the conservative estimate). The FIS military and political wings were calling for the implementation of (secret) agreements accepted by the Algerian regime.

Bouteflika dramatically ordered the release of more than 2,000 political detainees on 5 July 1999, Independence Day. Two months later, a referendum was held on one question: 'Do you support the President's general approach to achieve peace and civilian reconciliation?' Officially, the turnout was set at an unbelievable 85 per cent, with 98.6 per cent of the vote being positive. Bouteflika had managed to compensate for the (relative) humiliation of his presidential poll in April 1999 by having the population identify him the following September as the great defender of the elusive peace that so many Algerians had been longing for.

A presidential amnesty was offered to insurgents who agreed to lay down their weapons before January 1990. Government sources announced that some 5,500 Islamist guerrillas were disarmed and pardoned through this process.[24] Hardened terrorists were therefore treated with more clemency than some political opponents who remained in detention without ever having carried a gun. Abassi Madani and Ali Benhadj, the two civilian leaders of the ex-FIS, had been released from jail in 1997 only to be put under house arrest, while seasoned AIS combatants, once they were pardoned, were free to start a new life.

The Algerian Mamluks had forced their red line on president Bouteflika, even though he insisted on remaining his own minister of defence; the military were ready to accept the end of hostilities and to reintegrate their former enemies, but they would never tolerate the reconstitution of an Islamist party. This is why

Ahmed Taleb Ibrahimi's Wafa party was never authorized. The two most powerful generals, Lamari as chief of staff and Mediene as DRS chief, would not budge on that issue, and they imposed as minister of the interior 'Yazid' Zerhouni, who had run military intelligence from 1979 to 1982.

The political impasse was imposed at a heavy price on the Algerian public, with a monthly toll of some 200 killed. Local riots flared each time a defiant community sought to push its own demands or protest against the state. The traditionally restive Kabylia experienced a 'dark spring' in 2001, with dozens of protesters killed by the security forces. Even Algiers was rocked by violent demonstrations in favour of the Berber language and Kabylian autonomy.

The crisis of the Algerian state was even more shocking when hundreds of civilians died from devastating floods in Bab el-Oued in November 2001. Interestingly, this Algiers neighbourhood had been a stronghold of the FLN during the 'liberation war' against France, and Islamist cells had operated there during the 1990s. This led some observers to blame the catastrophic floods on the cementing of the sewage system by the security forces, anxious to close such 'terrorist' escape routes.

Ali Benflis, Bouteflika's prime minister since August 2000, was also leader of the FLN. When he visited Bab al-Oued after the floods, he was stoned and expelled by the furious population. Three weeks later, by contrast, Bouteflika mingled with the locals. However, the Algerian president had come with his French counterpart, Jacques Chirac, while excited youngsters shouted for 'Chirac' and for 'visas' (to France).

Bouteflika, hoping to appease the Kabylian unrest, encouraged an amendment to the Algerian Constitution that upgraded Berber as the 'national language' (Arabic being the 'official' one) in April 2002. This fell far short of stopping the cycle of riots and strikes in Kabylia, where the gendarmerie and the police were often loathed (and fought) as occupying forces. A bomb attack killed 35 people in Larbaa (25 km south of Algiers), marring the fortieth anniversary of Algerian independence; a tragic reminder of how terrorism was still a deadly threat.

The president sacked Benflis and chose Ouyahia as his new prime minister in May 2003. He knew that the top brass trusted Ouyahia, who had already run the government under Zeroual. Chief of staff Lamari felt bold enough to challenge Bouteflika publicly in the Egyptian press: 'our democratic experience is incomplete, but we are at the beginning of the path. Democracy is not a decision, it is the result of many years of struggle.'[25]

The defiant general claimed responsibility for the January 1992 coup against a 'suicidal process'.[26] He also endorsed three revealing figures: 150,000 killed in the civil war and a number of 'terrorists' reduced in a decade from 27,000 to 'around only 700, which does not represent a threat to the Republic and its institutions'.[27] Bouteflika, warned in such a blatant way, had to renounce any grand deal with the ex-FIS or Wafa. He could only liberate Madani from his house arrest. The released Islamist leader soon settled in Qatar, while Benhadj refused any presidential pardon.

For his second run as an 'independent' candidate in April 2004, Bouteflika had no more serious challenger than his former PM, Ali Benflis, the champion of the FLN. Bouteflika came out on top with 85 per cent of the vote against 6.5 per cent for Benflis, with a 58 per cent official turnout that nobody could be even bothered to satirise. Deprived of an electoral triumph for a second time, Bouteflika tried to reiterate his 1999 'concord' manoeuvre to reboot his personal legitimacy.

A 'charter for peace and national reconciliation' was drafted: reformed insurgents would be pardoned, except in cases of mass killings, bomb attacks and rape; but the FIS would remain banned and the 'missing' would disappear into official oblivion. Bouteflika had to concede this major denial of justice to his unrepentant top brass. In September 2005 a referendum was held on the charter, with 97 per cent approval (but official turn-out as low as 11 per cent, for instance in the Kabylian province of Tizi Ouzou).

A Presidential Mummy

The Algerian Mamluks had their quiet moment of glory when Bouteflika, acting as minister of defence, promoted three of them to the supreme rank of army general (*général de corps d'armée*) in July 2006. Mohammad Lamari was the only one ever to have attained this distinction, back in 1995. Retired, he advanced to the same lofty position his loyal successor as chief of staff, the Russian-speaker Ahmad Gaïd Salah. The two other promotions involved the main plotters of the 1992 coup: 'Tewfik' Mediene, the irremovable DRS chief, and Abbès Ghezaïel, the former gendarmerie chief, now in charge of 'coordinating' military operations from a modest office at the ministry. Guenaizia, their fellow plotter in 1992, had retired from the army long ago, but he had organized this game of musical chairs as ... deputy minister of defence.

People could vote, referendums could be held, laws could be passed. While Bouteflika could be president and minister of defence at the same time, the real decision-makers never loosened their grip on power (for instance, their protégé at the ministry of interior, 'Yazid' Zerhouni, retained this portfolio for eleven years under Bouteflika).

The military clique knew how to play on the president's (poor) health and (great) ambition. Bouteflika had spent December 2005 in Paris, where he was operated on for a stomach complaint at the Val-de-Grâce military hospital. Though the irony of the president being cured by the former colonial power did not go unnoticed among the Algerian public, Bouteflika had succeeded in being identified with the 'reconciliation' and the end of the nationwide bloodbath.

The president's brother, Said Bouteflika, had officially become his 'special adviser'. Said's rising influence clashed with Belkheir's clout, and the director of the cabinet had to leave the Mouradia Palace, the seat of the presidency, to become ambassador to Morocco. The resulting confusion between government affairs and family business eventually played into the hands of the intelligence apparatus, ready to document shady deals and dirty secrets.

Abdelaziz Bouteflika spent hours entertaining his foreign hosts at the Mouradia, and his long-winded speeches left his visitors with a disturbing feeling of unreality. The Algerian president was obsessed with his own re-election, while the constitution limited him to two five-year mandates. He therefore devoted considerable time and energy to having the constitution amended by a public vote in parliament (21 MPs dared to oppose the 'reform' measure against 500 who supported it) in November 2008.

Bouteflika could no longer pursue the fiction of running as an 'independent' so he was officially endorsed by the FLN for the April 2009 presidential contest. It was no surprise that he garnered 90 per cent of the vote, compared to 4 per cent for Louisa Hanoune, a veteran Trotskyite activist (who multiplied sixfold her 2004 result). The Algerian presidential plebiscites looked increasingly like the Tunisian ones, with Ben Ali's glory magnified by docile foils. In both countries, the real turnout was abysmal.

But Ben Ali was ruling Tunisia, while Bouteflika enjoyed only the appearance of power (along with substantial benefits for his relatives and himself). In 2010 a wave of unprecedented scandals rocked the Algerian nomenklatura and its major institution, the $56 billion SONATRACH petrochemical conglomerate (then the top oil company in Africa and twelfth biggest in the world). Chakib Khalil, appointed minister of energy by Bouteflika in 1999, had to resign after nearly eleven years in office (he settled in the US and remained there till an international warrant was eventually issued against him). Some analysts accused Mediene and the DRS of fuelling these 'SONATRACH scandals'.[28]

As chief of staff Lamari had declared as early as early as 2003, jihadi terrorism did not constitute a 'threat to the Republic'. The GIA had been swept away, leaving only his splinter group GSPC as an active outfit. Bouteflika's 'national reconciliation' had successfully drawn hundreds of fighters away from the insurgency. Meanwhile the GSPC commander (*émir*) Abdelmalek Droukdel abandoned his trademark 'Algerian jihad' and turned global by pledging allegiance to Usama Bin Laden on the fifth anniversary of the 9/11 attacks.

In January 2007, GSPC became officially al-Qaeda in the Islamic Maghreb (AQIM). It struck twice in Algiers, in April and December 2007, with coordinated suicide attacks that mixed 'local' (Algerian) targets and 'global' ones (the UN headquarters in Algeria). But the military managed to secure Greater Algiers in the following months, containing AQIM in the Kabylia mountains (the infamous 'triangle of death' between the three provinces of Boumerdes, Tizi Ouzou and Béjaïa).

Droukdel, cornered in his Kabylian stronghold, had to rely increasingly on his two subordinates in the Sahara region, Mokhtar Belmokhtar and Abdelhamid Abu Zeid, to keep AQIM 'global'. Both of them established their rear bases in Northern Mali, with Belmokhtar targeting Mauritania, while Abu Zeid's commandos were roaming from southern Tunisia to northern Niger. The Algerian army therefore succeeded in rolling back the jihadi threat at the cost of imperilling the security of the neighbouring states in the Sahel.

Bouteflika and the military leadership watched with absolute dismay as the Tunisian popular uprising washed away Ben Ali's dictatorship in January 2011. Algeria experienced a few days of urban riots that were soon quelled. The regime deflected the protest by lifting the State of Emergency (enforced since 1992), even though demonstrations remained banned in Algiers. Generous pay hikes were granted (up to 300 per cent for university professors), a $30 billion social plan was adopted and $150 billion were allocated to a gigantic and ambitious scheme of public works.

This impressive generosity was accompanied by a seemingly overwhelming media campaign that set out to refute the revolutionary character of the Tunisian and Egyptian upheavals. Algeria's liberation war against France was presented as the one and only 'revolution', while official pundits lamented repeatedly that Algeria had paid dearly for democratic experiments that were ultimately strengthening Islamist 'terrorism'.

The NATO air offensive launched in March 2011 against the Qaddafi regime was sharply criticized as the latest manifestation of a Western plot, with sinister ramifications in Israel and the Gulf. Algeria portrayed itself as the citadel of Arab nationalism and pride, besieged on all sides: by destabilized and 'jihadized' Libya and Tunisia in the east; by AQIM and its Malian partners in the south; and, of course, by US-friendly Morocco in the west.[29]

Algeria was more than ever determined to assert in Mali its role as the sole regional power. As in the domestic arena, civilians, in this case diplomats, occupied the front stage, while the DRS military were leading from behind. In the autumn of 2012 they favoured talks between the Malian government and Ansar Eddine, a jihadi Touareg group that had taken over the northern part of the country in alliance with AQIM. The Algerian intelligence believed that Ansar Eddine could be won back and split off from AQIM.

In January 2013, this gamble collapsed when Ansar Eddine and AQIM advanced towards Bamako. The Malian authorities demanded the immediate intervention of France. Bouteflika made offers (opening Algerian air space to French warplanes or effective Algerian closure of the southern border) that the army could not refuse. The French offensive, with a significant contribution from Chad, defeated Ansar Eddine and AQIM. Some 700 out the estimated 2,000 jihadi fighters died in combat, including AQIM commander Abdelhamid Abu Zeid.

Algerian militant Abu Zeid had managed to exclude his rival compatriot Belmokhtar from al-Qaeda in November 2012. While the French rollback was underway in Mali, the now dissident Belmokhtar masterminded a mass attack on the Algerian oil complex at In-Amenas in January 2013. The plant was run by Statoil, the Norwegian oil company, in a joint venture with SONATRACH. Never had hydrocarbon-related installations been attacked in two decades of Algerian terrorism.

The military reacted with predictable ferocity to this unprecedented challenge. An all-out assault involving helicopters and air-to-ground missiles left twenty-nine terrorists dead, but also forty hostages of ten different nationalities. Belmokhtar claimed responsibility for the disaster on behalf of a 'true al-Qaeda', before amalgamating his supporters with the survivors of the Malian debacle in a new jihadi outfit named Al-Mourabitoun.

The investigation report commissioned after the January 2013 assault was highly critical of the Algerian army, of its incapacity 'to detect and prevent the attackers'[30] and of its 'lack of imagination': 'an attack on In-Amenas should not have been entirely inconceivable', especially since 'there were strong economic incentives for the Algerian military to protect this critical national infrastructure'.[31]

The Algerian Mamluks had been caught off-guard and a merciless blame game ensued between the DRS and the armed forces. The former was accused at best of intelligence failure, at worst of having imposed a confrontational line that had proved fatal for the hostages.[32] 'Tewfik' Mediene, intelligence czar since 1990, had seen his fellow plotters of 1992 abandon the scene (like Nezzar) or die peacefully (Smaïn Lamari in 2007, Belkheir in 2010, Mohammad Lamari in 2012). He was left alone to face the chief of staff Gaïd Salah. The showdown between the two army generals was not about the future of Algeria, but about leadership within the military institution, in typical Mamluk style.

On 27 April 2013, Bouteflika was again admitted to the French Val-de-Grâce hospital, after a minor brain seizure. A total black-out was imposed on any information about the president's health. After forty-seven days, Bouteflika was shown on state TV receiving General Gaïd Salah and Prime Minister Abdelmalek Sellal in Paris. But it was another month before the now wheelchair bound Bouteflika could return to Algeria.

Gaïd Salah would however play the Bouteflika card for all that is was worth. In September 2013, he replaced Guenaizia as deputy minister of defence. He therefore became the real minister, since Bouteflika held the portfolio only in name. But the general remained chief of staff and even transferred a minor part of the DRS under his direct authority. 'Tewfik' was weakened, but far from defeated.

In February 2014, Amr Saadani, the FLN secretary general, launched a vicious attack against Mediene, demanding his resignation. Bewildered Algerians watched the secretive decision-makers lash out at each other for ten full days. A truce was reached on the basis of the re-election of Bouteflika in return for preserving the DRS's power structure. PM Sellal became campaign manager for the invalid president, communicating on his behalf in a surrealistic run-up to the elections.

Former PM Benflis enlisted as the main contender, just as in 2004, but he was much more pugnacious than a decade earlier. Activists also organized a protest movement called 'Barakat' (Enough), opposing a fourth mandate. Former president Zeroual, along with others, criticized Bouteflika's move. However strong the opposition, the president was re-elected with 81 per cent of the vote in April 2014. Benflis, credited with 12 per cent, denounced the state's fraudulent polls and even claimed victory. Bouteflika had cast his ballot from a wheelchair. It seemed that a puppet president was not enough for the Algerian Mamluks, who had now imposed a mummy as head of state.

*

Arab Mamluks have every reason to be fascinated by their Algerian counterparts. The 'decision-makers' (*décideurs*) never fell into the trap of promoting one-man rule after they deposed Bendjedid for the crime of accepting an electoral result. They succeeded in preserving the cohesion of their hard-core nucleus, maintaining the inevitable tensions at a level that would be sustainable by their regime as a whole.

In retrospect, the whole 1991–2014 cycle could be described as a generational transition from the generals promoted at the end of Bendjedid's mandate (the 'colonel' glass ceiling previously enshrined by Boumediene) to a new wave of officers trained during the 'black decade' of the 1990s. But the fact that seventy-four-year-old Gaïd Salah could embody this 'changing of the guard' also proved how the system had fossilized, exemplified by the 'living dead' Bouteflika at the helm.

No matter how loud they bragged about their nationalist credentials during the 'liberation war' against France, the 1992 coup-mongers did not have a tremendous military record to offer. By contrast, the newcomers had indeed fought and killed 'terrorists' for years, using incidentally the same terminology against the Islamist insurgents that the French military had coined for the nationalist guerrillas in 1954–62.

The horrendous tolls of the 'liberation war' (some 250,000 killed) and of the civil war (at least 150,000 dead, according to the chief of staff himself) were comparable. And the military clique that had grounded its legitimacy in the first bloodbath in 1962–5 had succeeded in reinvigorating the same anti-civilian ethos during this second Algerian catastrophe. Of course, the people were the chief victims of such collective dispossession.

The Algerian military would balk at the idea of being the true disciples of Berthold Brecht. But they achieved what the German playwright had jokingly envisaged after the 1953 riots in East Berlin: the people got it wrong, so change the people. The price that Algerian society paid for its massive vote against the system in 1991 (much more than a positive Islamist vote) was just staggering. Mass killings, forced displacements and generational exile transformed profoundly an Algerian public who had learned in the hardest manner possible how to stay docile and why it was best to do so.

Algerian GDP per capita approached the $5,500 target in 2012, making the country one of the richest of the continent. This bounty did not prevent more than a quarter of the population from dreaming of emigration:[33] 110,000 Algerians left their country during the 'black decade' of the 1990s, compared to 840,000 during the fifteen years following Bouteflika's election in 1999.[34] So the ongoing stagnation has proved more devastating for the long-term hopes of the Algerian youth than the horrors of the civil war.

Meanwhile, Algeria became the first African state to spend more than $10 billion a year on its military budget,[35] at an unprecedented 5 per cent share of GDP in 2013. So, no matter how distressed a country may be, Mamluks know how to take care of their constituency. And what is true of Algeria applies also to the other Arab kleptocracies.

5

THE RISE OF THE SECURITY MAFIAS

The Turkish military caste and the modern Arab Mamluks share the same in-bred feeling of ownership towards their nation, its resources and production, its political future and even the fate of their compatriots. They believe in their indisputable mission, no matter how obscure the historical roots of such a legitimacy narrative have become. Yet, as I have shown earlier in this book, Atatürk's epigones have much stronger nationalist credentials compared to their Arab counterparts, who have hijacked their independence from the hands of the actual, mostly civilian, freedom fighters.

In Turkey, the military ethos was celebrated as the supreme moral code, in order, initially, to fulfil the 'progressive' or 'socialist' promises of the nationalist 'revolution'. Soon this authoritarian credo served as a convenient whitewashing device for all the excesses in which the new masters indulged. Constitutional guarantees and legal restraints were good enough for a 'people' often caricatured as the 'masses'. Citizenship and its rights remained off-limits if they implied any curbing of the self-proclaimed elite, of its power and its greed. The new rulers were not above the law; they were, ultimately, the law.

Political scientist Steven Cook used the enlightening expression 'military enclaves'[1] to describe this relatively affluent counter-society, preserved and alienated from the rest of their fellow countrymen. The much-fabled Officers' Clubs are one of the privileged places where the security elite mingle, plot and rejoice. But military-only facilities can extend to exclusive kindergartens and boarding schools, to modern hospitals and private beaches, and they sometimes include whole residential areas in highly-guarded gated communities.

Hafez al-Assad or Ali Abdullah Saleh were only two among the thousands of lowly officers who made their way to the top, thanks to the military fast-track and various privileges. The class-based grudge of the underprivileged peasantry and their revengeful bias towards the former ruling class of businessmen and landowners should be given serious consideration.[2] Obviously, the hijacking of independence by the Arab Mamluks involved its own share of class struggle and retribution, through agrarian reform, land seizures and industrial nationalization.

Once the new militarized elite had consolidated its power, they became even more exclusive than the previous rulers. First, they locked the gates to social promotion and contained the swelling ranks of university graduates in an unnerving limbo (either underpaid, considering their academic qualifications, or unemployed, for lack of job opportunities). Second, they cemented a two-tiered army, where the conscripts were barely treated better than the 'mere' civilians (let us not forget how the Egyptian military massacred more than a hundred of rank-and-file recruits in February 1986).

The military enclaves could then flourish as a secluded oasis monopolizing national resources. Social endogamy became the norm, while political weddings were matched with the sons and daughters of the moguls of liberalization. Those privileged safe havens were increasingly connected with the hubs of globalization in the Gulf, Europe and USA, a process facilitating offshore transfer. Chapters 3 and 4 of this book have shown how the military clique could be divisive and unstable, yet they stood as one united body when their perceived core interests were attacked, wrapped up in ruthless defence of the 'regime'.

This is where the Turkish top brass diverged from the Arab Mamluks in the 1990s: the Deep State developed in Turkey as an antidote against the progressive empowerment of the civilian politicians, but it ultimately failed to thwart the AKP victory in 2002; the subsequent scandals involving the Deep State were therefore manifestations of its irreversible weakening, not of its resilience. During the same decade of the 1990s, Algeria showed an alternative path for the Arab Mamluks.

The Algerian 'decision-makers' managed to impose their rule and vision of power, at the cost of tens of thousands of civilian lives. They did not want to relinquish any substantial power, but nor did they wish to rule Algeria as a fully-fledged military junta. With five heads of state in seven years (including, in 1992, the deposed Bendjedid and assassinated Boudiaf), the Algerian Mamluks succeeded in clinging to power without risk of public exposure.

This leading from behind the scenes was more suited to a shadow state or a parallel state than a Deep State. That is where the 'fifth column' or the 'domestic enemy' narrative provides the Deep State with its mission and its resources. The counter-insurgency against the Kurdish PKK guerrillas buttressed the networks of the Turkish Deep State and the Algerian military waged an all-out war against 'terrorists', associated with a foreign existential threat, which helped them to revamp their power structure.

During the 1990s, the Egyptian security apparatus also had to face a jihadi campaign, even if its intensity was much lower than the Algerian one and than the Syrian insurgency of the previous decade. But all those big or small 'civil wars' were crucial to the rejuvenation of the repressive apparatus. President Saleh in Yemen confronted the Southern separatists in 1994, and his victory gave much more gravitas to his presidency of unified Yemen than the formal reunification of 1990.

In reference to Charles Tilly's famous argument according to which 'War makes states',[3] one might add that for the Arab Mamluks 'civil wars make (and strengthen) Deep States'. The issue of war financing, at the core of Tilly's reasoning, is also key to the Arab civil wars and the repressive apparatus that they fed and magnified. War is costly, especially when it is waged against a significant section of the local population, labelled as 'terrorist' and/or 'separatist'.

Thus the seemingly endless Arab domestic conflicts cannot be understood without a proper perception of the income financing them, in a war economy that sometimes became its ultimate objective. The military cliques have morphed into multi-faceted protection networks, far beyond the realm of security concerns. The oil bounty has been essential in the successful upgrading of the repressive structures through civil wars. But geopolitical income has also played a key role in stabilizing the worst forms of domination.

The Arab Dons

I have heard this same joke told dozens of times in Algiers, Cairo or Damascus. It always spins off a similar theme, one Arab leader visiting another, before his former host returns the visit. I heard it told of Hafez al-Assad, Husni Mubarak, Moammar Qaddafi, Zine al-Abidine Ben Ali, Chadli Bendjedid or Ali Abdullah Saleh as the two main characters (since the guest is supposed to outwit his host, a vast series of combinations is possible). But the punchline relied on the two presidents, their grandiose palaces... and a bridge.

Since this story could go on at length, I'll take the fun out of it and summarize it as follows. Leader A visits leader B and is awed by the magnificence of his palace. The tour of the presidential facilities ends up on a grand balcony where A asks B for the secret of all this wealth. B answers shrewdly 'The bridge', before showing an unfinished bridge in the middle of the landscape and smiling towards one of his pockets.

Later, B is invited back by A, who treats him to a private tour of his own presidential palace, even more luxurious than B's residence. At the end of the visit, the two leaders rest on a panoramic balcony where B interrogates A about all this munificence. A: 'The bridge!' B: 'But what bridge? There is no bridge in sight.' A: 'Well, you are absolutely right.' Then A smiles knowingly and taps his suit pocket.

The Arab Mamluks have certainly not unleashed their predatory instincts overnight. They often set out as a bunch of dedicated and patriotic officers, with a compelling sense of mission and the urge to dismantle what they perceived as a decaying system. But the very dynamics of conspiracies and patronage forced them to reward allegiances and redistribute largesse. We saw, for instance, how Field Marshal Amer behaved like some sort of Santa Claus for his military clientele, in order to challenge Nasser's presidential authority.

The opacity of the military budgets, and of the security structure as a whole, also paved the way for major personal or collective appropriations. 'National defence' had only to be mentioned to bypass any kind of administrative monitoring. In Algeria, the much-coveted status of veteran (*mujahid/in*) of the anti-French liberation war gave access to vacant property and multi-faceted privileges. The summer of 1962 therefore witnessed a dramatic swelling of the army ranks, after the ceasefire with France, but during the fierce struggle with the domestic resistance. Even if some of these veterans had impeccable nationalist credentials, a great number of them were profiteers, who had merely to bribe officials in order to join the military elite.

The disastrous Egyptian expedition in Yemen, from 1962 to 1967, offered unexpected opportunities for individual enrichment and social promotion.[4] There was no customs control for returning servicemen, which opened the way for large-scale smuggling. Veterans from Yemen were given absolute priority for land allocation, housing attribution and car acquisition. Student scholarships and special medical care were often attached to questionable 'battlefield' promotions. Amer's personal military secretary was even arrested in 1966 for reselling goods acquired under the fake names of supposed widows of Egyptian 'martyrs' who had fallen in Yemen.[5]

One decade later, the Syrian occupation of most of the Lebanese territory proved far more beneficial for the expeditionary force than the Egyptian adventure into impoverished Yemen. The local population, bewildered by their Syrian 'brothers'' inextinguishable greed, routinely described them as 'locusts'. Hafez al-Assad took good care to ensure regular rotations of combat units in Lebanon, in order to maximize the placating impact of such a bounty. This proved crucial to securing the loyalty of the main Alawi generals during the 1984 showdown with Rifaat al-Assad, the president's brother.

On a more legitimate side of the economy, the military apparatus opened new avenues for large scale heavy industry and the construction business. They benefited from cheap manpower, their skills in mass engineering, their control over key infrastructures and their monopoly over strategic trade. Diversified conglomerates expanded during the 1980s, like the Syrian Milihouse (standing for Military Housing establishment, but involved in a wide scale of industries), the Egypt-based Arab Organization for Industrialization (AOI)[6] and the Egyptian National Service Projects Organization (NSPO).

During the Iran–Iraq conflict of 1980–88, the Egyptian armament industry was boosted by Saddam Hussein's war effort. Egyptian officers were employed as military 'advisers' since Arab solidarity would not sanction the word mercenary. Field Marshal Abu Ghazala controlled these very profitable networks, in addition to the AOI and the NSPO. But the end of the Gulf War terminated this golden era and brought the demise of Abu Ghazala himself. Field Marshal Mohammad Hussein Tantawi became the new minister of defence in 1991.

When President Mubarak disposed of Abu Ghazala, not only did he marginalize the most popular man in Egypt, but also masterminded the incorporation of the top brass into crony capitalism. Abu Ghazala had repeatedly justified the enlargement of the military economy by the 'self-sufficiency' motto.[7] In fact, those new economic activities were heavily subsidized and they consumed a significant share of the public finances. The armed forces as a whole benefited from this ambitious upgrading and expansion.

On the contrary, Tantawi privileged the army hierarchy in his attribution of the 'loyalty allowance': a retiring top officer would not only benefit from this substantial premium, but also augment his military pension with lucrative positions in state-owned companies, in civil bureaucracies or in the 'consulting' business. Political loyalty was explicitly connected with the prospect of this second career, financially far more attractive. Any dissent, even minor, would be sanctioned by early retirement and/or absence of promotion over the rank of major.[8]

The Mamluks' grip over Egypt therefore grew even tighter during the 1990s. Presidential appointees, such as provincial governors, largely came from the top brass[9] and key 'civilian' ministers usually had a military background, for instance in aviation or local development. The 'privatization' of state-owned companies did not foster a free-market logic, but a more intimate co-optation between retired officers and their protégés. Just as the military hierarchy had been connected to crony capitalism in the past, now it amalgamated a new generation of globalized capitalists—prospering under the comfortable umbrella of the Egyptian state—into its patronage networks.

Dancing with the Mob

In Yemen during the 1990s, 'privatization' took the form of dismantling the socialist regime prevailing in the former Southern

Republic. Ali Abdullah Saleh's victory in 1994 against the Southern separatists, associated with the Yemeni Socialist Party (YSP), ended up in Aden with a massive confiscation by the presidential clan not only of YSP properties, but also of the private assets of the exiled YSP leaders.[10]

Using the 'restoration' of private property in the South as an excuse, President Saleh's henchmen launched a major campaign of brutal expropriation. The office of land registry in Aden was locally described as the 'office of plunder and theft'.[11] Public records had to be copied and hidden to prevent their destruction or alteration by greedy bureaucrats. A gang of Northern tribesmen went so far as to forge a three-century-old deed of property, claiming a part of Aden's harbour... that was at that time deep under water![12]

The Algerian civil war of the 1990s had the unexpected effect of fostering job creation (mainly, but not exclusively, in the security sector), of boosting investment in the oil and gas industries, and of nurturing the 'grey' zone of *trabendo* activities (even though an increasing number of these import–export companies were legal).

Algerian Mamluks and their clients were the main victors in this murderous game, even though Islamist warlords had their share of conflict-generated bounty. One of the main challenges of the 'dialogue' under president Zeroual, then of the 'reconciliation' under his successor Bouteflika, was in fact the integration and the co-optation of reformed insurgents, as soon as their war-related financial resources could be 'laundered'.[13]

Political scientist Luis Martinez explained that the so-called 'black decade' has 'favoured conditions for a "plunder economy" from which warring elites and leading personalities profit'.[14] He added: 'the civil war has been accompanied by a privatisation of violence which has led to the private accumulation of economic goods'.[15] However, the military hierarchy was quick to disband the local militias, once the main insurgent threat was over, in order to avoid losing control over this 'privatization' process.

The land border between Algeria and Morocco was opened in 1988—the year the one-party system collapsed in Algiers—and closed again in 1994. Unable to challenge the Moroccan military victory in the Western Sahara (with a ceasefire observed since 1991 by the Polisario guerrillas), the Algerian Mamluks had found this devious way to put pressure on their western neighbour. But the main casualties were among the Moroccan population of the border provinces, who depended heavily on Algerian cross-frontier trade.

What began as a tit-for-tat act by Algiers against Rabat has frozen into a twenty-year border closure. The repeated calls by Morocco and the various international pleas (including from the World Bank) left the so-called Algerian decision-makers unnerved, since they discovered how sponsored smuggling with the neighbouring kingdom could become extremely profitable.

Oil is the main smuggled product, but subsidized medicines and basic commodities also find their way into Morocco. Considering that the Algerian military outposts are only a few km away from each other,[16] organized networks have to pay some form of protection in order to cross this densely patrolled border. They are therefore less vulnerable than the individual oil-smugglers (called *helaba* on the Algerian side of the border[17] and *kamikaze* on the other side,[18] because of the amount of inflammable material they transport at high speed).

So even in times of peace, the state-imposed restrictions on a strategic border can generate sizeable profits for military leaders. But all these shady deals fade in comparison with the crime industry the Syrian army directly sponsored in occupied Lebanon. Plundering the neighbouring country was the main Syrian activity in the 1980s, but the next decade saw a growing (and highly profitable) bipolarity between the state-fettered Syrian market and the free-for-all Lebanese land of opportunity.

The Assad clan and the top-ranking generals controlled both sides of the border and adjusted the discrepancies between the two economic zones in order to maximize their patronage revenues. Military-only roads were 'rented' by the hour to criminal networks. *Shabbiha* (ghost-like) smugglers, loyal to prominent Alawi gang-leaders, drove their fast cars along the Mediterranean coast.[19] Tobacco soon appeared too cheap a commodity and drugs then became the new focus.

We have seen how the Turkish Deep State coalesced, at the same period, around intelligence officials and criminal dons, united in fighting the Kurdish separatist guerrillas of the PKK. But the main Syrian military intelligence service, led by general Ali Duba, not only protected Abdullah Öcalan, the PKK chief, in the very city of Damascus; they also extracted a significant profit from the heroin laboratories that the PKK had established on the Lebanese plain of the Bekaa, on the Syrian border.[20] So the clash between Turkish and Syrian intelligences over the PKK only exacerbated the existing Kurdish turf war over drugs.

In October 1998, Ankara massed troops on its southern border to force the Syrian regime to abandon Öcalan. Bashar al-Assad, the heir apparent, convinced his father Hafez to drop such a risky Kurdish 'card'. The PKK leader was removed to Moscow. From there, he moved to Greece, then to Kenya, where he would eventually be captured by Turkish intelligence. Bashar al-Assad, fully backed by the declining Syrian dictator, had defeated Duba in this inter-Alawite showdown.

When Hafez al-Assad died in June 2000, Bashar succeeded his father as planned (and was 'elected' as the sole candidate for the presidency with 97.3 per cent of votes cast). He then cajoled the Western powers with unprecedented calls for a 'modernizing' of Syria. Trained in London and married to a financial consultant, the new 'Lion of Damascus'[21] was well versed in the international lingo of 'liberalization'. However his model was far from

California. Rather, it was explicitly China, where a one-party system had generated formidable wealth without relinquishing absolute power.

This is how the second-generation of Syrian Mamluks started to 'privatize', one decade after their Algerian, Egyptian and Yemeni counterparts. The Duba-led criminal pattern had been seriously hampered by the October 1998 crisis with Turkey. The Syrian dons had to move into 'legitimate' business, the key word becoming 'partnership'. Just as their fathers had played on both sides of the border with Lebanon, their Syrian heirs benefited from the 'privatization' bounty on one side, and from their new 'partnerships' in the private sector on the other.

The beacon of this crony capitalism was Rami Makhlouf, the most prominent of Bashar al-Assad's many cousins. He was a 'partner' in nine out of the twelve new private banks. His multi-faceted empire, from real estate to mobile phones and import–export, was valued at some $3 billion.[22] But in this opening decade of the millennium, Makhlouf had emulators throughout the ruling class in Syria. And the fabulous wealth he accumulated mirrored the fortunes siphoned off by second-generation Arab Mamluks. 'The bridge! What bridge?'

Blood for Oil

There is much written about the 'oil curse': some authors raise the argument that the oil-induced redistribution-state is a fertile ground for corruption and civil strife per se, while others extol the counter-examples of Norway, or even Indonesia, to undermine this thesis.[23] The Arab Mamluks did not rely on the oil bounty in order to hijack the post-colonial independent states and establish their military dictatorships. Questioning the historical trajectory of the process may help clarify this crucial issue.

Chapter 2 showed how Wahhabism provided the Saud family with an ideology on which to establish their 'Saudi Arabia'. This state-building creed was also sharply hostile to the Arab Nahda and its dynamics of collective emancipation. So the oil-induced bonanza, after the Second World War, was largely invested by Riyadh in undermining nationalist regimes, with a special focus on Syria. (During the 1950s, major fluctuations in the Damascus gold market were often connected to the arrival of an airplane from Saudi Arabia!)[24]

The Egyptian expedition into Yemen transformed the southern neighbour of Saudi Arabia into the main battlefield of the 'Arab cold war' raging between US-backed King Faysal and Soviet-supported Nasser. While the Egyptian forces were until 1967 directly involved in combat, the Saudis mainly acted through generously paid protégés. The oil-related largesse was key to this war by proxy. Once the Egyptian forces had withdrawn, the nationalist dynamics empowered the Republican leadership, besieged in Sanaa, to sustain and repel the Saudi-sponsored onslaught.

So oil alone could not win the day. In 1970 King Faysal had to recognize the Yemen Arab Republic (YAR) in Sanaa. He even had to live with the 1974 'corrective' coup that saw YAR join the military club already staffed by Algeria, Syria and Egypt. And even if Saudi influence was denounced in the 1977 killing of President Hamdi, the shock of this murder did not derail the Mamluk logic now at work in Sanaa.

Characterized by his survivor mentality and his deceptive manoeuvres, Ali Abdullah Saleh proved a difficult partner for Riyadh. Saudi largesse would not buy his loyalty, but he worked effectively to channel and oversee most of it, thereby diverting it from his rivals. Saleh let Saudi-inspired Salafist groups operate, only to counter-balance them with the Muslim Brotherhood. He also diversified his Gulf connections by attracting into Yemen the newly independent United Arab Emirates. (Sheikh Zayed, the ruler, considered the Yemeni province of Marib as the cradle of his family.)

The discovery of oil in the region of Marib, in 1984, enabled President Saleh to be less dependent on Saudi Arabia. Without oil-related revenues, the Yemeni leader would probably never have succeeded in unifying the country under his authority in 1990 and later absorbing the trauma of the Saudi sanctions (Riyadh wanted then to punish Saleh for supporting the Iraqi occupation of Kuwait). Two years later, the discovery of oil in the Southern province of Hadramaut—the so-called Wadi al-Masila—further strengthened the Yemeni president's power.

Saleh was adamant about controlling the oil resources for his own benefit and in redistributing it in a classical patron/client relationship. This monopolizing of oil revenues certainly fuelled the flames of Southern separatism and of the 1994 civil war. But Saleh's victory only tightened his control on the Wadi al-Masila oil field. Canadian Occidental (Canoxy), the production operator, had to transfer its headquarters from Aden to Sanaa, while Mohammad Ismail, one of the president's uncles, became military commander of the oilfield sector.

Ismail pressured Canoxy, first into contracting him as their security provider, then in hiring a large number of Northerners instead of the local employees.[25] This exclusion naturally led to increased tension with the local population, an unprecedented number of incidents, and even sabotage, which in turn aggravated Ismail's 'protection' fees. We shall explore below when discussing the jihadi nemesis how the Wadi al-Masila pattern might serve as a metaphor for the Arab Mamluks' blackmail of Western powers, in order to extract a 'protection' bounty against a threat that they largely generated themselves.

Before the end of the 1990s, oil production had reached a level of 400,000 barrels a day, with one fourth for local consumption. While Yemen remained a small oil producer, from 2000 to 2009 the hydrocarbon sector accounted for 20–30 per cent of GNP, 80–90 per cent of Yemeni exports and 70–80 per cent of government revenues.[26] More than 50 per cent of these revenues were spent on the presidential office, armed forces and security services, all tightly connected to Saleh's closest circle. On top of that 'official' hijacking, Yemeni specialist Stephen Day considers that 'President Saleh and his family raked in billions of dollars' from oil revenue, before it was even included in government accounts.[27]

Oil was not only the main official and unofficial resource for the Yemeni Mamluks. It was also the key factor in government spending, generating another source of parallel revenues, since subsidies on fuel and diesel represented one fifth of official expenditure. In 2008 political scientist Sarah Philips estimated that half of this subsidized gasoline was pumped and smuggled into 'illegal' yet well-protected networks.[28] Even programmes designed for the underprivileged ended up benefitting the military elite and its clients.

Contrary to Yemen, Algeria had been a long-term major player in the international oil market. The first oil shock in 1973 gave President Boumediene the financial means of his 'socialist' policy, as the second oil shock in 1979 kept Bendjedid's 'liberal' policy afloat. We have seen how the 1986 oil counter-shock contributed to the collapse of the one-party system, two years later, with civil war raging during the 'black decade' of the 1990s.

In 1999, the hydrocarbon sector accounted for 95 per cent of export receipts and 60 per cent of government resources.[29] At the same time, the offshore assets of the Algerian billionaires were estimated at $40 billion.[30] Political scientist Luis Martinez concludes that the Algerian 'military clique',[31] 'instead of negotiating an "exit from authoritarianism" or imploding', morphed into a 'mafia regime', since 'mafias emerged and ensured security for the new rules of the game'.[32]

The issue of the 'oil curse' is therefore less relevant than the tenacity of the Arab Mamluks in exploiting their country's national resources after they hijacked the post-colonial independent state. The mafia paradigm is thus a useful means of underlining the predatory ferocity of the forces unleashed in times of armed challenge (by the Islamist guerrillas in Algeria or Southern separatists in Yemen): even though this was a civil war, the war bounty was to be monopolized by the sole victors.

Oil consolidated President Saleh's power far beyond his wildest expectations and oil kept the Algerian 'military clique' prosperous and affluent all through the 'black decade'. But national oil was only a minor resource for the Egyptian and Syrian Mamluks (with three to five times less oil production than Algeria). For Mubarak in the 1990s and Assad junior after his father's death in 2000, expanding crony capitalism was the main prize.

Let us then escape the 'oil curse' and follow the mafia lead. The former single parties suffered in all the Mamluk regimes from an existential and structural crisis that led to their losing the political monopoly and/or becoming hollowed out shells, dedicated to the nostalgic recitation of long-discredited slogans. This crisis of the 'mass parties' laid bare the regime's apparatus of repression, which was only too keen to ensure that everyone followed the new rules of the game.

This is how, here with oil, there without it, security services and praetorian guards took the front line in defending not only the Mamluk regimes, but their day-to-day plundering of the country. 'Privatization' went hand in hand with increased interference in the state's political policies in the public sphere and in the private sphere of oppressed individuals. But the 'security mafias' in Egypt and Syria, to coin a colourful oxymoron, came to rely on a fascinating source of income that was much thicker than oil.

The Israeli Jackpot

We have seen how the Arab Mamluks established their ruthless regimes on the ruins of the anti-Israeli resistance. Husni Zaim opened the sequence of military coups in 1949, followed three years later by Nasser, Amer and the so-called Free Officers. In Syria as in Egypt, the power struggles among the ruling clique were far more absorbing than the actual confrontation against the 'Zionist enemy'. This is a key factor in understanding the disaster of the June 1967 war, which ended with the Israeli occupation of the Egyptian Sinaï and the Syrian Golan (along with East Jerusalem, the West Bank and the Gaza Strip).

The Black September conflict in Jordan in 1970, between loyalist forces and the PLO guerrillas, was the turning point towards the two 'corrective' movements in Egypt and Syria. Nasser collapsed and died after sponsoring a ceasefire that was a cover-up for the Palestinian defeat. His successor Sadat was adamant in his resolve to regain Sinaï, even at the cost of Palestinian rights. Assad was far more hostile to the PLO, since he had ascended to supreme power by backstabbing the Black September Palestinians.

Sadat and Assad both led their countries into the October 1973 joint offensive against Israel. They enjoyed the full backing of King Faysal of Saudi Arabia, who considered he had won the 'Arab cold war', now that Sadat had expelled thousands of Soviet advisers from his country. After initial setbacks on both fronts, Israel retook the initiative and reversed the course of the battle. Incensed by the United States' unconditional support for the Israeli counter-offensive, King Faysal decided to cut Saudi oil exports by 10 per cent, with an additional 5 per cent monthly reduction until an effective Israeli withdrawal was completed.

The Saudi embargo was soon enforced by the other Arab oil producers. Oil prices quadrupled in a matter of weeks. This first 'oil shock' was partly psychological, since non-Arab producers, especially Iran, compensated for some of the slashing of production. This game-changer brought unprecedented wealth to Saudi Arabia, Kuwait and the four Gulf states that had reached full independence as recently as 1971. Billions of dollars were allocated to Syria and Egypt as a pledge of 'Arab solidarity'.

The Arab Mamluks knew quite well how to exploit this incredible bounty for their own personal benefit. It did not need much sophistication to plug into Gulf largesse. For instance, Assad sent his vice premier for economic affairs to Riyadh, just after the conflict with Israel. King Faysal benevolently asked for 'a list of projects with some figures'.[33] So the vice premier, who had come empty-handed, drafted a document based on calculations he did on site with his pocket calculator and went home with a virtually blank cheque!

The oil embargo was eventually lifted when Henry Kissinger brokered two parallel disengagement agreements between Israel and Egypt on one side, and Israel and Syria on the other. The demand for a full withdrawal from the territories occupied in 1967 had been forgotten, even though the Gulf money kept flowing in: King Faysal promised an additional $350 million to Syria during his visit to Damascus in January 1975.[34] (Two months later, the Saudi monarch was killed by a distant relative, a murder routinely attributed to an Israeli plot by Arab conspiracy fans.)[35]

That is where Sadat and Assad parted ways: the former considered that only a fully-fledged *Pax Americana* could bring back the Sinaï, while the latter abandoned any hope of recovering the Golan, contending himself with the US guarantee extended to his regime through the Syrian–Israeli ceasefire. This is why the Syrian Mamluks reacted with such ferocity to the challenge of the PLO forming an alliance with the leftist militias in neighbouring Lebanon.

Such a revolutionary coalition could jeopardize the triangular deal on the Golan Heights involving Syria, Israel and the USA. So those two countries approved tacitly, with the corresponding 'red lines', the Syrian invasion of Lebanon to crush the PLO–leftist forces, in the summer of 1976. The agreement reached in Riyadh the following October secured two victories for Assad: the confirmation of the Gulf's financial support; and the Arab endorsement of the Syrian occupying force in Lebanon, under the flag of a so-called Arab Deterrence Force.

The Syrian regime benefited to an even greater extent from the Gulf oil bonanza following the US-sponsored Camp David peace talks between Egypt and Israel. In November 1978, the Arab summit held in Baghdad sharply condemned the negotiations. A delegation led by the Lebanese PM was sent to Sadat with the proposal of a massive Arab aid plan to Egypt, in compensation for the termination of the Camp David process. Sadat answered that 'all the billions in the world could not buy Egypt's dignity'.[36]

The truth was that Sadat was advantageously replacing Arab 'billions' by American 'billions': over $2 billion in civilian aid and more than $1 billion in military aid were pledged by Washington in the Camp David package (with parallel generosity towards Israel). Meanwhile, in Baghdad, Syria reaped the lion's share ($2 billion) of Arab financial support for the 'confrontation states'.

Those mind-boggling figures demonstrate how the Egyptian and Syrian Mamluks had succeeded in transforming their relationship with Israel into a grandiose form of moral blackmail in order to generate a stream of unprecedented income from their outside sponsors. The fact that Egypt was at 'peace' with Israel while Syria was at 'war' (with not a single shot fired since 1974) was less important than the belief in both countries that this foreign support was their due. The Syrian regime even dared to threaten some Gulf states, through Damascus-friendly terrorist organizations, when the aid pledged in Baghdad was not disbursed in time.[37]

All this re-alignment occurred while the Islamic revolution was shaking Iran, cutting oil production there by 75 per cent. Such turmoil provoked great instability on the international markets and caused a second 'oil shock' in 1979. Syria, now firmly hooked on Gulf cash reserves, was a main beneficiary from these oil price hikes.

Far from tilting the Assad regime towards 'confrontation' with Israel, this affluence allowed it to finance a merciless campaign against the Muslim Brotherhood: the military re-conquest of Aleppo went on for many months in 1980 and caused thousands of casualties; in March 1982, some 12,000 soldiers crushed an Islamist uprising in Hama and destroyed one third of the historic city.

The Israeli invasion of Lebanon in June 1982 was basically all about targeting the PLO and its local allies. A ceasefire was quickly reached between Israel and Syria, even though some 3,000 Syrian soldiers were trapped and besieged in Beirut (where they conspicuously left the Palestinian guerrillas to defend the front lines). But the 'new cold war' that the Likud government pretended to wage in the Middle East, with the support of the Reagan administration, prompted Moscow to upgrade dramatically its help to Damascus.

Thousands of Soviet advisers were dispatched to Syria, with a large number assigned to man the latest generation of Warsaw Pact missiles. The number of Syrian tanks swelled from 3,200 to 4,400, with a comparable increase in combat aircraft (from 440 to 650) and air defence sites (from 100 to 180). From 1982 to 1986, the Syrian armed forces doubled in size, reaching 400,000[38] (for a population of some 11 million).

Hafez al-Assad completed this dramatic consolidation of his regime while consistently avoiding any direct hostility with Israel (he even fought and expelled PLO guerrillas from Northern Lebanon at the end of 1983, thereby concluding the anti-Palestinian cleansing campaign inaugurated the previous year by the Likud government in Beirut and southern Lebanon). He played rough and dirty, but through various proxies, without ever exposing himself. And he forged a strategic alliance with Ayatollah Khomeini and his Islamic Republic of Iran.

This unholy alliance between Damascus and Teheran proved how deceptive the 'Arab nationalist' discourse of the Syrian

Mamluks could be. Assad had designed a complex web of 'partnerships' where his regime was always on the receiving end: oil from Iran, weapons from the Soviet Union and cash from the Gulf, where the Iranian bogeyman worked superbly to stimulate 'generosity' towards Syria.

The Lebanese 'Party of God' (Hezbollah) was created in 1982 through a joint venture between Syrian and Iranian intelligence. This Shia militia eliminated its local rivals to secure the monopoly of its 'Islamic resistance' over the anti-Israeli insurgency. Therefore, Assad could safely fuel the flames of armed struggle in south Lebanon, while enforcing an impeccable ceasefire with Israel on the Golan Heights.

Compared to the sophistication of Syrian 'protection', the Egyptian Mamluks looked pretty straightforward. When Mubarak succeeded Sadat after his assassination in October 1981, he had yet to oversee the Israeli evacuation of the last sector of occupied Sinai. Egyptian sovereignty was fully restored in April 1982, which gave Israel a free hand to invade Lebanon two months later. But Mubarak had secured considerable US military aid, essential for the ruling clique.

The Egyptian president, while being far less proactive on the civilian side of the American largesse, made sure that his armed forces would receive $1.3 billion each year from Washington. This incredible sum was supposedly based on a 2/3 ratio between US military aid to Egypt and to Israel.[39] The calculation was far more complex, but the net result was that Mubarak defended his top brass with a dedication that probably explains how he could with little fuss eventually marginalize Field Marshal Abu Ghazala.

During the autumn of 1990, the Egyptian and Syrian Mamluks, who had gone their separate ways for the past fifteen years, joined ranks again on Saudi soil: this 'defence shield' was aimed at deterring Saddam Hussein's menacing moves towards the Gulf countries and served as the Arab fig-leaf for the US-led

'Desert Storm' campaign to liberate Kuwait. Once again, the Israeli dimension was crucial, with Egypt and Syria fighting (at least symbolically) Iraq in Kuwait, while Iraqi SCUD missiles fell on Israeli territory.

The stage was then set for the 1990s, with a return to the paradoxical stability of the pattern adopted by the Egyptian and Syrian Mamluks. Despite the collapse of the Soviet Union in 1991, the mutual recognition between Israel and the PLO in 1993, and the Israeli–Jordanian peace treaty in 1994, Husni Mubarak kept cashing in $1.3 billion a year of military aid, while Hafez al-Assad played off shrewdly his Gulf, Iranian and Russian backers. Bashar al-Assad would follow in his father's footsteps, compensating for his minor talent through his tenacious greed.

*

Arab Mamluks have demonstrated an exceptional capacity to survive at any cost, especially when this cost is paid by their own population. After having hijacked the post-colonial independent states, they secured their (quasi) monopoly of national resources and their ubiquitous patronage over the public sphere. Later, they succeeded in expanding their domination through a 'privatization' that would benefit their protégés or themselves. Egyptian Mamluks were the pioneers of this crony capitalism, but soon their Arab counterparts joined the fray.

'Security mafias' emerged in the 1990s as the key actor in this process, amalgamating the intrusive power of the repressive apparatus and the aggressive solidarity of the mafia networks. The resilience and robustness of such regime-inspired violence could only be fuelled by significant income, whether indigenous or imported. This is why Tunisia remained a police state under Ben Ali, unable to play in the Mamluk league, since it kept on racketeering its own citizens, without a substantial income to live off.

As discussed earlier, this income could be multi-faceted and heterogeneous. Oil alone would not have saved the Algerian 'decision-makers' from the trials of the 'black decade'. Ali Abdullah Saleh needed more than oil to complete his two 'unifications' of Yemen, the peaceful one in 1990, and the military one four years later. This is the main difference with the Libyan and Iraqi totalitarian systems, which relied essentially on oil to avoid breakdown during the international embargos of the 1990s.

The largesse of foreign donors might not be sufficient either, even though it was clearly crucial to the prosperity of Assad and Mubarak's regimes. The Mamluks enjoyed the ability to blackmail their patrons, be it directly in the Syrian case, or more subtly in the Egyptian one. Vulnerable Jordan, a major recipient of international generosity, could never dream of achieving such a feat, and King Hussein had to swallow his pride repeatedly to placate angry donors.

So the 'security mafias' needed a no-strings-attached income to operate, to redistribute and, ultimately, to reproduce themselves. The cash dimension of this income was indexed on the geopolitical environment that was supposed to optimize its value for the Mamluks' benefit (European vulnerability towards energy and immigration for Algeria, security of Israel for Egypt, and so on). But this century opened with a strategic earthquake that proved immensely profitable for the Arab dictators.

6

THE 'GLOBAL TERROR' NEXT DOOR

Arab Mamluks have fought and survived armed insurgencies inspired by their Islamist opponents. From 1979 to 1982, the Syrian regime resisted, suppressed and ultimately eliminated a military uprising led by the local branch of the Muslim Brotherhood. Their liquidation convinced not only the Syrian Brotherhood, but also the organization as a whole in the Islamic world that ballots should prevail over bullets in order to reach power.

This legalist aggiornamento alienated the mainstream Islamist movement from a galaxy of radical groups for whom 'jihad' against the 'infidel' regimes remained the guiding imperative. One of these jihadi outfits managed to assassinate President Sadat in Cairo, in October 1981, but the subsequent uprising in Upper Egypt was thoroughly crushed. It would take more than ten years for the jihadi militants to reconstitute a critical mass and launch a new terror campaign, in March 1992.

The Gamaa Islamiyya (Islamic Group), inspired by the US-based Egyptian sheikh Omar Abderrahmane, vowed to topple Mubarak's regime. It targeted government officials, security forces and secular intellectuals in a string of assassinations that brought the expected armed response from the military. The Christian Coptic minority and foreign tourists were also victims of this terror campaign.

This low-intensity conflict in Egypt also had major international ramifications, with Arab jihadis trying to turn their struggle 'global'. Sheikh Abderrahmane was arrested and sentenced to life imprisonment in New York after an attack on the World Trade Center (six were killed in a car bomb attack in February 1993). This detention prompted Ayman Zawahiri, the leader of a rival group called the Egyptian Islamic Jihad, to try to surpass the Gamaa in high-profile terrorism.

Zawahiri was based in Sudan and, already a close associate of Usama Bin Laden, he was considered his deputy in the top-secret al-Qaeda organization. The dictatorial regime in Khartoum, a mix of Islamist radicals and military adventurers, provided a safe haven for a large number of terrorist groups of various shades. The Sudanese diplomatic service even offered the cover of its immunity for a major attack in neighbouring Ethiopia.

On 26 June 1995, President Mubarak landed in Addis Ababa to participate in an African summit. General Omar Suleiman, whom he had appointed head of the General Intelligence Department (GID) two years earlier, had insisted that the president travel with his own armoured car. Suleiman had prevailed upon the Egyptian diplomats and their Ethiopian hosts.[1] This decision saved Mubarak's life when he fell into a jihadi ambush (two Egyptian bodyguards and three attackers were killed).

This foiled regicide brought the full wrath of the Egyptian regime down on the jihadis, while international sanctions were voted against Sudan. Zawahiri spent the next two years on the run all over the world, before he reunited with Bin Laden in May 1997: the two jihadi leaders had found a new shelter in Taliban-run Afghanistan. In Egypt, the repression increased, with thousands of arrests (according to some commentators, the figure may have reached 20,000) and the predictable iron fist counter-insurgency.

The toll became so unbearable on the Gamaa Islamiyya that in July 1997 they convinced the jailed sheikh Abderrahmane to endorse their call for an end to violence. But Zawahiri managed to lure a military leader of the Gamaa into organizing, along with his ownIslamic jihad, the massacre of fifty-eight Swiss tourists in Luxor in Islamic jihad in November 1997. The public shock generated by such slaughter, instead of re-igniting the jihadi flame, had the opposite effect of terminating the insurgency.

More than a thousand people were estimated to have been killed in Egypt during this 1992–7 jihadi trial by fire. These figures pale beside the horrendous toll of the parallel Algerian 'black decade', with one hundred times more casualties in a country whose population numbered only 40 per cent of that of Egypt. But Egyptian jihadism had proved to be intimately woven into a 'global jihad' that would gain its full meaning with the 9/11 attacks on New York and Washington, masterminded from Afghanistan by Bin Laden and Zawahiri.

Egyptian and Algerian leaders rushed to say that they had been fighting al-Qaeda for the past ten years and that they had felt pretty isolated in their own private wars. The assertion was certainly far-fetched since, with the exception of the Zawahiri's minor contribution to the 1992–7 terror campaign, the jihadi insurgency in both Algeria and Egypt was basically indigenous. But such discourse struck a deep chord with the George W. Bush administration as it braced itself for a 'global war on terror'.

Arab Mamluks would also take advantage of a softer oil shock that would—though without the dramatic impact of the two previous ones—bring back affluence whether directly (as in Algeria) or indirectly (through the Gulf largesse). 'Security mafias' had extended their clout all over the public sphere, but the global war on terror gave them the unexpected privilege of international integration. 'Black holes' were not only tolerated, they became part of a world web of 'dirty wars' against 'terrorists'.

Egypt rose as a main partner in the rendition programme and the torture by proxy it involved on behalf of the USA.[2] Algeria collaborated more in information-sharing and adjusted its inputs on its preferred domestic targets. Intelligence barons became regular guests at Western think tanks and meetings held by the sensitive 'security sector', while their American and European counterparts competed for their cooperation. This was the high tide for the Mamluk 'security mafias'.

Back to the Past in Yemen

Al-Qaeda was something of a family story in Yemen. The Bin Ladens originated from the Southern Yemeni province of Hadramaut before emigrating into Saudi Arabia and settling in Jeddah, Usama's birthplace. Just after he founded al-Qaeda in Pakistan, Bin Laden ran his first operations in 1988 on behalf of his secret network against South Yemeni officials, especially in Hadramaut.[3] This covert anti-communist guerrilla operated with the full knowledge and support of both the North Yemeni and Saudi intelligence apparatus.

The unification of the country under Ali Abdullah Saleh in April 1990 led al-Qaeda's sponsors to force it to terminate its activities in Yemen, now that the Marxist straw man had been incorporated into a Sanaa-run Republic. This was the first crisis between Bin Laden and the Saudi security services that had until then facilitated his operations, without being fully aware of the clandestine dimension of al-Qaeda. The breach became unbridgeable after Saddam's invasion of Kuwait in August 1990, when Bin Laden condemned both the Saudi alliance with the USA and Yemeni support for Iraq.

He was expelled from Saudi Arabia to Pakistan, from where he resettled in Sudan. There Bin Laden devoted al-Qaeda to an ambitious anti-US jihad, but the opening salvo of such a grand design was rather a flop: in December 1992, a bomb attack on a 5-star hotel in Aden missed the intended target, namely American servicemen en route to Somalia, instead killing an Austrian tourist and a Yemeni employee.[4]

However, rather than turning against al-Qaeda, Yemeni security jailed a high-profile Afghanistan 'veteran', Tareq al-Fadhli, whose anti-communist activism in the Southern province of Abyan had become a nuisance since the 1990 reunification. But when the 1994 civil war erupted, Fadhli was swiftly released and his tribal shock troops played a significant role in the victory of President Saleh against the Southern separatists.

In genuine Mamluk style, Fadhli was rewarded with a key position in the ruling party, the General Congress of the People (GCP). Saleh commissioned his own strong man (and fellow tribesman) General Ali Mohsen al-Ahmar to deal with Fadhli and the other Yemeni 'veterans' from Afghanistan.[5] But this arrangement did not involve al-Qaeda, who carried out a major suicide attack in the harbour at Aden in October 2000, destroying USS Cole and killing seventeen American servicemen.

Saleh granted only limited cooperation to the FBI investigation team after the attack, in order to maintain full control over the Yemeni chessboard. But he understood the global impact of 9/11 and enthusiastically enrolled in the US-led global war on terror. George W. Bush received his Yemeni counterpart in November 2001 at the White House. US advisers and advanced weaponry started pouring into Yemen, where 'suspects' were rounded up by the thousands, sometimes deported, and most of the time brutalized.

The Republican Guard was the main recipient of American largesse. Nobody seemed troubled in Washington that the spearhead of the 'counter-terrorism' campaign was also the regime's praetorian guard, commanded by the son of the Yemeni ruler, Ahmed Ali Saleh. The Political Security Organization (PSO), or Yemeni intelligence, founded in 1992, had been sidelined after the USS Cole fiasco by a new National Security Bureau (NSB), whose deputy director (and real chief) was Ammar Mohammad Saleh, one of the president's nephews.

Therefore the 'globalization' of the war on terror led to the Saleh family tightening their grip on an ever-expanding security apparatus. Ahmed Ali Saleh's Republican Guard grew rapidly from ten to eighteen brigades. The Jordanian special forces that were the backbone of the monarchy (King Abdullah II had commanded the Jordanian special forces before succeeding his father Hussein in 1999) served as a model.

Yahya Mohammad Saleh, Ammar's brother, and another of the president's nephews, boosted the paramilitary Central Security Forces (CSF) at the ministry of the interior. The counter-terrorism branch of the CSF was generously supported by the USA.[6] In the Republican Guard even more than in the CSF, higher wages, better weaponry and various benefits were credited to Saleh's clan,[7] ensuring the personal loyalty of those elite fighters.

US generosity brought some results in the anti-al Qaeda struggle. In November 2002, the leader of the local branch of the jihadi network, Qaïd Sinan al-Harithi, nicknamed Abu Ali, was killed in a drone strike in the Marib desert. (The official version was that his car exploded carrying a bomb, but the Pentagon could not help bragging about this CIA success in its 'covert war'.)[8] Over the next three years, no fewer than twenty-three major al-Qaeda operatives were captured and taken to Sanaa central prison.

Yemeni Mamluks seemed to have designed the best formula to extract the most from this monopolized income. They had found an antidote for the declining oil bonanza, soon to be depleted by the absence of significant reserves, now that they had plugged into the US global war on terror. They had escaped the ordeal suffered by their Saudi neighbours, who were confronted in 2003–4 by a fully-fledged terror campaign by al-Qaeda in the Arabian Peninsula (AQAP). And in Yemen, defending the Saleh regime was the top priority for these newly trained and equipped 'special forces'.

This income-upgrading process could have gone astray, in February 2006, when the twenty-three top al-Qaeda detainees all managed to escape together from Sanaa central jail. The prison breakout was monitored by US satellites, and the CIA was incensed that a 140m long tunnel could have been dug out of the facility. Accusations of corruption and deception flew between Sanaa and Washington. Saudi Arabia, anxious that there were eleven of its nationals among the runaway jihadis, relieved the tension.

Eventually, President Saleh benefited from this jail break: the Gulf Cooperation Council (GCC) states pledged to Yemen a $5.5 billion aid package, and the USA resumed its security cooperation. Even though only ten per cent of the mooted GCC aid was actually disbursed (for want of any transparency),[9] the Yemeni anti-terror show was back on the road. Al-Qaeda in Yemen focused its attacks on foreign tourists, Western expatriates and embassies, contrary to the insurgency dynamics of AQAP in Saudi Arabia[10] which extracted a heavy toll on the local security forces.

In January 2009, the disbanded Saudi networks regrouped in Yemen, where they merged into the indigenous jihadi outfit to form a revamped AQAP. Nasir al-Wuhayshi (aka Abu Basir), one of the Sanaa jail escapees, became the first Yemeni leader of this Yemen-based AQAP, with a Saudi deputy at his side. The jihadi discourse went vibrantly revolutionary and attacks started targeting security services.

President Saleh then faced major challenges from all sides. Most of the parliamentary opposition had coalesced into the Joint Meeting Parties (JMP) and forced the ruling GCP to cancel the 2009 elections. The Southern Movement (*Hirak*, in Arabic) opposed the presidential clan's predation in the former PDRY. Tariq Fadhli quit the GCP after fifteen years and joined *Hirak*. And last but not least, a Zaydi insurgency was devastating the northernmost Saada province, with Saleh launching a 'scorched earth' offensive against this so-called Houthi movement (the guerrilla was entitled 'Believing Youth', but was led by the Houthi clan).

The Yemeni president stubbornly held his ground and reaped an unexpected benefit from an AQAP-foiled terror attack on a US airline. On Christmas Eve 2009, a Nigerian carrying a bomb was arrested on board an Amsterdam–Detroit flight. It was soon proved that the terrorist had been trained, equipped and instructed by AQAP in Yemen.

Less than a year into office, the Obama administration decided to dramatically increase US support for Yemeni security: military aid boomed from $67 million in 2009 to $155 million in 2010.[11] British Prime Minister Gordon Brown called for a top-level international conference about Yemen in January 2010, and a 'Friends of Yemen' group was then constituted in London under the auspices of the USA and Britain.

President Saleh's propaganda succeeded in associating his political rivals with the jihadi menace, for instance playing on Fadhli's joining the Southern separatists. With insecurity reaching unprecedented levels in Yemen, Western intelligence agencies were finding it increasingly difficult to screen the regime's allegations. The Yemeni president could also revert to his Gulf donors, where the jihadi straw man always worked his magic, along with the alleged links between Zaydi Houthis and pro-Iranian Shia hardliners.

The economy was in a shambles, while civil strife and armed insurgencies had impoverished Yemen even more. Jihadi commandos, cornered in the Marib region a decade earlier, were now active in the Shabwa, Abyan and Hadramaut provinces as well. Ali Abdullah Saleh was determined to conclude the succession plan that would—as in 2000 Syria—benefit his heir apparent Ahmed Ali, head of the Republican Guard.

An outrageous failure in Yemen, the so-called global war on terror had nevertheless served the Yemeni Mamluks extremely well. They had even managed to create a two-tier army, with a privileged presidential stratum lavishly supplied by foreign donors under the 'anti-terrorist' rubric, as against an ill-equipped mainstream army, bearing the brunt of the merciless counter-insurgency in the far North.

Two decades earlier, we saw how one of President Saleh's uncles had imposed his 'protection' regime on a Canadian oil company operating in the southern province of Hadramout. This blunt blackmail only worsened the security environment for oil production, since excluded Southerners retaliated through sabotage. As a consequence of this deterioration, protection taxes rose to unprecedented heights.

The global war on terror saw the Yemeni Mamluks replicating this operation on a far larger scale, oil now being replaced by 'anti-terrorism' as a strategic commodity for the Western leaders. The more this global war was waged in Yemen, the greater the jihadi threat became, largely fuelled by the exclusive sectarian policies of the 'anti-terrorist' warlords. This pattern would prove even more perverse in Syria.

The Syrian Triple Game

Bashar al-Assad could also play the al-Qaeda tune to Western decision-makers after 9/11: Usama Bin Laden, whose mother was Syrian, had been inroduced to radicalism by a Syrian Islamist in Jeddah;[12] Abu Musab al-Suri, the Syrian 'architect of global jihad',[13] was the chief trainer at the main al-Qaeda camp in Afghanistan, while being an 'adviser' to Mullah Omar, the Taliban leader.[14] The Assad regime traded on its past history and claimed to have been fighting the same terrorist enemy during their 1979–82 insurgency as the one who had now struck New York and Washington.

No lie was too big for the Syrian Mamluks. Decades of involvement in international terrorism, with Hafez al-Assad granting his protection to Carlos or Abu Nidal, left some scars. In 1986, a Jordanian operative of Syrian air force intelligence (the one in charge of overseas operations) was jailed in London for an attempted bomb attack against an Israeli passenger aircraft. But the West had rehabilitated Assad senior when he joined the US-led coalition against Iraq in 1990. So far, Assad junior was given the benefit of the doubt.

Syrian security officials, like their Algerian and Egyptian counterparts, were more than eager to share information with the CIA about 'high-value targets', as al-Qaeda militants were labelled, either dead or alive. Bashar al-Assad also relished seeing the global war on terror aimed at his regional rivals: in Palestine, Yasser Arafat was vilified as 'Israel's Bin Laden'[15] by Prime Minister Ariel Sharon; in Iraq, Saddam Hussein was top of the US list of the 'Axis of Evil'.

In September 2002 George W. Bush addressed the UN General Assembly, accusing Iraq of 'supporting terrorist organisations', adding that 'al-Qaeda terrorists who escaped Afghanistan are known to be in Iraq'.[16] These jihadis had in fact found shelter in the Kurdish northern region, out of reach of Saddam's regime, but the US president needed this al-Qaeda 'smoking gun' to force his way into the war. Two months later, Syria joined the unanimous vote of the Security Council in passing resolution 1441, warning against 'any further material breach of Iraq's obligations'.[17]

However, Bashar al-Assad did not support the US invasion of Iraq in March 2003, since he feared his regime would be next in the so-called democratizing campaign of the Middle East. His various intelligence agencies started cooperating with the rising Sunni insurgency on the other side of the 600-kilometre Syrian–Iraqi border. Of course, Damascus claimed to an angry Washington that controlling such a porous border was beyond its capabilities.

This was a 'win–win' game from the Syrian Mamluks' point of view: the American occupying force was stuck in Iraq proper and would not dare to extend its operations towards neighbouring Syria; Assad, through his unofficial support of the Iraqi insurgency, had a new card to play with in the regional and international arena (mainly with the Gulf states and with the USA); and all the fighters and weapons being smuggled through Syria to Iraq were heavily taxed by intelligence officials.

This Iraqi bonanza became even more palatable for the Syrian godfathers when they were forced out of Lebanon by the Spring 2005 'Cedar Revolution', after nearly three decades of plundering occupation. Just as when Bashar al-Assad had absorbed the blow of the US invasion of Iraq before retaliating through radical proxies, so now he swallowed the humiliation of his ousting from Lebanon, but let numerous jihadi activists sneak into Tripoli, the main city of northern Lebanon.

In August 2006, a new organization named Fatah al-Islam appeared in the Palestinian refugee camp of Nahr al-Bared, close to Tripoli. Only a fraction of those jihadi militants were Palestinian (there was for instance a strong Saudi contingent), but many of them had already fought in Iraq. They discussed with the al-Qaeda senior leadership (AQSL) the prospect of becoming its branch for the Levant (*bilad al-Shâm*), as a logical follow-up to the establishment of the Islamic State in Iraq (ISI), the local al-Qaeda franchise.[18]

Fatah al-Islam provoked the Lebanese army into a siege of the Nahr al-Bared camp, which continued from May to August 2007. Hundreds of casualties fell in the battle, but the remaining jihadi nucleus managed to escape safely. This could only be explained by intervention on the part of Syrian intelligence, which later rid itself of Fatah al-Islam's leader. As political scientist Bernard Rougier underlined, Assad's regime needed the jihadi threat both to exist and to be controlled, since 'a key component of its [the regime's] survival stems from the comparison he nurtures abroad with a worse threat than itself'.[19]

Syria's playing with jihadi fire proved costly in October 2008, when the US army, infuriated by Damascus's support for the Iraqi insurgency, raided one of its bases near the Syrian town of

Abou Kamal. Bashar al-Assad got the message loud and clear: during the following years, the Syrian security barons kept a low profile, even though they never suspended their active cooperation with the jihadi networks.[20] The rising star in Baghdad was the Syria-friendly PM Nouri al-Maliki, a former exile in Damascus during Saddam's dictatorship, which also contributed to this deceptive manoeuvre.

Assad's regime had handled with cool-blooded sophistication the global war on terror on its own doorstep, making the most of this threatening development. It had demonstrated that dedicated Mamluks could use the al-Qaeda bogeyman against their domestic opposition without even halting their continuing collaboration with authentic jihadi networks. This was a lesson that Bashar al-Assad would soon put into practice on a much larger and more devastating scale.

*

The Arab security mafias were the best equipped to benefit from the post 9/11 international reshuffle. They had the anti-terrorist discourse, the operational background, the sensitive files and, most important of all, the required absolute absence of scruples. Chapter 4 showed how the Algerian Mamluks had managed through this new environment to extricate themselves from their black decade in isolation. However, their Yemeni counterparts remained unmatched in their ability to extract foreign support and expand their power against the backdrop of a parallel expansion of the local jihadi menace.

The US invasion of Iraq (and the ensuing chaos it generated) allowed Bashar al-Assad and Husni Mubarak to play on nationalist sympathies (and the popular fear of instability) to resist any pressure for change. In 2005, the Egyptian autocrat had to run against other challengers, for the first time since his accession to power in 1981 (neither Nasser nor Sadat ever had any contender). Mubarak still won 88 per cent of the vote, while his police harassed opposition leaders, despite official and repeated US protests.

The colossal material aid that Washington was granting to Cairo played into the hands of the Mubarak regime rather than the reverse, since it was earmarked to buy US weapons and other goods whose producers were lobbying in DC on behalf of Egypt. When in 2005 Congress discussed the mere prospect of allocating part of the $1.3 billion military aid to development projects, the self-righteous uproar of the Egyptian Mamluks was impressive (and effective).[21] A few months later, the Muslim Brotherhood got 88 supposedly independent MPs elected (out of 454), but the regime made it clear that this was the upper limit of what it could tolerate.

In Syria, more than a million Iraqi refugees had crossed the border during America's post-Saddam occupation, and these became de facto the best propagandists for the Assad regime. Their heart-breaking accounts of civil war, widespread looting and unbridled crime made the Syrian population shiver at the prospect of such a disaster hitting them. In addition to that, the historical Iranian breakthrough in relations with the new regime in Baghdad, under the cover of the American protectorate, convinced Gulf donors to enhance their generosity towards the Mamluks in Syria, and even more so in Egypt.

But the global war on terror would not last for ever, and the newly elected President Obama wanted to withdraw from Iraq first, and then from Afghanistan. Arab Mamluks were still able to rely on the oil bonanza, either produced locally or derived from outside sponsors. At the end of the 1980s the first (aborted) wave of democratization in the Arab world had coincided with the demise of the Soviet Union and the oil counter-shock. Now stability was the name of the game in the diplomatic lexicon, and oil prices reached historical highs.

This explains why the dynamics of the second wave of democratization were much more indigenous and durable: a new Arab generation went on the streets to demand the end of the *nizâm*, meaning both the ruling 'regime' and the corrupted 'system' it nurtured. Some called it the 'Arab Spring'. Yet an Arab revolution would be more appropriate, since the regime/system was deemed unable to reform itself. A leaderless and non-violent uprising was threatening the very foundations of the most entrenched dictatorships.

This movement started at the end of December 2010 in Tunisia, where the security mafia was too centred on the presidential family (Ben Ali and his Trabelsi in-laws) and too police-oriented to see off the challenge of civilian protests. Once the armed forces had refused to crush the demonstrations, the Tunisian autocrat was forced to flee to Saudi Arabia on 14 January 2011.

It took only twenty-seven days to topple the twenty-three-year old Ben Ali regime. In every Arab country the situation seemed unpredictable. However, the Mamluk cliques were the most vigilant of all: they were aware of the revolutionary menace and were ready to absorb its initial impact. They were also preparing to strike back with all their might.

7

THE STORY OF TWO SQUARES IN EGYPT

Husni Mubarak could not but feel supremely confident in his thirtieth year of presidential rule. The November 2010 parliamentary elections were so conspicuously controlled by the security apparatus than all the opposition parties eventually boycotted them. Even the Muslim Brotherhood, which had initially expected to reiterate its 2005 electoral breakthrough, had opted out after the first round, blatantly marred by government manipulation.

Mubarak had succeeded Sadat in 1981 because he was his deputy, but he never designated a vice president himself. He was keeping an alternative open between his son Gamal, a living symbol of crony capitalism, who had built his own base inside the ruling party (NDP/National Democratic Party), and Omar Suleiman, the military head of the General Intelligence Department (GID). The security czar had increased his power through the US-led global war on terror, while 'Mubarak Junior' was charming foreign investors and Davos Forum guest stars.

The Egyptian president did not want to choose his own successor, since he had no wish to alienate either constituency (the security apparatus associated with Suleiman or the compradore bourgeoisie rallied behind Gamal). In the Mamluk handbook the safest bet was the spymaster option, because Suleiman combined the domestic and international clout that were key to the ruling clique. But the Egyptian despot was obviously tempted by the dynastic scenario, first implemented at Hafez al-Assad's death in 2000 on behalf of his son Bashar (in Yemen, Saleh was forcefully pushing in favour of his son Ahmed, commander of the Republican Guard).

Gamal Mubarak's main weakness in this Mamluk-run world was his lack of any military credentials. That was also what he boasted about when he claimed to be able to reform Egypt. In fact, such 'reform' was only intended to maximize the profits of the tiny minority of Egyptian businessmen plugged into the global economy. For the overwhelming rest of the country, it was survival as usual. As economist Samer Suleiman put it: 'Egypt's story in the last quarter century had been the story of regime success and state failure.'[1]

This regime victory over national interests was the main driving force for the takeover of Tahrir Square in the middle of Cairo by tens of thousands of peaceful protesters on 25 January 2011. Inspired by the Tunisian revolution, they shouted that 'the people want to topple the regime', and Tahrir (Liberation) became a collective aspiration as much as an urban centre. Despite a violent crackdown involving live ammunition, the opposition activists held their ground and the demonstrations extended countrywide.

Mubarak sacked his prime minister on 28 January 2011, replacing him with Ahmed Shafiq, a former general from the air force like himself. The next day, he appointed Omar Suleiman as vice president. But the police had lost control of the streets and tried to regain them in an unprecedented way: criminals were released from eighteen prisons and dozens of police stations[2] in order to scare the population away from revolutionary protests.

On Tahrir Square, waves of police-supported hoodlums, named *baltaguiyya*, attacked the demonstrators, often on camel or horseback. This 'Battle of the Camel', waged on 2 February, turned out to be a revolutionary success. Everywhere, the security forces, already blamed for their brutal repression, were now accused of having betrayed the country by unleashing criminal violence against the population, instead of protecting it. Police stations were attacked, sometimes looted and burnt, along with NDP headquarters. Neighbourhood vigilantes organized local patrols and checkpoints.

The Mamluk top brass contemplated with horror their whole system on the verge of collapse because of the stubbornness of the 82-year-old president, who insisted on remaining in power until the end of his fifth term in September 2011. The armed forces had managed to dissociate their public image from the police bogey-man, even though they had been actively engaged in the repression of the protests (and abuses carried out against detaineees).

Local accounts of fraternization between demonstrators and soldiers contributed to this enhancing of the military's popular credentials. 'The people and the army are united like fingers of one hand' was a common rallying cry. On 6 February, Suleiman opened a 'national dialogue' with various opposition parties, including the Muslim Brotherhood, but the protesters on Tahrir demanded nothing less than Mubarak's ouster.

Mubarak reluctantly agreed to transfer most of his powers to Suleiman and to relinquish leadership of the army on the evening of 10 February. The Supreme Council of the Armed Forces (SCAF) therefore convened without the president. At dawn, on 11 February, a human wave of protest surrounded the presidential palace. Suleiman went on state TV to announce that Mubarak 'has entrusted the SCAF to administer the nation's affairs'.[3] The now deposed president was flown from Cairo to the Sinai resort of Sharm al-Sheikh.

A Not So Revolutionary Coup

Although the Tunisian revolution has been celebrated on 14 January, the date Ben Ali fled the country in 2011, interestingly the

Egyptian revolution has been associated with 25 January, the first day of the anti-Mubarak protests on Tahrir Square. For the Egyptians themselves, their uprising has been perceived as an open-ended process at best and at worst as an aborted liberation struggle. Mubarak's fall was not just a dramatic achievement, but also a total game changer.

The Egyptian Mamluks stood ready to remain the major beneficiaries of the new rules, the way their Algerian counterparts had maintained their upper hand at the cost of a fully-fledged civil war. The parallel between Bendjedid's deposition in January 1992 and Mubarak's in February 2011 has seldom been drawn, but it deserves attention. In both cases, a military coup was implemented against the constitutional head of state. But the so-called Algerian decision-makers preferred to remain in the shadows, while the Egyptian SCAF came out as the official executive power.

Field Marshal Mohammad Hussein Tantawi, minister of defence since 1991, chaired the supreme military council through his seniority over the twenty plus other members (SCAF membership has oscillated between 20 and 25, according to the reshuffle of the top brass). The main players in the SCAF seemed to be Generals Sami Hafez Anan, the Chief of Staff, and Sedki Sobhi, commander of the Third Army. The SCAF's most junior member was Abdelfattah Sisi, director of military intelligence since 2010.

The SCAF could first count on an exceptional unity of views among its components (or at least, on their shared resolve to keep any dissent silent).[4] The Mamluk elite's behaviour matched its belief that its collective fate was at stake. (The same process occurred in Syria, but with President Assad still in power, while the Yemeni Mamluks would soon split between pro-Saleh and his opponents, bringing the country to the verge of civil war, and therefore prompting direct Saudi interference.)

This strong cohesion within SCAF contrasted sharply with the power struggles that had plagued the Free Officers six decades earlier. It was also a significant advantage for the Egyptian Mamluks in a country agitated by revolutionary fever, with activists of all shades exploring the possibilities of free speech at last. The only Egyptian body that could match the military's discipline was the Muslim Brotherhood (MB). Therefore one should not be surprised about the polarization of the post-Mubarak scene—be it positive or negative—between the SCAF and the MB.

The myth of a 'clean' and 'patriotic' army as opposed to a 'dirty' and 'repressive' police force was also key to consolidating the prestige of the new rulers. Contrary to the non-Mamluk Tunisian army, they had not deposed the dictator to pave the way for democratic transition. They had moved in to protect their domination and privileges. Their preferred formula was to have a civilian front, Algerian-style, yet they made it very clear that they were ready to go all the way in their power bid.

During three long weeks, the Shafiq government that Mubarak had appointed just before his fall was kept in place. However, popular pressure grew so strong that the SCAF designated Essam Sharaf as the new prime minister on 3 March 2011. Sharaf, a respected professor who had joined the anti-Mubarak Tahrir protests, soon had to admit that the real power remained in the hands of Tantawi and his fellow generals.

The SCAF had no problem in sacrificing civilian leaders of the security apparatus to appease the public's outrage. It was also settling long-term accounts with police chiefs who had benefited from Mubarak's bias (police budgets had soared sevenfold during the previous decade, compared to a 'mere' doubling of the armed forces' spending).[5] Habib al-Adly, minister of the interior from 1997 to 2011, was soon charged with embezzlement (but significantly not for having ordered the killing of protesters).

Meanwhile, Omar Suleiman disappeared from the official stage after two weeks of being vice president. The SCAF had no interest in him now that he had fulfilled his only mission, the announcement of Mubarak's resignation. The new head of the GID was a SCAF member, General Murad Muwafi, previously governor of Northern Sinaï. Israel, who had betted until the last day on Mubarak's remaining in power, was relieved to find long-time partners in leadership positions.

The adamant commitment of the SCAF to the peace treaty with Israel was also crucial for the US renewal of the $1.3 billion military aid package, disbursed annually. The Egyptian revolution had not raised the Camp David issue and the Muslim Brotherhood only promised to hold a referendum on the treaty, but the SCAF's warmth towards Israel facilitated the continuation of associated income flows to the Mamluk regime.

It took the popular assault on various State Security posts, in the early days of March 2011, to force the SCAF to act against the much-hated political police. However, State Security was simply renamed National Security and its powers remained nearly intact. The much-publicized purge of State Security was just cosmetic, since most of the 'purged' officers were eligible for retirement (or were transferred to other police departments).[6]

So the Egyptian Mamluks had restored their hegemony over the security apparatus, while sending all the right signals to the USA and Israel in order to safeguard their strategic income. With the limited cost of deposing Mubarak, they had managed to absorb the worst shock of the revolutionary protests. Now they needed a constitutional formula that would consolidate their upgraded power structure.

Paradoxically, the Muslim Brotherhood became the SCAF's closest ally during this volatile period. The Islamist organization had proved ready to strike a deal with Suleiman, to the dismay of the Tahrir activists, days before Mubarak's fall. They were now open to a tacit agreement with the top brass in order to hold general elections that they were confident of winning. In this fool's bargain, the MB dreamed of turning the clock back to 1952–4, when Islamist support for the Free Officers was aimed at securing Neguib's presidency, only to have this plot crushed by Nasser.

The Egyptian Mamluks had not doubts about the MB long-term objective, but they eagerly welcomed their help in curbing the revolutionary fervour throughout the country. One prominent MB lawyer from Alexandria was appointed by the SCAF to the eight-member committee in charge of drafting constitutional amendments. In a record ten days, this committee proposed strictly functional amendments: judicial monitoring of the elections, limitation to two successive four-year terms of the presidency, and the obligation to appoint a vice president in the first two months of the mandate.

Those limited amendments were presented to a popular referendum on 19 March 2011. The MB joined the SCAF in actively campaigning for a *yes* vote. The revolutionary coalition, on the other hand, called for a totally revised constitution and argued that a *no* vote would be the safest means to establish a new Republic. This path was the one that would be followed in Tunisia, with a public commitment to convene early elections for a Constitutional Assembly.

The Egyptian Mamluks had no intention of loosening their grip on power, and as long as they could elicit Islamist support, they felt confident about the success of their restoration plan. The referendum saw a sweeping victory of the *yes* contingent (77 per cent) with an estimated 60 per cent turnout. No major incident marred this electoral triumph for the SCAF, now officially legitimized as the supreme executive authority over the 'transition' period.

Bullets and Ballots

One month after the referendum, a military court passed a three-year jail sentence to an Alexandria blogger who had accused the armed forces of active participation in the repression. This was a clear warning to the 'revolutionary youth', which the SCAF was still praising on its Facebook page, the official mouthpiece of the collective leadership. In one of its many 'letters to the Egyptian people', the SCAF claimed 'all the legal measures taken lately were only directed toward thugs who terrorize the people of Egypt'.[7]

After having pledged to protect the protesters from any harm, the military leadership reversed its policy and left a puzzling security void during the next wave of demonstrations. In late May 2011, tens of thousands of people again gathered in Tahrir Square to call for a 'second revolution'. A minority of them were shouting for Tantawi and the SCAF to resign. Liberal and nationalist forces were worried about the rapid convening of general elections that would boost the well-organised MB (with its new legal political branch, the Freedom and Justice Party).

One basic demand of the Tahrir protesters had been the repeal of the State of Emergency (imposed after Sadat's killing in 1981, it had been renewed every three years ever since). But the SCAF retorted that its repeal could only be considered once the streets were cleared of protesters. The military top brass dismissed as mere 'rumours' the accusations made by human-rights activists of the reported detention of up to 12,000 political prisoners.[8]

On 8 July 2011, an open-ended sit-in was convened in Tahrir Square to press for dramatic changes. Tantawi's deputy at the ministry of defence, the SCAF member Mohsen al-Fangary, went on TV to address the protesters in a 'threatening' manner that was received very negatively. A disillusioned protester commented: 'Statements always come very late, just like with Mubarak, and are not satisfactory. We are not thugs, we are revolutionaries demanding justice.'[9]

The paternalistic tone of SCAF leaders towards the 'revolutionary youth' was indeed a caricature[10] reminiscent of the mix of benevolent cajoling and stubborn scolding of the last speeches of Mubarak. But direct violence soon followed these paternalistic admonitions. On National Day, 23 July 2011, hundreds of protesters were injured while marching to the SCAF headquarters at the ministry of defence. The infamous *baltaguiyya* that the Mubarak regime had unleashed on Tahrir were back on the streets, now posing as SCAF supporters.[11]

Two months later, Wael Ghonim, one of the icons of the Egyptian revolution, published an open letter to Marshal Tantawi: 'Accusations of treachery have targeted individuals who oppose SCAF policies under the premise that they are trying to sabotage the trust between the people and the army. However, some of the accused were at the frontlines of a revolution that the SCAF has described as one of the historical moments in the life of our nation.'[12]

With the State of Emergency still enforced, activists were now routinely condemned by military courts on criminal grounds. Despite these widespread human rights abuses, fifteen parties met on 1 October 2011 with Chief of Staff Anan to grant their public support to the SCAF. Among the main signatories of such an endorsement was Mohammad Morsi, the leader of the MB political branch. The newly-founded Salafi Nour Party was also part of the move, which deepened the divide between SCAF-friendly Islamists and Tahrir revolutionary militants.

The ghost of a military–Islamist alliance haunted post-Mubarak Egypt during autumn 2011. On 9 October, Christian Coptic activists demonstrated in front of state TV against the official cover-up of sectarian violence. The military crushed the rally and killed twenty-five protesters with live ammunition. The anchor-woman on air called Cairo residents to come and assist the soldiers 'under attack by the Christians'.[13]

The SCAF Facebook page published no 'letter to the Egyptian people' during the month following the massacre. It was even more of a shock when a cabinet office published a list of 'supra-constitutional principles' enshrining how the SCAF were above the law. Moreover, the military hierarchy could select 80 out the

100 members of the future Constitutional Assembly, and it was declared that the defence budget would remain undisclosed.

The slogan 'The people want the downfall of the marshal' (Tantawi) became increasingly popular in the subsequent protest marches. Meanwhile, the Muslim Brothers were campaigning for the parliamentary elections, scheduled to take place from 28 November 2011 to 11 January 2012. Their main rivals were the Salafi Nour Party that had enlisted a new generation of militants, contrary to the 'veteran' members of the MB-run Freedom and Justice Party (FJP).

The contrast could not have been greater between downtown Cairo, where anti-SCAF protesters were falling every day under security force firing, and the rest of Egypt, where elections were being held under an appearance of normality. Revolutionary groups, increasingly fragmented, were now weaker on Tahrir than the Ultras, the generic term to designate the battle-hardened soccer fans, who had a long record of clashes with the police, rather than with the army.[14]

General Sisi, who was the SCAF's most junior member, was in charge of the relationship with the young activists. Empowering the director of military intelligence with such an outreach mission was typical of the Mamluk mentality. And when the revolutionary delegates complained about the victims of the repression in a closed meeting with Sisi, they were appalled at his reply: that he lost more men whenever he went on military manoeuvres.[15] The time for courtesy calls, let alone authentic dialogue, was obviously over.

The first round of legislative elections saw a sweeping majority in favour of the Muslim Brothers (37 per cent) and the Nour-led Islamic Bloc (24 per cent). Shortly afterwards, the SCAF sacked Sharaf and appointed as head of government Kamal Ganzouri, who had already been prime minister under Mubarak from 1996 to 1999. The ministry of information was preserved, thereby ignoring one of the most popular revolutionary demands, and a retired general who had run the armed forces morale department inherited the portfolio.

When the three rounds of parliamentary procedure were completed, the Islamists confirmed their initial victory with 37 per cent to the MB/FJP and nearly 25 per cent for the Salafi Bloc. With 235 MPs out of 498, the Muslim Brotherhood got the secretary general of its political branch, Saad Qatatni, elected as the new Speaker. While the cycle of Tahrir violence had alienated the revolutionary youth from the general public, the tacit agreement between the Islamists and the SCAF seemed to have been mutually beneficial.

Between a Rock and a Hard Place

The military top brass was very clear in issuing its red lines to the elected parliament, despite the latter's democratic legitimacy based on a 54 per cent official turnout. SCAF member General Mukhtar al-Mulla announced that the legislative majority would 'not have the ability to impose anything that the people do not want'.[16] The government remained responsible only to the SCAF, and when Prime Minister Ganzouri addressed MPs on 31 January 2012, it was to stress the need to maintain the State of Emergency.

The following day, in Port Saïd, a football match between the Cairo club Al-Ahly and its local rival Al-Masry ended up in a massacre: seventy-four people, mostly Cairo Ultras, were killed when Al-Masry supporters attacked them, with the security forces standing by. Police passivity together with staunch support of the SCAF by Al-Masry fans led quickly to accusations that the revolutionary Ultras had fallen into a merciless trap.

Some Tahrir shock troops had indeed died in the bloodbath. And this tragedy, occurring one year after Mubarak's fall, proved that the Egyptian security remained unfit to handle mass movements without provoking catastrophic outcomes. Ultras and revolutionary activists now shared the same hatred for the SCAF and accused the Islamists of passively endorsing military repression.

Tantawi suggested deploying two helicopters to evacuate the injured victims, revealing his incapacity to grasp the magnitude of the slaughter. He then proclaimed a day of national mourning, but when returning to Cairo, the soccer stars of the Al-Ahly team refused to greet him at the airport. The SCAF leader eventually went on TV with a threatening and elliptical statement: 'The people know the culprits.'[17] The ministry of the interior was besieged in Cairo by Ultras calling for revenge, while some radicals even shouted 'Death to Tantawi'.

Not only had the Egyptian Mamluks been unable to restore calm in the country after one year in command, but they had also erected so many stumbling blocks on the way to a decent political transition that they had generated an institutional impasse. The Muslim Brotherhood seized the opportunity by appointing a 100-member constitutional commission with two-thirds of its members being Islamists (and only six women). The liberal members soon withdrew from the commission, nipping it in the bud. The escalating showdown between the SCAF and the MB had thus paralyzed the post-Mubarak political order. Both rival forces now simply hoped for victory in the presidential elections scheduled for the end of May 2012.

The SCAF's delaying tactics had denied the constitutional process its original meaning and deprived the elected assembly of effective power. They contributed directly to the polarization of politics through the presidential elections. The MB had repeatedly pledged not to have a candidate of its own, and had even excluded one of its top officials, Abdelmoneim Aboul Foutouh, when he declared his candidacy. But the failure of the Islamist constitutional manoeuvre led the MB to reverse its presidential stance entirely.

Brotherhood strongman Khayrat al-Shater was nominated as their official candidate. An alternative challenger, Mohammad

Morsi, was also registered to avoid any military veto on Shater, who had been jailed for years under Mubarak and pardoned in 2011 by the SCAF. This jail record, even though it was political rather than criminal, was indeed used to reject Shater's application. The main Salafi contender, Hazem Abu Ismail, was also vetoed because of the alleged dual citizenship (American and Egyptian) of his mother.

The SCAF had therefore excluded from the presidential race the two charismatic leaders of the MB and the Salafi movement. The remaining Islamist contenders were the MB dissident Aboul Foutouh and the unglamorous apparatchik Morsi. The military favourites were the retired general Ahmed Shafiq, who had been Mubarak's last PM (and first SCAF head of government), along with former foreign minister Amr Moussa. One outsider, Hamdin Sabbahi, claimed the Nasserist legacy.

On 23 and 24 May 2012, 46 per cent of the registered voters went to the polls. The drop in the electoral turnout, compared to the 54 percent of the legislative elections, could largely be explained by the dissatisfaction of the public after the disempowerment of the members of parliament. Morsi gained 24.8 per cent of the vote, followed by Shafiq (23.6 per cent), Sabbahi (20.7 per cent), Aboul Foutouh (17.5 per cent) and Moussa (11.1 per cent). A revolutionary coalition between Sabbahi and Aboul Foutouh could have easily topped the competition, but the divisions between nationalists, liberals and non-MB Islamists had paved the way for a dramatic showdown between Morsi and Shafiq.

The SCAF could still rely on its constitutional watchdog, a redoubt of Mubarak nostalgia, whose mission was to protect the constitution adopted under Sadat in September 1971 and amended by referendum in March 2011. All the members of the Supreme Constitutional Court (SCC) had been designated by Mubarak and its president was specially chosen by the deposed president to smooth the way for a dynastic transmission of power between Husni and Gamal.

On 14 June 2012 the SCC deemed unconstitutional the legislative electoral law and therefore dissolved the parliament elected five months earlier. The MB-dominated constitutional commission was also dissolved on the grounds of being the creation of a supposedly illegal parliament, in the same way as the recent law banning Mubarak's dignitaries from political office had been abrogated.

To cut a long story short, the SCAF had simply erased through this *coup de force* sixteen months of political transition, depriving the country of a parliament and a viable constitution. Egyptian Mamluks were now concentrating all the executive and legislative powers in their own hands. They were betting on popular fear of the unknown to secure the victory of their champion Shafiq. But their cynical gamble backfired.

On 16 and 17 June 2012, the official turnout fell to 35 per cent, more than ten points fewer than during the first round. Many disillusioned voters rejected the proposed alternative offered to them: either Islamist or military candidates. This popular disaffection favoured the militant networks of the Brotherhood, while disgruntled revolutionaries, like Aboul Foutouh or Ghonim, voted for Morsi to force Tantawi's clique out of office. Just after voting closed, the SCAF issued a 'constitutional declaration' that granted the military the upper hand in any dispute with the future president.

Morsi was eventually proclaimed the winning candidate with 51.7 per cent of the ballots (13.2 million votes, which meant 0.8 million more than Shafiq). He was sworn in on 30 June 2012 by the Supreme Constitutional Court and appeased the SCAF with his first statements. But once in power the new president moved quickly: on 9 July, he reinstated the dissolved MB-dominated constitutional commission; one month later, he reshuffled the military hierarchy, appointing Tantawi and Enan as 'presidential advisers' (the SCAF's leading duo was granted immunity through this move).

Abdelfattah Sisi, the head of military intelligence, became minister of defence, while Sedki Sobhi was promoted to chief of staff. The various top generals were replaced by their deputies (including Murad Muwafi, leaving the GID to Rafaat Shehata) and were generously compensated by public sinecures. The Muslim Brothers were duped into believing that they had finally subdued the Egyptian Mamluks. But the Deep State was soon busy undermining the first democratically elected president of the country.

Ten Months of Covert War

The Egyptian Mamluks were tempted to 'suspend' the electoral process in June 2012, as their Algerian counterparts had done in January 1992. But they were convinced that their constitutional manipulation had ensured iron-clad guarantees on the preservation of their power. More important, they were deeply aware of the formidable task any new government would have to face, with the Egyptian economy in shambles, and they were probably relieved to leave the domestic frontline to a civilian authority ready to pay the political price of making long-awaited and painful reforms.

One presidential source described Tantawi and Enan trapped in an office, their mobile phones deactivated, while Sisi, until then head of the military intelligence, was sworn in as minister of defence by Morsi in a nearby room.[18] This daring move occurred on 12 August 2012, a few days after a major security breach in the Sinai (sixteen Egyptian soldiers had been killed by a jihadi combat cell in Rafah, which then travelled 15 km on Egyptian territory, before being eliminated as soon as it had crossed the Israeli border). Tantawi and his chief of staff could reasonably be held responsible for such a fiasco. Israel and the USA therefore stayed calm when Tantawi and Enan were deposed.

But the parallel image of Tantawi out and Sisi in, portrayed as Morsi's masterstroke, could also be interpreted as a generational changing of the guards among the Egyptian Mamluks. Tantawi, born in 1935, and Enan, born in 1948, were replaced by promising generals in their late fifties. Contrary to the October 1973 generation, Sisi and his peers had no combat record. In true Mamluk endogamous style, Sisi transferred his command of military intelligence to his fellow general Mahmoud Hegazy, whose daughter had married one of Sisi's sons.

A former military attaché in Saudi Arabia, Sisi would soon prove to be a shrewd politico. He even duped the local and foreign media into believing he was a 'notorious Islamist'.[19] Meanwhile, he kept channels open with the opposition that had coalesced into a National Salvation Front (NSF). He also remained popular among the dignitaries and beneficiaries of Mubarak's era, designated by the pejorative term *fouloul*.

Last but not least, Sisi kept the armed forces out of domestic security, while the Islamist government appeared as insensitive as the SCAF had been to human rights abuses (during the first 100 days of Morsi's office, 34 people were reported killed by the police, and 88 cases of torture registered).[20] Keeping behind the scenes, while the Muslim Brotherhood was taking all the blame, proved both smart and efficient.

There was another reason for this ostensible low profile: the reshuffling and rearming of the Deep State. This concept, imported from the Turkish public debate, had become a popular point of discussion in the Egyptian media during the winter of 2012. When Nasser, Sadat or Mubarak were in power, there was no need for the Mamluk-run state to go 'deep'. The January 2011 mass protest forced the military top brass, rebranded as the SCAF, to pay lip service to the 'revolutionary youth' and to play political games with the newly legalized parties, most prominently the MB-led FJP.

Issandr al-Amrani, one of the most astute observers of the Egyptian scene, summarized SCAF's performance through the first year of the revolutionary process as follows: 'Apart from gross incompetence, the army's actions have another explanation: reassertion of a "Deep State" that was badly bruised during the January 2011 uprising and took some time to regain its footing.'[21] The dissolution of the former presidential party (NDP)and the public rejection of Mubarak-era figures forced the Mamluks to run 'deep' into alternative partnerships.

One ally to contain and eventually roll back the revolution was obviously the judicial hierarchy, which did a great job of sabotaging the democratic transition by any means necessary. The other more unexpected partner was the delinquent *baltaguiyya*. Instead of being hired by party bosses, as was the standard practice in the heyday of the now defunct NDP, the 'loyalist' hoodlums were controlled more or less directly by the 'security' agencies, especially the 'civilian' GID (led by a general, a member of the SCAF).

This tripartite alliance between militarized intelligence, politicized judiciary and criminal gangs that slowly emerged in Egypt in 2011–12 is reminiscent of the nefarious triad that was the trademark of the Turkish Deep State during the 1990s. In both instances, the priority target was at first the leftist movements (Kurdish or Turkish in Turkey, 'revolutionary youth' in Egypt). But this was perceived as the easiest part of a struggle that would eventually be waged against the Islamist threat.

In June 2012, the Deep State threw all its weight behind Shafiq in the presidential campaign, and was defeated. This left the Egyptian Mamluks in a state of shock, blaming Tantawi, Enan and Muwafi for such a failure. This might also explain why Morsi's ousting of this military trio did not generate a stronger reaction from the other SCAF members. In purging the top brass, Morsi helped it to absorb the traumas of January 2011 and June 2012 with a renewed aggressiveness.

Sisi had only to wait for Morsi to make mistakes, and the Egyptian president wasted no time in that respect. On 16 November 2012, Morsi sent his prime minister, Hisham Qandil, into the Gaza Strip, for the past two days under bombardment during the Israeli offensive codenamed 'Pillars of Smoke'. This unprecedented move contributed substantially to deterring an Israeli ground assault on the Hamas-run enclave. A ceasefire was brokered under Egyptian auspices on 21 November, since Israel and Hamas would not talk face to face.

Barack Obama called his Egyptian counterpart twice during the Gaza crisis and 'commended President Morsi's efforts to pursue a de-escalation'.[22] This American blessing, combined with pressure from MB hardliners, convinced the Islamist head of state that the time was ripe for a bold move. On 22 November 2012, he published a 'constitutional declaration' that gave him exceptional powers and immunized him from the judiciary. One week later, the constitutional commission, although boycotted by the liberals, hastily finalized a constitutional draft that incorporated most of the Islamists' demands.

Mohammad al-Baradeï one of the leaders of the NSF opposition coalition, accused Morsi of 'appointing himself Egypt's new Pharaoh'.[23] Tens of thousands of protesters soon rallied in Tahrir Square to denounce Morsi, while MB offices were attacked in Alexandria and in several other cities. In Damanhour, for instance, a fifteen-year-old Muslim Brother was celebrated by the Islamists as a 'martyr' because he died defending the party's local headquarters. But the opposition accused local gangs of being responsible for the killing that deeply divided the city between pro and anti-Morsi.[24]

What happened in Damanhour was experienced in many other places in Egypt. The Deep State had only to cunningly encourage the growing splits that were isolating the Islamists in power from the people, even though it is impossible to claim it actually took part in murderous provocations. On the contrary, Sisi called publicly for national reconciliation and pledged that the armed forces would never support one camp against the other.

Morsi's decision to push the MB-drafted constitution through a referendum ignited Egyptian politics. On 5 December 2012, waves of protesters marched to the presidential palace of Heliopolis. Military tanks moved in, but stayed put. Thousands of MB activists gathered to defend Morsi's palace and attacked the peaceful protesters. Increasingly violent clashes went on all night, with at least ten people killed by live firing, mostly Islamists. In Ismaïliya and Suez, MB party offices were attacked and looted.

The following day, Morsi, who had escaped from his besieged palace during the night, accused the protesters of being 'hired thugs'. He based this claim on their 'confessions', admitting that dozens of them had been illegally arrested and abused by MB members. Islamist activists had even established a makeshift detention centre at one of the gates of the presidential palace.[25] Morsi appeared increasingly as a party leader, covering up the illegal activities of his fellow Islamists, instead of ruling as a president for all Egyptians.

Morsi's 'constitutional declaration' of November 2012 mirrored the SCAF 'constitutional declaration' in June 2012. But the Egyptian Mamluks had been defeated by the polls, while the Muslim Brotherhood could bet on a victory through the referendum. The turnout on 15 and 22 December was just 32.9 per cent, revealing the constant and puzzling diminution in popular participation. But the constitution was approved by 63.8 per cent of those who voted.

The divisive legality on which Morsi was building his power proved fatal to his popular legitimacy. The more the Muslim Brotherhood believed it was 'winning', the more confrontational the relations between their supporters and the rest of the population became. Even the Salafi militants, who had actively backed the MB-drafted constitution, were now antagonized by Morsi's party tactics.

The liberal opposition had downgraded its hopes and was now hoping to get a mere one third of parliamentary seats in the coming elections, just enough to block any constitutional reform (that had to be approved by two-thirds of the MPs). The repeated call for a 'national dialogue' fell on deaf ears, with activists on both sides clashing in the streets in what looked increasingly like a blind vendetta. Morsi denied the formula of a national unity government that Baradeï was proposing, and which the NSF thought was the only way out of the crisis.

The political impasse and the confrontational environment generated the perfect conditions for the Deep State's operations. Historians of the next generation will no doubt be able to reconstruct with documented sources the exact chronology of this covert destabilization. And maybe they will have the benefits of filmed research, echoing the landmark *Spirale* that Armand Mattelart made about the carefully planned campaign against Allende's Popular Union in Chile in 1973.[26]

At this stage, one can only point to the successive indicators of a mounting escalation of subversion against the Muslim Brotherhood. In a country where conspiracy theories abound, it would be inappropriate to try to invest irrelevant meaning into the sequence. But by merely outlining the various stages of military mobilization is indeed revealing, given that most of the attention at that time was devoted to the political showdown between the MB and the NSF, now joined by the Salafis.

For obvious strategic reasons the Suez Canal had always stood at the core of the Mamluks' priorities. The Brotherhood's headquarters had been repeatedly attacked in that part of the country and Port Saïd witnessed the massacre of the revolutionary Ultras. The second anniversary of the Egyptian revolution, on 25 January 2013, saw violent anti-MB protests, especially in Suez, where the army was deployed to 'secure strategic institutions'.[27] Protesters routinely condemned 'the Brotherhoodization of the state' and the government's alleged 'begging to Qatar'.[28]

Qatar had indeed pledged generous financial help to Egypt, doubling its aid package from $2.5 to $5 billion.[29] However, the Gulf emirate was perceived not as a neutral partner, but rather as the political patron of the Muslim Brotherhood throughout the Arab world. The increased polarization between Qatar and Saudi Arabia, despite the two monarchies being Wahhabi, had also contributed to repeated crises between Cairo and Riyadh, alienating even further the Saudi-backed Salafis from the Qatar-supported MB.

The day following the 'second anniversary' riots, the political flames were fiercely fanned when a Cairo court condemned to execution twenty-one Port Saïd residents accused of taking part of the anti-Ultra massacre. The extreme severity of the verdict, in a country where few security personnel responsible for pro-testers' death had ever been convicted during the past two years, was received with outrage in Port Saïd.

Immediately after the verdict, the prison in Port Saïd where the defendants were detained was attacked by gangs armed with firearms. Police stations were also assaulted in other parts of the city. By that evening, at least thirty people had been killed, including two policemen. Contrary to Suez where the army had moved in swiftly after the first clashes, in Port Saïd the military kept a low profile. On 27 January 2013, an enraged Morsi imposed a curfew in Suez, Port Saïd and Ismailiya.

The local population openly defied the curfew, expressing their vocal hatred for both the police and the Muslim Brothers. The military sent clear signals as to where they stood (they even organized evening soccer competitions with the residents in Suez).[30] The slogan 'One hand' celebrating the alliance between 'the army and the people' became ubiquitous again. Thousands of Port Saïd residents went so far as to sign a petition calling explicitly for the military to topple Morsi.[31]

In Cairo, the brutality of the Port Saïd verdicts at least had the effect of appeasing the Ultras, who toned down their attacks against the Muslim Brotherhood. But they were soon replaced by masked activists who called themselves Black Block and whose aggressiveness was totally focused on the Islamists: 'We will fight until victory, which means Morsi and his regime have to go. Then, we do not care who will be president, as long as he takes care of the country.'[32]

It was the first time in post-Mubarak Egypt that a 'revolutionary' force had preached both anonymity and all-out war against the Brotherhood. In Port Saïd, after weeks of clashes between local gangs and the police, the army took full control of the city in early March 2013. The military were welcomed by the relieved population, while opposition officials openly bet on a showdown between the army and the MB: 'The army is back at the table. We have to be careful that the military does not eat all the cake. But nothing stops us using them to prevent the Muslim Brothers eating all the cake either.'[33]

Secret meetings were then held at the Navy Officers Club in Cairo, between top generals and opposition leaders. Their conclave led to a daring conclusion: 'if the opposition could put enough protesters on the street, the army would step in, and forcibly remove the president'.[34] Mubarak-era loyalists joined the talks, including Hany Sarie el-Din, the lawyer of the imprisoned magnate Ahmad Ezz, who symbolised Gamal-inspired crony capitalism.

This inclusion of wealthy businessmen in the anti-MB coalition was crucial, as Morsi tried desperately to secure a long-awaited deal with the IMF on a $4.8 billion loan. But IMF demands to cut government subsidies on basic commodities would have been politically suicidal for the Muslim Brotherhood. So the downward spiral meant a constant deterioration in living standards of Egyptians (25 per cent youth unemployment, rising inflation, combined with 10 per cent wage cuts).[35]

Parallel to the Navy Officers Club top-level meetings, the General Shehata-run GID had done its homework on the grassroots organizers. They 'identified young activists unhappy with Morsi's rule' since they thought the army and ministry of the interior were 'handing the country to the Brotherhood'.[36] The first working sessions started in mid-March 2013. Six weeks later, the 'Tamarod' (Rebellion) movement was launched.

Mahmoud Badr and the four other liberal founding members decided that the movement's target would be collecting 15 million signatures on a petition calling for Morsi's resignation. The self-proclaimed purpose was to challenge the legitimacy bestowed on the elected president by more than 13 million voters in June 2012. This was quite a strange approach to democratic process and institutions, to say the least, since nobody could check the validity of the signatures thus collected.

The five founders of Tamarod came from the Baradeï-linked opposition to Mubarak, as did Wael Ghonim and some of his associates from the January 2011 uprising. But the Tahrir activists had then called for a fully-fledged 'revolution', while the 'rebellion' goal of Tamarod could placate the Mubarak-era grandees, many of whom supported Tamarod financially.[37]

Meanwhile, a powerful group of 'independent' media were attacking not only Morsi's rule, but his very legitimacy as an elected president. The Arabist blog described a 'relentless media machine demonizing and delegitimizing the Morsi administration far beyond its self-inflicted damage'.[38] The Muslim Brotherhood felt under attack from all sides and reacted by a renewed aggressiveness that in turn sharpened its political isolation and its militant rhetoric.

This positioned Sisi and his fellow Mamluks at the very heart of the political scene, just where they wanted to be. On 15 May 2013, the minister of defence issued no less than five public messages, all posted on his Facebook page, that were avidly commented on throughout the political spectrum. The first message was a solemn denial of any personal ambition: 'the notion of inviting the army into the country's political life again is extremely dangerous, it could turn Egypt into another Afghanistan or Somalia'.[39]

Sisi also warned the media against any attack on the military establishment: 'the army follows what is published about it and it does not like to see its officers and soldiers offended'.[40] So much for freedom of expression. But the military supremo was also keen on stressing that the Mamluk grand design of a pharaonic 'Suez Canal Development Axis Project' would go ahead as planned under the supervision of the armed forces and the GID.

Morsi's supporters felt reassured that the top brass would stick to its corporatist interests and its neutral stand. One of the Islamist officials declared: 'in the Muslim Brotherhood, we did not believe that the army would act against a government that has revived Egypt's prestige home and abroad'.[41] Interestingly, pro-Morsi activists were stating his 'prestige', not his democratic credentials, as his main asset. The stage was set for the final showdown.

A Summer of Blood

The Tamarod campaign was now going at full speed, with police and administration officials openly supporting it. Anti-Morsi activists claimed they had now reached their target of 15 million signatures. A mass protest march was scheduled for 30 June 2013. One week ahead of this much-anticipated deadline, Sisi's tone turned far less benevolent than it had been in mid-May.

'We have a week during which a great deal can be accomplished. This is a call that is just motivated by the love of the nation.' The minister of defence urged 'understanding, consensus and genuine reconciliation', before adding in an ominous threat that the military 'will not remain silent while the country slips into a conflict that will be hard to control'.[42]

On 29 June 2013, Tamarod announced that it had gathered the unverifiable number of 22 million signatures. The following day, millions of people took to the streets of Egypt. Impressive pictures of the human tide were taken from the air by military planes (Air Force planes also performed elaborate stunts, painting smoke hearts and Egyptian flags above the protesters). Morsi showed no sign of backing down, even though the 'one hand' of the military–Tamarod alliance was now looming over his own head.

On 1 July 2013, Sisi issued a 48-hour ultimatum to Morsi, urging him to reach an agreement with the opposition. Mahmoud Badr, on behalf of Tamarod, called publicly for the army to step in.[43] There were strong indications that the military were ready to move anyway.[44] On 3 July, three of the Tamarod founding members met with Sisi, to the dismay of the two others. Soon afterwards, the first democratically elected president of Egypt was arrested and held incommunicado by the military. MB leaders were targeted in a sweeping campaign.

The military coup was described, consistently with the Tamarod narrative, as a 'revolution', while Sisi declared, in true Orwellian style, that he was still not seeking power, at the very moment when he was grabbing it brutally: 'The armed forces could not close their eyes to the movement and demands of the masses calling them to play a national role, not a political role, as the armed forces will be the first to proclaim that they will stay away from politics.'[45]

Once he had paid lip service to his repeated promises to 'stay away from politics', Sisi went on with an explicit warning: the army 'will confront with all its might, in cooperation with the ministry of interior, any violation of public peace'.[45] The Tahrir dream of the army defending the people from the police was gone; it was now the entire security apparatus that was united against any dissent. Such a public address was broadcast live, with the military, administrative and judiciary hierarchy sitting around a standing Sisi, along with the sheikh of Al-Azhar, the Pope of the Coptic Church … and the leader of the opposition front (NSF).

Mahmoud Badr fully endorsed Sisi's coup on behalf of Tamarod, alienating a significant sector of the liberal activists who had hoped for a peaceful solution. One of the five founding members of Tamarod was in shock: 'What state TV read was as if it had been written by the army, it threatened the Brother-hood, told them they would use force if necessary.'[47] Tamarod's state of grace had been as short as the 48-hour ultimatum Sisi issued to Morsi.

Adly Mansour, whom the deposed president had nominated as head of the Supreme Constitutional Court in May 2013, became the interim president. He soon chose the opposition leader Baradeï as deputy. This civilian front left all real power in the hands of Sisi, who had announced the suspension of the con-stitution. The power cuts and gas shortages that had aggravated Morsi's unpopularity disappeared with a speed that gave credit to the thesis of an organized destabilization.[48]

Sisi appointed Shehata as Mansour's security adviser and replaced him at the head of the GID with one of his closest asso-ciates: General Mohammad Farid al-Tohamy had been Sisi's men-tor when he was director of military intelligence and, after 2004, of the Administrative Oversight Authority. This neutral title hid a Nasser-founded secretive bureau that kept the security apparatus in line through so-called 'anti-corruption campaigns'.

Morsi had ousted Tohamy in September 2012, after repeated accusations that he had covered up massive financial irregulari-ties on behalf of Mubarak's cronies, including the presidential family. One Western diplomat described Tohamy as 'the most hard-line, the most absolutely unreformed. He talked as though the revolution of 2011 had never even happened.'[49] Tohamy's appointment indicated that Sisi was seriously considering not only a crackdown on the Muslim Brothers, but also their com-plete eradication now that the coup was over.

On 5 July 2013, twenty-five people died during clashes between pro-Sisi and pro-Morsi activists all over the country. Thousands of supporters of the former president gathered for an open-ended sit-in in front of the Republican Guard Club, in the North-East of Cairo, where they believed Morsi was detained. Before dawn on 8 July, the sit-in was attacked by the military and police with live ammunition. At least fifty-one people were killed. Most of the local media did not even bother to report the massacre.

A few hours later, Mansour published a 'constitutional declaration' that prepared the ground for drafting a new constitution. Legislative elections would then be organized, prior to a presidential vote. It was obvious that the 'interim president' was only Sisi's mouthpiece, since even Mansour's deputy had not been informed of such a declaration. The army remained explicitly above the law in this proclamation.

In Damascus, Bashar al-Assad warmly congratulated Sisi for having deposed Morsi (one of the last decisions of the Islamist president had been to sever diplomatic relations with the Assad regime, relations that resumed immediately after the coup). In Algiers as well, Bouteflika and his government lent their full support to Sisi's coup. The icon of the Yemeni revolution (and Nobel Peace Prize winner in 2011) Tawakul Karman was barred from entering Egypt by the military leadership. This was a clear signal of their support for Ali Abdullah Saleh, even a year and a half after he had left office in Sanaa.

Saudi Arabia, the United Arab Emirates and Kuwait announced an exceptional aid package of $12 billion to Sisi's Egypt. Qatar—the main financial backer of the Muslim Brothers, especially in Egypt—was now vilified by the Cairo media. The Doha-based Al-Jazeera satellite TV was even accused of 'intoxicating' the Egyptian people on behalf of the Brotherhood. The Egyptian Mamluks could therefore combine the endorsement of their Syrian and Algerian counterparts with the unlimited generosity of Saudi Arabia and its Gulf allies.

On 26 July 2013, Sisi called the 'Egyptian people' to demonstrate their support for his fight against Muslim Brotherhood 'terrorism'.[50] Millions took to the streets that day, also celebrating the anniversary of the Free Officers' coup in 1952. Dozens were killed in clashes with Islamist supporters. A 'museum of the revolution' was now erected in Tahrir Square, but it was dedicated only to the struggle against the Muslim Brothers, under the symbolic patronage of Nasser, Sadat and Sisi.[51]

Hunted away from Tahrir, tens of thousands of pro-Morsi demonstrators, including entire families, were now regrouped in two mass sit-ins, one in Rabia al-Adawiya, in Madinat al-Nasr, the other on Al-Nahda square, near the university of Cairo. They kept demanding Morsi's reinstallation to power. The ministers of foreign affairs of the USA (John Kerry) and of the European Union (Catherine Ashton) tried to broker the resumption of a 'national dialogue' between the Sisi and Morsi camps. But on 7 August 2013, the new regime rejected any concessions, thereby ending any hopes for international mediation.

One week later, the two sit-ins were forcefully broken up, with hundreds of people killed in Rabia al-Adawiya. Armoured tanks and indiscriminate sniping cleared the mass gatherings at a horrendous cost. Human Rights Watch denounced 'the most serious incident of mass unlawful killings in modern Egyptian history'.[52] From 14 to 18 August 2013, more civilians were killed than during the 18 days of the January 2011 revolution (at least 928, compared to 846 in 2011).[53]

Most of the casualties occurred in Cairo, while Islamist activists 'retaliated' against Coptic citizens and buildings (twenty-five churches were attacked in ten of Egypt's twenty-seven provinces on 14 and 15 August 2013).[54] There was also evidence of armed resistance to the crackdown, since the number of policemen killed in those five days of bloodshed was three times higher than in January 2011.[55]

Baradeï resigned from his vice presidency, in protest against the massacre. But a lawsuit was soon filed against him for 'betrayal of (the people's) trust'.[56] Baradeï knew first-hand how the judiciary worked hand in glove with the armed forces, and he therefore fled Egypt. The liberal fig leaf on the military coup had served its purpose from Sisi's point of view and could now be utterly discarded.

A police general interviewed on the record by the French newspaper *Le Monde* was very candid about the targets of the repression: 'We need six months to liquidate or jail all the Muslim Brothers. It is not a problem for us, we already did that in the nineties.' He added that 'we have to detain or kill their leaders, thirty top leaders and 500 mid-rankers, and then the others will go home'.[57] The police and the army threw all their forces into this 'war', with a constant link drawn between the then still legal Brotherhood and the jihadi groups that had been defeated two decades earlier.

One might wonder if the international community's passivity in the wake of the Egyptian slaughter did not convince Bashar al-Assad that he could escalate the war against his own population without significant risk. In the early hours of 21 August 2013, pro-regime forces bombed insurgent-held neighbourhoods of Damascus with a combination of gas-loaded and conventional rockets. Around 1,400 people were killed in the attack, most of them through chemical strikes.

Sisi's Egypt, along with Bouteflika's Algeria, dismissed the accusation of war crimes against the Syrian dictator and stood firmly opposed to any 'aggression against Syria'.[58] Mamluks vowed to close ranks in order to protect one of their own, no matter how horrendous the massacres he had committed. Interestingly, Sisi did not shy away from contradicting his generous Gulf backers when it came to solidarity with his fellow Mamluk from Damascus.

In Egypt, the dynamics of the all-out repression soon exceeded its initial target. Some 2,000 alleged 'Brothers' were detained in the course of a month. On 23 September 2013, the Egyptian justice declared the Muslim Brotherhood illegal and confiscated all its properties. Two weeks later, an ecstatic pro-Sisi crowd celebrated the fortieth anniversary of the 'October War' on Tahrir Square. Dozens of pro-Morsi demonstrators were killed when trying to access Tahrir. The bloodshed was barely reported in the local media. The square associated with the anti-Mubarak revolution was now firmly back in the hands of the Egyptian Mamluks.

Sisi the Superstar

'In Sisi we trust.' This banner was waved by a 50-year-old Cairo fan of the minister of defence, who said in October 2013: 'Sisi is the best. He knew how to rid us of the Muslim Brothers and how to confront the United States.'[59] The schizophrenic idea that the Egyptian military were a model of anti-American steadfastness had spread as fast as the conspiracy theories describing the MB as a CIA puppet. One of the SCAF mouthpieces went as far as threatening live on TV to 'slaughter Americans in the streets' if Sisi were harmed in any way.[60]

Sisi mania was running wild in an Egypt that had forgotten that the pale Mansour was still, nominally, its president. Al-Ahram celebrated the saviour general in understated prose: 'Yes, the eagle has landed. His bronze, gold skin, as gold as the sun's rays, hides a keen, analytical fire within. He challenges the world not with bellows and bravura, but with a soft, sombre reproach.'[61] T-shirts, posters, mugs and souvenirs appeared on sale as the full paraphernalia of a personality cult swept across Egypt.

A hero always needs a villain. Morsi, the deposed president, still claiming his legitimacy from within his defendant's cage, was accused of spying for Qatar, conspiring with Hamas, and, on top of that, of incitement to murder, looting and destruction of the economy. Meanwhile, Mubarak was released and even praised Sisi in a rare interview: 'the people want Sisi and the people's will shall prevail'.[62] Luminaries of the Mubarak era were lining up behind Sisi, while exiled 'businessmen' reached 'reconciliation' agreements (settling corruption charges against cash compensation) in order to return to their homeland.[63]

The fierce crackdown against the Muslim Brothers continued and was also extended to the remnants of the 'revolutionary youth' who refused to join Sisi's fan club. Since neither the mainstream Islamist nor the leftist protesters had fallen into the trap of armed violence, they were systematically linked with the growing jihadi threat. The Egyptian military had launched massive anti-jihadi campaigns in the Sinai Peninsula, codenamed Eagle in August 2011, Sinai in August 2012 and ... Desert Storm in August 2013. But, far from curbing the militant surge, those operations had further alienated the local Bedouins and consolidated the popular base of the jihadi groups.

Ansar Beit al-Maqdis (ABM, literally the 'Champions of Jerusalem') had emerged as the strongest of those groups. Originally active in the Sinai, with Israel as its main target, it had increasingly begun to attack the security forces in a retaliatory logic for their alleged 'crimes'. ABM had also extended its reach into downtown Cairo, where it attacked the minister of the interior, Mohammad Ibrahim, on 5 September 2013. He escaped the assassination attempt, but on 24 December ABM claimed the suicide bombing of a police station that killed sixteen people in Mansoura in the Nile Delta, 120 km north of Cairo.

The following day, the Muslim Brotherhood was officially labelled a terrorist organization. Egypt therefore joined the exclusive club of countries who had branded as terrorist the historic matrix of Islamism, along with Israel (towards Hamas), Syria (where mere membership of the Muslim Brotherhood had been punishable by death since 1980), Saudi Arabia and the United Arab Emirates (in the escalation of their feud with Brotherhood-friendly Qatar). Egyptian security alleged they could demonstrate the links between the MB and ABM, but those claims were never substantiated.

A fifty-member constitutional committee drafted a new charter, the third since Mubarak's fall, in which the concept of 'civilian regime' was replaced by 'civilian government' (leaving full rein to the military). The text was referred to as a 'recipe for civil war' by one European think tank,[64] while the political scientist

Nathan Brown described it as 'a security state with a democratic face', since it 'grants military courts the rights to try civilians' and 'the military budget is effectively insulated from the political process'.[65]

On 14 and 15 January 2014 the constitution was approved, with an official turnout of 38.6 per cent (compared to 32.9 per cent in December 2012) and an overwhelming 98.1 per cent positive votes (63.8 per cent under Morsi). The Salafis, who had endorsed the MB-drafted text, now supported the junta-inspired constitution, gambling that the military would have need of a loyal Islamist partner. Indeed, the attacks on Christians, Shias and non-believers remained frequent under Sisi, since Salafis were often more sectarian than the Muslim Brothers.[66]

Soon after the constitutional plebiscite, the docile Mansour promoted Sisi to the rank of field marshal. The SCAF commented that 'the popular demand for Sisi is an order'.[67] This momentous display of Mamluk discipline was naturally followed by the official candidacy of 'Super-Sisi'. Nobody spoke any longer about holding parliamentary elections before the presidential poll, contrary to what Sisi himself had promised after his coup.

During the run-up to the elections, the judiciary, whose help had been crucial to Sisi's ousting of Morsi, asserted their sympathies in the most unambiguous manner. The justice department was thoroughly purged of any Islamist sympathizers. A court in Minya, 250 km south of Cairo, sentenced to death no less than 529 alleged Islamists in March 2014 (then commuted the death penalty to life imprisonment for 492 of them), and 683 the following month. This grisly parody of justice sent shockwaves worldwide, but left Sisi and his supporters unmoved.

Meanwhile, the military were now dealing directly, without formal tender, with billion-dollar-worth projects funded by the United Arab Emirates, ranging from colossal wheat silos to vast housebuilding programmes ($40 billion for one million units with the Dubai-based Arabtec).[68] The ministries of health, transportation, housing and youth also gave commissions to the ministry of defence for ambitious infrastructure projects.[69] The Mubarak-era magnates were aware that they would have to take into full consideration the demands of their military business partners.

Sisi resigned from the ministry of defence and retired from his recent Field Marshalship in order to preserve the illusion of a 'civilian' candidacy. He did not campaign much, officially due to his innate humility, more probably for security reasons (the jihadi threat was indeed growing, instead of receding). His only challenger, the Nasserist Hamdin Sabbahi, was prevented from waging a serious campaign, notably because of the media blackout on his programme and performances.

Presidential elections were scheduled for 26 and 27 May 2014. The turnout was so low on the first day that the government panicked and declared May 27 a public holiday, while shutting down commercial malls, encouraging the private sector to let their employees vote and threatening abstainers with fines. As the turnout remained dismally low, the elections were prolonged for a third day and free transport was offered to voters.

In these circumstances, the official turnout of 47.5 per cent seemed highly improbable, since the official media had claimed it was 35 per cent, before 'upgrading' it to 40 per cent in the final hours of the vote. The 4 per cent proportion of invalid votes proved that a significant number of voters had been forced to the polls and reacted with a defiant gesture. Sabbahi managed to secure only 3 per cent of registered votes, compared to 97 per cent for Sisi. But the tarnished presidential consecration had all the traits of a shameful remake of the worst Mubarak-style plebiscite.

The elected president did not wait long before asking the Egyptian people to prepare for two generations of sacrifice until the country's economy could be restored. In July 2014, he took the bold step of announcing a progressive cut in fuel price support (accounting for 20 per cent of overall government expenditure), as part of a comprehensive plan to reduce all public subsidies.

The hot summer was then plagued by power outages lasting up to six hours in Cairo and sometimes twice as long in Upper Egypt. The minister in charge admitted that the situation would remain unsatisfactory for the next four years, until large-scale investment in new power stations and renewable solar energy came to fruition.[70] But the extra amount of water discharged to generate more hydroelectric power carried the risk of potential drought.[71]

More troubling for the (former) marshal-president was his inability to curb the rising tide of jihadi violence. The military crackdown on the Muslim Brotherhood, despite their electoral victories, had vindicated ABM and other militant factions, like Ajnad Masr (Soldiers of Egypt), in their choice of armed jihad as the only option against the 'infidels'. They targeted security forces, but also tourism facilities, aggravating the collapse of the tourism sector, a major currency-earner during the previous decade.

In three consecutive days in January 2014, ABM struck at three different locations, with a string of bombings in Cairo, the shooting down of a helicopter in Sinai and a deadly ambush of an army bus. The military increasingly retaliated with air strikes in the Sinai Peninsula. Such a nailed fist policy towards the local population, coupled with mass arrests and forced deportations, fuelled Bedouin hostility against the security forces. This is how, for instance, the Sawarka tribe, south of Rafah, became even more supportive of ABM.

The perception of the Egyptian military as an occupying force only enhanced the profile of jihadi groups as the armed protectors of the local tribes.[72] Israel understood the danger well and allowed the Egyptian air force into the border region for the first time since 1967. But an increasing proportion of jihadi attacks occurred in mainland Egypt now, a trend that underlined the failure of this bellicose approach. Despite such failure, President Sisi delivered the staunchest warning one year after his coup:

'Egypt is in a state of war, many are hostile to it within and out-side the country who do not want this country to be saved.'[73]

Mamluks United

The first official trip made by the newly-elected Egyptian president was to his Algerian counterpart, on 25 June 2014. Both Sisi and Bouteflika knew better than anybody else what it had taken to get them into the presidential seat, so they could skip the preliminaries. Their joint statement focused heavily on their shared concern about Libya and so-called terrorism. In the past, Algerian and Egyptian Mamluks alike had joined in branding as "terrorist" any kind of serious domestic opposition But their convergence of views on Libya was a recent development.

When Benghazi rose against Moammar Qaddafi in February 2011, the Egyptian military supported with intelligence and supply the Libyan insurgency in the eastern part of the country. The Egyptian Mamluks were eager to take revenge for a four-decade cycle of provocation, since the Libyan dictator boasted of being more Nasserist than Nasser had ever been. They loathed the Jamahiriyya system that had enslaved the professional army to Qaddafi's praetorian guard.

Retribution came with the Benghazi uprising and the defection of the Libyan minister of interior, General Abdelfattah Younes, who led his special forces with him on the revolutionary side. The split inside the Libyan armed forces seemed a harbinger of the collapse of Qaddafi's regime for the Egyptian Mamluks, who looked at their institution as a watertight one, ready to defend itself against all odds.

However, Younes, who was appointed commander-in-chief of the anti-Qaddafi forces, failed to live up to those expectations. Egypt backed his demand for a NATO-enforced no-fly zone that eventually led to an air campaign against the regime forces in the second half of March 2011. Benghazi was saved from an all-out

assault, but a protracted desert war absorbed much of the revolutionaries' energies and blocked their advance westward.

In late July 2011, Younes was detained on his way back from
the front by a disgruntled Islamist warlord and summarily executed.[74] This murder came as a shock to the Egyptian military:
they tried to fall back on Khalifa Haftar, who had been Qaddafi's governor of Tobruk from 1981 to 1986, before defecting
to the CIA in Chad in 1987. But this veteran nationalist opponent had a far too confrontational attitude, which killed his
chances of becoming Younes' successor. And Egyptian intelligence lost the advantage, as its Qatari and Emirati counterparts
intensified their involvement in western Libya, around Misrata
and Zintan, respectively.

The Algerian generals had warned against any foreign intervention in Qaddafi's Libya from the very beginning. They condemned
this 'plot' against Arab nationalism and stoked the wildest conspiracy theories about Israel, Qatar and NATO. They feared the
impact on Algeria of a revolutionary precedent in Tunisia and
they now denounced the growing jihadi threat in Libya. Algeria's
military also lent covert support to Qaddafi's regime until its
overthrow, and then welcomed some of the dictator's family and
senior associates after Tripoli's fall in August 2011.

The Algerian and Egyptian Mamluks were relieved therefore
when the Libyan Muslim Brotherhood fared poorly at the first
free elections held in July 2012 (they won 17 out of 80 party
seats, on top of the 120 'independent' MPs). This was a reassur-
ing message for the SCAF, recently humiliated by the defeat of
his protégé, Shafiq, in front of Morsi. The same went for Algeria's so-called decision-makers, wary as they were of the success
of an Islamist-run Tunisia. In eastern Libya Egypt increased its
support for Haftar, while Algeria did likewise for the Zintan
militias in the west.

Haftar had indeed opposed the jihadi militia of Ansar al-
Sharia (the Supporters of Sharia) in Benghazi. Yet the main

rivals of Zintan for control of Tripoli were the militias of Misrata who were by no means Islamist, despite their tactical alliance with the Muslim Brotherhood. These local nuances were naturally irrelevant for the Egyptian and Algerian Mamluks, advocating in their own country a fight against 'Islamic terrorism' which had to be replicated with the same brutality in Libya.

In February 2014, Haftar appeared on TV in a general's uniform, calling for a presidential commission to organize new elections. He had then been accused of attempting a Sisi-style coup, but three months later, emboldened by the political impasse and by Egyptian support, Haftar launched his 'Dignity' offensive, along with air raids, against jihadi and Islamist groups in Benghazi. This was followed by a parallel move on the part of the Algerian-backed Zintan militias in Tripoli.

The violent clashes that followed, with dozens killed in Benghazi and Tripoli, compelled the authorities to convene new elections, in which only 42 per cent of the registered voters took part in June 2014. The new assembly met in Tobruk, but was deemed illegal by the previous parliament, which refused to be dissolved. Libya now had two governments, each responsible in front of its own parliament: in Tripoli for the Misrata–MB coalition, in Tobruk for the Haftar–Zintan alliance.

It is important to note that, contrary to the dominant narratives, this was neither an East versus West conflict (Zintan actively supported the Tobruk government) nor a 'nationalist' versus 'Islamist' struggle (Misrata's militias were no more Islamist than Zintan's). But Sisi, even more than Bouteflika, pushed for the anti-jihadi discourse, which encouraged Haftar to new extremes.

Fighter bombers from the east targeted Misratan positions in Tripoli twice in August 2014. Those unprecedented air strikes did not prevent the Misratans capturing Tripoli airport from the Zintan militias. US sources soon confirmed that Emirati airplanes flying from Egyptian air bases had carried out the bombings.[75] Egypt denied any intervention of the part of its air force, without elaborating on its logistical support, while the United Arab Emirates stayed silent.

Those joint Egyptian–Emirati air raids, perhaps coordinated with neighbouring Algeria, and backed by Saudi Arabia, had a brutal counter-revolutionary flavour. The Misratan targets were neither Islamist nor jihadi, but they happened to have entered a political alliance with the Muslim Brotherhood. Saudi Arabia and the United Arab Emirates had already joined forces in crushing the popular protests in Bahrain as early as March 2011. They had struggled in the whole region against Qatari support for the Muslim Brotherhood in particular, and revolutionary activism in general.

In Egypt, the Saudi and Emirati authorities had contributed billions to Sisi's coup. They were also supportive towards his Libyan avatar Haftar. Since Qatar still backed the Misrata militias, the Emirates had intensified their aid to the Zintanis. However, the August 2014 bombings did not prevent the ejection of the Zintanis by the Misratans from the capital city. And the Cairo-backed Tobruk government still carried less weight than the Tripoli one, since Haftar had been unable to conquer Benghazi.

Beyond the post-Qaddafi power struggle, it is fascinating to see how the Egyptian Mamluks joined the fray in a very dubious battle in Libya, but refused to enter the anti-jihadi coalition in Syria. Sisi, while visiting the USA in September 2014, answered smilingly to a question about his absence from the Obama-led bombing campaign against the self-proclaimed jihadi 'caliphate' in Syria: 'Give us back our F-16 and Apache warplanes first.'[76] Washington had indeed suspended the delivery of four F-16 fighter jets and some combat helicopters as a consequence of Sisi's coup. But the Egyptian supremo insisted on reclaiming them as his, just as the Egyptian Mamluks considered the $1.3 billion annual American aid as a due. To date they have rejected intervening in the sphere of their fellow Mamluks in Syria. Thus it was that Sisi could combine his dependency on America with a vibrant nationalist rhetoric. Nothing was new in that regard under the Arab counter-revolutionary sun.

*

The Egyptian Mamluks had managed with far more talent than their Algerian counterparts, two decades earlier, to contain, roll back and eventually crush the democratic wave. While the Algerian decision-makers were still fanning the flames of their 1954–62 'revolution' against French colonialism, the Egyptian top brass had succeeded in associating themselves with two 'revolutions' against two presidents: the first against Mubarak in January–February 2011, the second against Morsi in June–July 2013.

In both instances, the Egyptian Mamluks had operated a coup that had hijacked the popular movement into fulfilling the grand design of the military hierarchy: sabotaging any decent democratic transition under the SCAF in 2011–12, and restoring absolute power on the ruins of the Muslim Brotherhood in 2013–14. In Algiers, the presidential mummy was a sinister tribute to his fellow 'founding fathers' of independence, but in Egypt, Sisi was playing his part as a reincarnated Nasser—with obvious delight.

The fossilized ruling clique in Algeria had demonstrated its inability to accept even a minimal dose of real change, while the Egyptian Mamluks had gone through a generational changing of the guard, from Tantawi to Sisi, that proved beneficial in the long run for the whole corporation. This greater adaptability in Egypt stemmed from the fact that the local Mamluks were not dependent solely on oil income, like their Algerian counterparts, but on a geopolitical cash injection, originally American and Camp David-induced, then increasingly transferred from the Gulf.

The Algerian nomenklatura was hooked on hydrocarbons, with all the pathologies produced by such a fifty-year addiction. The Egyptian Mamluks had gone through two essential metamorphoses to preserve the bulk of their privileges: from the vibrant Arab nationalism of Nasser to the peace-making credo of Sadat; from the crony capitalism of Mubarak to the arrogant restoration of Sisi. Algerian rulers had been absorbed in their domestic intrigues at a time when the masters of Egypt had consistently played their international cards very well, thereby cashing in the kickbacks that flowed from sustained involvement in 'anti-extremism'.

Algerian Mamluks could not, even in their wildest dreams, pledge that they were fighting on behalf of others; while their Egyptian fellows had successfully posed as the line of defence for stability in the Gulf. This militant narrative was consolidated by the ferocity of the Arab counter-revolution at a regional level. With the horrors reported daily from Syria and, to a lesser extent, Libya, it was easy to hammer home to the Egyptian public the benefits of a military-enforced security. Sisi was a far more credible 'father of the nation' than Bouteflika.

This does not imply that Egypt would be wholly insulated from a tragedy of the magnitude of the Algerian civil war in the 1990s. Under the disguise of a misleading 'stability', the country had already, since the 2013 coup, reached the highest level of political violence in its modern history: in the eight months following Morsi's deposition, some 2,500 civilians had been killed in the crackdown, some 17,000 wounded and more than 16,000 arrested.[77] In October 2014, the number of political detainees exceeded the unprecedented figure of 40,000.[78]

Universities in particular have become a major stage for political violence. In the academic year 2013–14, no fewer than sixteen students were killed and over 3,000 arrested.[79] When classes resumed in October 2014, campuses had fallen under the control of a private contractor, Falcon, previously in charge ... of Sisi's presidential campaign. University presidents also admitted having recruited 'patriotic students' in order to monitor activities on the campuses.[80] Despite this unprecedented infringement of academic liberties, incidents occurred on a regular basis in the Egyptian universities.

When it came to jihadi terrorism, Sisi's record was already ten times worse than Morsi's (twenty-eight deaths, mostly in Sinai, from July 2012 to June 2013; against 281 victims, 40 per cent of them on the Egyptian mainland, in the following eight months).[81] The Egyptian Mamluks had displayed in the past a far better control of the security situation, even in the heydays of the jihadi campaign of 1993–5.

They had however succeeded, in their own manner and style, in the same operation that had served their Algerian counterparts so well two decades earlier: amplify the jihadi menace to such an extent that it kills the democratic process. Once it was achieved, the ruling cliques, a modern version of the medieval *khâssa*, were far less vulnerable than the humble *'âmma* to the upsurge of violence or to more mundane troubles, like power cuts and water shortages. A steady cycle of plebiscites would suffice to keep this paternalistic social contract in place.

Tahrir, or Liberation, Square was occupied in January 2011 in a revolutionary wave that forced the Egyptian Mamluks into their first coup. During the following two and a half years, openly under the SCAF, or more viciously under Morsi, the military elite struggled to retake control of Tahrir from the 'revolutionary youth'. They were helped in that war of attrition by the sectarian party politics of the Muslim Brotherhood who dreamed of conquering Tahrir, before withdrawing to another Cairo square, Rabia al-Adawiya.

Very few people in Egypt were aware that Rabia al-Adawiya had been a female mystic and an emancipated slave in southern Iraq, during the second century of Islam. Rabia (Fourth) was associated with the four-finger symbol that became the rallying sign of the repressed Brotherhood. The massacre of hundreds of protesters on Rabia al-Adawiya Square, in August 2013, was indeed met with limited pockets of armed resistance. But this bloody outcome was exactly what the Egyptian Mamluks wanted to precipitate.

It was far easier for the military clique to handle civil strife than peaceful demonstrations. They knew how to shoot to kill, not how to restrain their forces to allow protests to take place. When Rabia al-Adawiya Square was eventually 'cleared' of all opposition, the dream of Tahrir/Liberation seemed less attainable than ever. The local Mamluks, meanwhile, could promote the most gifted among them as a new pharaoh. The jihadi menace was not conceived as an existential threat; it was extolled as a collective bond. Them or us. Shoot to kill. This deadly polarization would prove even more deadly in Yemen and Syria.

8

EVIL TWINS IN YEMEN AND SYRIA

Throughout the 1990s, Algerian Mamluks proved their readiness to plunge their country into horrendous civil war rather than relinquish even a portion of their collective power. Again, the absolute priority given to the regime's interests rather than the nation's played into the hands of jihadi groups, who grew out of the Islamists' inability to build a sustainable alternative. The Algerian military had effectively strengthened the jihadi monster by closing the door to any authentic political transition.

The same gamble produced the same results in Egypt during the 1990s, albeit on a much smaller scale: the Egyptian Mamluks could rely on resources, namely the dividends of the US-sponsored peace with Israel, which their Algerian counterparts lacked, while the NDP's hegemony was still a commanding reality in Egypt, long after the FLN's one-party rule had collapsed in Algeria.

Following the 9/11 attacks on New York and Washington, the Algerian and Egyptian regimes banked on their anti-jihadi credentials with success. Their discreet, but substantial contribution to the US-inspired 'global war on terror' was extremely rewarding for their security bureaucracies (especially through the rendition programme in Egypt). Initially caught off-guard by the rise of al-Qaeda in the Islamic Maghreb (AQIM) in 2007, the Algerian

Mamluks soon managed to marginalize the jihadi insurgents, either in the mountains of Kabylia or in the border areas.

When the Tunisian revolution terminated Ben Ali's rule in January 2011, the jihadi threat remained at an ideal level for both the Algerian and Egyptian Mamluks: strong enough to justify foreign support to the security apparatus, but too weak to really jeopardize any core interests of the ruling clique. The ban that the Algerian security had imposed on the Islamist party two decades earlier remained absolute; and in the same vein, as we have seen, the Egyptian Mamluks eventually toppled the Islamist president, jailed him and declared the Muslim Brotherhood a terrorist organization.

The Yemeni and Syrian Mamluks would use the jihadi joker in an even more mischievous way. Ali Abdullah Saleh boosted the jihadi menace to deter any form of political transition and, once he had been forced to resign, he would fan the jihadi flames in order to avoid dismantling his family's control of the security apparatus. Bashar al-Assad went further by paving the way for the self-proclaimed Islamic State in his offensive against the nationalist opposition and the revolutionary forces. The evil twins of the dictators and the jihadis agreed on one basic thing: popular protests had to be liquidated at any cost... for the protesters.

The Jihadi Payback of a Presidential Ouster

During the decade following the 9/11 attacks, the jihadi threat had grown as steadily in Yemen as had the US largesse towards Ali Abdullah Saleh's regime. Al-Qaeda in the Arabian Peninsula (AQAP) had been revamped in 2009 as a Yemeni outfit far more dangerous than the original Saudi organization: AQAP maintained only urban underground networks in major Saudi cities in 2003, while, eight years later, it controlled large swathes of the Yemeni provinces of Marib, Shabwa, Hadramaout and Abyan.

President Saleh had found in AQAP the ideal justification to consolidate a two-tier army, with a praetorian guard run by his own kin and footsoldiers left to fight the jihadi guerrillas. Western support was mainly absorbed by the regime's inner circle, while the regular army was ill-equipped and frequently ambushed by AQAP (178 Yemeni soldiers were killed in combat against jihadis in 2010).[1]

Despite the growing protests in Sanaa and Taez, the Houthi insurgency in the extreme North and the separatist trend in the South, Saleh pushed forward a reform of the constitution that would enable him to cling to power even after 2013. The Syrian-style dynastical scenario of his son Ahmed Ali Saleh, chief of the Republican Guard, succeeding him gained traction with every day. The threat from AQAP was the main counter-argument deployed in Washington or Riyadh when the regime's foreign backers expressed their worries about the despotic tendencies of Saleh and his clique.

Mubarak's overthrow in February 2011 generated an unprecedented wave of popular protests all over Yemen. Young demonstrators were harassed, brutalized and sometimes killed by an ominous mix of plain-clothes policemen and armed hoodlums (the same *baltaguiyya* that the Egyptian regime had launched on the street protesters). On 'Bloody Friday', 18 March, more than fifty peaceful demonstrators were shot by government snipers in Sanaa.

This bloodbath was the turning point in a crisis that became openly revolutionary. The armed forces split when Ali Mohsen al-Ahmar, commander of the first armoured brigade (*Firqa*), joined the opposition and vowed to protect the demonstrators. The defection of one of the closest military associates of President Saleh, a prominent member of his own Sanhan tribe, proved how the 'national' army was turning against the 'regime' forces.

Clashes escalated in Sanaa and the countryside, involving military units and tribal militiamen. The situation had grown so volatile that it forced the Gulf Cooperation Council (GCC) to work actively for a political transition. But Saleh was adamant in his resolve to complete his presidential mandate until 2013. When outside pressures increased, the Yemeni dictator played his jihadi joker.

At the end of May 2011, loyalist forces withdrew from the coastal town of Zinjibar, leaving it defenceless against AQAP-friendly militants.[2] Jihadi activists soon proclaimed an Islamic emirate of Abyan, since Zinjibar was the capital city of this Southern province. But shrewd Saleh had this time unleashed an overpowering demon: a few days after Zinjibar's 'fall', the Yemeni ruler was gravely injured in a bomb attack within his presidential complex.

Ahmed Ali Saleh, commander of the Republican Guard, stood in for his father while the Yemeni president, badly burnt, was evacuated for treatment in Saudi Arabia. The dynastical scenario was met with strong resistance from the president's own tribe, and GCC had more leverage on the ailing Yemeni ruler. In September 2011, a coalition of military brigades, loyal to the president or to the opposition, joined forces in expelling the jihadi fighters from Zinjibar.

Soon after, Saleh returned to Sanaa and claimed that his resolve to stay in power was intact. Timely intelligence was then provided to US forces which enabled them to kill Anwar al-Awlaqi in an drone strike: this Yemeni–American imam was accused by the Obama administration of having inspired the failed terror attack of Christmas Eve 2009. In this context, the American president approved the unprecedented targeting of a US citizen.[3] Saleh appealed to Washington, citing Awlaki's elimination, in order to alleviate pressure from the GCC on his dictatorship.

But the Yemeni ruler had played his final card and was forced to relinquish executive power in November 2011. His deputy, the Abyan-born Abd Rabbo Mansour Hadi, was endorsed as the sole presidential candidate by both the ruling party and a major-ity of the opposition in the February 2012 election, when he won an unsurprising 99.8 per cent of the vote, with a 65 per cent official turnout. Such statistics proved how this democratic transition was heavily influenced by the dictatorial legacy of twenty-one years of Ali Abdullah Saleh's rule (thirty-three years over North Yemen).

The former president was granted full immunity, while his son and nephews remained in their commanding position in the military apparatus. New presidential elections were to take place after a two-year transitional period during which a 'committee on military affairs for achieving security and stability' was supposed to 'integrate the armed forces under unified, national and professional leadership, in the context of the rule of law'.[4] This military committee managed to lift checkpoints and reduce tensions, but did not make significant breakthroughs in the Saleh family's security structure.

An ominous warning against any attempt to rock the military apparatus came just one week after the transfer of power from Saleh to Hadi: 185 soldiers were massacred, many of them in their sleep, in an AQAP night attack against the Al-Kawd military base near Zijinbar. This devastating blow was most certainly based on detailed inside information. The transitional period thus began with the worst defeat ever suffered by Yemeni forces in their decade-long battle against the jihadis.

President Hadi's first move, in April 2012, was aimed at removing one of his successor's half-brothers from the command of the air force and one of his nephews from a senior position in the Republican Guard. Both generals balked at the presidential order and openly resisted this change. They eventually backed down from a direct confrontation. But the retribution was horrendous: a hundred soldiers, practising for the National Day parade, were killed on 21 May by a suicide bomb attack, next to the presidential palace.

The terrorist was wearing an official uniform, so AQAP was relying on inside intelligence as well as complicity, just as for the assault on Al-Kawd that had occurred two and a half months earlier. Hadi reacted strongly by demoting two of his predecessor's nephews, Ammar Mohammad Saleh (chief of the National Security Bureau) and his brother Yahya (commander of the Central Security Forces). The Saleh clan protested at being singled out after the 'National Day' massacre, but eventually accepted their fate.

In August 2012, Hadi formed a special presidential protection unit, generating a significant reshuffle of the Republican Guard. This action against Ahmed Ali Saleh's military constituency triggered a retaliatory murderous assault by some of the former heir apparent's gunmen on the ministry of defence. The following month, the minister himself escaped assassination. The Yemeni president felt the heat and struck a major blow in December, by dismantling both the Republican Guard and the pro-opposition *Firqa*, as the first armoured brigade was popularly known.

Through this daring move, President Hadi demonstrated his will to promote a national army, and not to trade the Saleh bias for an opposition one. This restructuring was resented among activists on both sides, but was generally welcomed by the Yemeni public. It was the best prologue to the 'national dialogue' that opened in March 2013. However, AQAP kept threatening the transition process, with a major plot against the Hadramaout oil facilities uncovered five months later.

The 'national dialogue' closed after ten months of deliberation with the approval, in January 2014, of a constitutional document that only the Houthi insurgents refused to endorse. This democratic achievement was followed by a string of jihadi attacks. The escalation led, in April, to the launching of the Yemeni army's largest ever ground offensive against AQAP, in the provinces of Abyan and Shabwa. The jihadis struck back in the heart of Sanaa, attacking twice in 48 hours a checkpoint guarding access to the presidential palace.

The Yemeni transition remained fragile, two years after Saleh's departure. The playing with jihadi fire had prevailed on the former dictator's side, only changing in its form and maliciousness. But AQAP networks with privileged access to restricted intelligence and facilities had not managed to derail the democratic process. So Saleh turned to his arch-enemies in the Houthi insurgency and struck a deal with them in order to undermine his successor's government.

There were several reasons for this seemingly contra-natural alliance. First, the Saleh clan had been progressively ousted from its powerful position in the security apparatus over the course of 2012, and it could conveniently divert the Houthi armed retribution against its rivals from the Ahmar family. Second, the Houthi movement had officially turned into Ansarullah (Partisans of God), developing its cooperation (and even identification) with the Lebanese Hezbollah and supporting the Assad regime in Syria: the Yemeni Mamluks were therefore siding actively with their Syrian counterparts.

This counter-revolutionary dynamic gained momentum in July 2014 when the Yemeni government decided to cut fuel subsidies, a major Mamluk resource through institutionalized smuggling, as discussed in Chapter 5. Riots flared in the city of Sanaa, with the open involvement of Saleh's supporters. Ansarullah combat units started to move southwards in a blitzkrieg that was facilitated by more inside information.

On 21 September 2014, a combined force of 2,000 Houthist and 3,000 Saleh's supporters moved into the capital city. The offensive was coordinated by Ammar Mohammad Saleh, one of Ali Abdullah Saleh's nephews, and the former chief of the National Security Bureau.[5] The UN managed to mediate a ceasefire between loyalists and insurgents, who took over the government seat, the ministry of defence and the central bank.

President Hadi was now forced to share his own capital with an armed rebellion that was publicly supporting the Assad dictatorship. Homes and offices of revolutionary figures were assaulted and looted in Sanaa.[6] The formation of a new technocratic cabinet had to be painstankingly negotiated with Ansarullah, whose columns were now advancing towards the port city of Hodeida. But Saleh could bide his time, since his perverse manipulation had restored him to being Yemen's main powerbroker.

Ansarullah offensives out of the Zaydi strongholds ignited both anguish and anger among the major Sunni tribes, who felt abandoned by Hadi and his government. An AQAP call for an all-out sectarian war was followed, on 9 October 2014, by a terrorist bloodbath in the heart of Sanaa, with fifty-three people killed.[7] The jihadi menace that had been arduously contained during the previous spring was rising again. Saleh's playing with jihadi fire became so alarming that on 7 November the UN Security Council adopted sanctions against the deposed president.

The case of Yemen proves that even ousted Mamluks are prepared to do anything to abort a democratic process they treated and fought as a deadly threat. The jihadi bogeyman is a trump card that can prove lethal to any political process, especially when it is mixed up with other armed insurgencies. This should end the recurrent debate about the virtues of the 'Yemeni solution', the oxymoron coined by diplomats to designate a 'smooth' transition where the despot retains certain powers, along with absolute immunity.

A Syrian Self-Fulfilling Prophecy

Since the beginning of the US occupation of Iraq, in 2003, the various Syrian intelligence agencies cooperated with the Iraqi Sunni insurgents along the 600-km international border. Damascus was the main entry point for international volunteers eager to join the Iraqi jihad.[8] In this war by proxy, one of the main partners of the Assad regime has been the Iraqi branch of al-Qaeda that took the name of Islamic State in Iraq (ISI) in 2006.

There were two reasons for the Syrian Mamluks and the ISI jihadis to collaborate even more closely: the 2007 US-inspired 'surge' against al-Qaeda generated an unprecedented Sunni coalition that divided the insurgency and isolated ISI; and large numbers of former intelligence officials from Saddam Hussein's regime joined ISI, their Baathist-security background smoothing the relationship between Syrian intelligence and the Iraqi jihadis.[9]

Bashar al-Assad denied the very existence of popular protests when they began in Syria in March 2011. His state propaganda machine hammered away that the Assad regime, supposedly supported by the Syrian people, was the target of an al-Qaeda terrorist campaign, launched by a bizarre coalition of Israeli, Saudi, US and Western intelligence forces. Meanwhile, Syrian officials kept claiming worldwide that they were the sole bulwark against al-Qaeda and were defending the frontline in the global struggle against the jihadi threat.

Even by the Orwellian standards of the Assad regime, such a blatant denial of reality was hard to sustain: peaceful marches occurred in the streets of Deraa, Homs and Latakia, with slogans such as 'God, Syria, Freedom and nothing else'; protesters sometimes carried olive branches as gestures of peace and stripped to the waist in order to show the security forces that they did not have concealed weapons. But the bloody repression went on unabated as state TV started to broadcast live 'confessions' by captured 'terrorists'.

Since most of the jihadis present on Syrian soil were actually in jail, the Assad regime had no other means of sustaining its own propaganda than by releasing them. This highly selective amnesty took place through the spring and summer of 2011. It coincided with a merciless attempt to crush the non-violent opposition: thousands of civilian activists were rounded up, hundreds went missing, often dying under torture; the city of Hama, where hundreds of thousands of people had demonstrated against the regime in July 2011, was the target of a military offensive that killed hundreds.

Mohammad Abou al-Fateh al-Jolani (literally, from the Golan) was one of the jihadi leaders discreetly pardoned by

Assad. After his release he went straight into Iraq to join ISI, which was led by Abu Bakr al-Baghdadi (literally, from Baghdad) since 2010.[10] ISI no longer had a territorial base in Iraq proper, due to the successful US-led 'surge', so Baghdadi sought room for manoeuvre in Syria, from where he could build up enough potential to strike back in Iraq.

The non-violent strategy of the Syrian revolution had run into a deadly impasse, with Assad unconditionally supported by Russia and Iran, and the West wary of a repetition of the Libyan crisis. During the autumn of 2011, groups of military defectors and self-defence local militias coalesced into a Free Syrian Army (FSA). This army lacked everything, from armaments to supply lines, and even a chain of command. This structural weakness reduced it to purely defensive operations.

Murderous suicide attacks rocked Damascus and Aleppo through the winter of 2012. They were vehemently condemned by all shades of opposition, while the regime denounced the so-called terrorist plot behind any form of protest. In February 2012, Jolani officially established his Nusra (Support) Front, while Zawahiri declared jihad against Assad on behalf of al-Qaeda. Nusra was in fact the Syrian affiliate of ISI, but the Iraqi Baghdadi used the Syrian Jolani as a front to appease Syrian nationalism.

In March 2012, the neighbourhood of Baba Amr, the FSA stronghold in Homs, fell to an all-out assault by the Assad regime. At least 7,500 civilians had been killed during the first year of the government's offensive against the revolutionary protests.[11] Nevertheless many segments of the opposition resisted the growing militarization of their movement. The Assad regime was also abandoned by some long-term allies: Hamas, the Palestinian Islamist movement whose Political Bureau had been based in Damascus since 1999, left Syria to relocate in Egypt and Qatar.

Paralysed by the Russian and Chinese vetoes on Syria, the UN Security Council eventually endorsed the peace plan presented by former UN Secretary General Kofi Annan, in March 2012. Annan had the support on the ground of a 300-strong UNSMIS (UN Supervision Mission in Syria). Those unarmed military observers had no power to enforce truces and could only monitor the increasing escalation of violence. A series of mass killings by government soldiers and pro-regime militiamen (*shabbiha*), especially in Houla and Koubeir in May–June 2012, laid bare the impotence of UNSMIS. The mission was soon suspended, then terminated, while Annan resigned.

The FSA, which was reinforced by a wave of defections, launched a joint offensive on Damascus and Aleppo in July 2012. This military gamble was a strategic blunder for the Syrian revolution, since it polarized the country in an increasingly merciless civil war. The balance of power was overwhelmingly in favour of the Assad regime, which had sole use of planes, helicopters, heavy artillery and tanks. The insurgency got bogged down in costly battles for one checkpoint, one hilltop or one street block.

No Western power was ready to give significant assistance to the rebels. Nor did Saudi Arabia want a democratic Syria to emerge either, since it would threaten the status quo within the Wahhabi kingdom. The support Qatar provided to the FSA only made the Saudis more eager to fund Salafi, and even jihadi, groups. The situation was aggravated when the Qataris tried to challenge Saudi influence over these extremists, while private donors and Salafi networks actively raised funds in the Gulf to support these fringe groups.

Naturally, this vicious circle was exploited by the Nusra Front. Yet the Syrian insurgents, who were tragically under-equipped and often inexperienced, took the risk of inviting more and more jihadis to the front line. While fighting for its mere survival, the Syrian revolution lost its focus on its priorities and underestimated the lethal threat of the jihadi groups. Nusra was exploiting the advantages of its compact structure in relation to its divided rebel partners.

The provincial capital of Raqqa, in the Upper Euphrates Valley, was an open city where Assad supporters, surrounded on all sides, laid low. The Syrian revolutionaries needed this tacit agreement to prevail in Raqqa, as a key supply centre and a crucial way station between Aleppo and Deir Ezzor. So Raqqa had been spared the horrors and destruction that had already disfigured these two other cities. But Jolani wanted a town he could call his own and Baghdadi felt the time was right, with a Sunni uprising in the making in Iraq.

Since the summer of 2012, the Assad regime had decided to cut its losses in the Kurdish periphery in the north-east and the north-west, in order to focus its war effort on central and coastal Syria. The government therefore did not put up a fight to defend Raqqa against the Nusra offensive in March 2013. The new jihadi stronghold was not even bombed, while everywhere else the armed forces were pounding FSA positions and rebel-held cities.

Notwithstanding, the Raqqa saga was far from being over. In a spectacular move, Baghdadi proclaimed in April 2013 the Islamic State of Iraq and *Sham* (ISIS) (*Sham* was the Greater Syria that jihadi propaganda had been hailing for years). ISIS absorbed Nusra in Raqqa, which became the main city under its control on both sides of the border. But Jolani refused this forced merger and called for Zawahiri to arbitrate this unprecedented inter-jihadi feud.[12]

The al-Qaeda supreme leader backed Jolani's claims and acknowledged Nusra as his official affiliate in Syria. Baghdadi was ordered to withdraw and focus on Iraq, but he took no notice, since he had never pledged allegiance to Zawahiri after Bin Laden's death in 2011. Syrian jihadis deserted ISIS to join Nusra, while foreign volunteers, more attracted by Baghdadi's global ambitions, made the reverse move.

Assad could not have dreamt up a more favourable scenario. Not only had his 2011 self-fulfilling prophecy about al-Qaeda become real, but the jihadis, who had contributed so much to the backstabbing in the revolution, were also fighting each other with unbridled ferocity. The Syrian dictator felt then he could deliver the final blow to the insurgency in Damascus: combined with artillery bombardments, the gas attacks of August 2013 killed some 1,400 people. The rebel-held positions, initially overwhelmed by casualties, eventually held fast.[13] Yet despite the Obama administration's strongly worded speeches against such carnage, they did nothing. And we saw how Sisi's Egypt and Bouteflika's Algeria consistently fought any mooted 'aggression' against Syria.[14]

The Caliph of Terror

For two and a half years, the USA and the European Union had justified their refusal of military support to the Syrian insurgents by the fact that this could play into the hands of the jihadis. Russia, for her part, echoed from the very start Assad's anti-jihadi narrative. But, contrary to what was assumed on both sides of the international divide, abandoning the Syrian revolution had only consolidated the jihadi threat and extended its capacities.

During my field research trip to the rebel-held areas of Aleppo in the summer of 2013, I was struck by how the opposition activists seemed trapped between the Assad 'regime' (*nizâm*) and the Islamic 'state' (*dawla*). There was a tragic irony to this grass-roots revolution fighting a 'regime' and a 'state', both of which embodied the brutal negation of popular aspirations. But, even at that late stage, young militants still considered the jihadis to be the lesser of two evils compared with Assad's regime.[15]

Tensions were however brewing all over the 'liberated' territories of Syria. ISIS had suppressed any dissent in Raqqa and was implementing its rule of terror through public executions or punishments. The intolerance of foreign jihadis precipitated frequent clashes with the local population. Violent encounters with the FSA became commonplace. Vengeance and retribution spilt their trail of blood, while Assad's regime conspicuously spared ISIS, in order to target its rivals.

In January 2014, a heterogeneous coalition of opposition militias launched the 'second revolution' against ISIS. After sustaining thousands of casualties, they managed to expel Baghdadi's supporters from the rebel-held parts of the northern Aleppo and Idlib provinces. That was the first time that ISIS had not only been defeated, but repelled. Assad's answer was a massive bombing campaign of the jihadi-free districts of Aleppo. After some 2,000 died in those bombings, the population in 'liberated' Aleppo plummeted from more than a million souls to fewer than 300,000.

While the Syrian revolutionaries were paying such a terrible price for their victory against ISIS, Baghdadi had quickly compensated for his Syrian defeat in the Iraqi theatre. The sectarian policies of Prime Minister Nouri al-Maliki, a staunch ally of President Assad, had alienated Sunni leaders and exacerbated their protests, especially in Western Anbar province. The army siege and bombing of Falluja, in January 2014, allowed ISIS to take the lion's share of this symbolic stronghold.[16]

There was an obvious parallel between the two allies Assad and Maliki, both supported by Iran, and both bombing with blind brutality the very forces that could have stood against ISIS. The fact that Russia backed Assad in the same way that Washington had backed Maliki made only more apparent the two superpowers' gamble on 'national armies' that were little more than sectarian militias, with relatively limited operational capabilities, despite the enormous arsenal delivered by their foreign patrons.

Both Assad and Maliki needed to rejuvenate their 'electoral' credentials in spring 2014. More than 3,000 people had been killed in Iraq in the four months preceding the legislative elections of late April. But Maliki could claim victory with his Daawa party winning 92 of the 328 parliamentary seats. The

Iraqi PM knew there was widespread hostility to him renewing his mandate, so he bet on the jihadi bogeyman to force reluctant partners into a government coalition.

This is how, at the beginning of June 2014, Iraq's armed forces simply collapsed in face of the ISIS assault on Mosul. Whole units disbanded, senior officers vanished, weapon caches were left wide open, along with half a billion dollars in the city's various banks.[17] Such a rout was not the result of betrayal, but the logical consequence of the fact that this 'national army' was national only in name. It was trained, financed and indoctrinated to defend the regime, not the people, and had already garnered a sinister reputation oppressing Iraqis opposed to this regime.

Meanwhile in Syria, the Assad regime held its first ever 'multi-party' presidential election, with two loyalist candidates running as a pluralistic fig leaf for the dictator. The organization of such a vote in a war-ridden country, with more than 160,000 dead and 3 million refugees, was condemned by the UN Secretary General, whose special envoy to Syria resigned. President Assad was supposed to have claimed 88.7 per cent of the vote, which meant 10.5 million voters with a 73.4 per cent official turnout.

Those figures are frankly farcical. Since some 40 per cent of Syrian territory (and 60 per cent of its population) was under full government control, only a maximum of 7 million people could have participated in the presidential elections.[18] No vote took place in Turkey, where most Syrian refugees resided, and even in Lebanon only 40,000 voters were registered at Syrian consulates (out of 1 million refugees).[19]

Assad could claim to have been less greedy for his citizens' votes than, in recent weeks, his Egyptian counterpart (97 per cent for Sisi), but more than his Algerian fellow Mamluk (81 per cent for Bouteflika). And, contrary to the former Egyptian Field Marshal, Assad was not compelled to extend the voting period to boost a turnout that nobody would trust anyway. In this tragic parody of elections, the Iraqi poll looked the least rigged and the only substantial result.

Maliki soon appeared less worried about the capture of Mosul than about the possibility of losing the prime ministership.[20] He gave free rein in Baghdad to the sectarian militias that were harassing any opponent as a potential ISIS operative. He ignored every call to step down, even from the Najaf-based Grand Ayatollah Ali Sistani, the most respected Shia religious authority. When Washington refused to deliver fighter-jets to Baghdad as long as Maliki was clinging to power, he turned to Moscow and Putin delivered Sukhoï-25 warplanes in record time.

Russia was still blindly adhering to the *them or us* narratives peddled by both Assad and Maliki to consolidate their dictatorships via the jihadi threat. The fact that Baghdadi lacked a territorial base in 2011 and that, after three years of ruthless counter-revolution, he now controlled significant swathes of both Syria and Iraq did not affect the Kremlin's thinking. But the fall of Mosul had worked as a belated wake-up call to the White House.

On the first day of Ramadan (29 June 2014), ISIS announced the restoration of the Caliphate. The following Friday, Abu Bakr al-Baghdadi proclaimed from a mosque in Mosul that he was now Caliph Ibrahim and that all Muslims worldwide had to pledge allegiance to him. The call went viral on the social networks that had become the main echo chamber for jihadi propaganda. The self-appointed caliph also announced that ISIS was now an 'Islamic State' with no territorial denomination. Thus, he expressively claimed his expansionist strategy far beyond the Middle East.

For Assad and Maliki, however, it was business as usual. Their main targets remained the domestic opposition, not distant jihadis. Dozens of fighters fell in July 2014, during the battle between the Syrian army and ISIS over a gas facility in central Syria. But this turf war did not prevent the jihadi smugglers from trading part of the production of the oil fields they controlled in the Euphrates Valley ... to proxies of the Syrian government.[21]

It would take another two months after the fall of Mosul before the outside powers decided to bypass the local Mamluks in order to confront directly the jihadi challenge. ISIS had brutally expelled the Christian population from its Iraqi territory and moved, in the first days of August 2014, against the Sinjar range. This precipitated an exodus of several hundred thousand people to the areas controlled by the Kurdish Regional Government (KRG). But even the KRG fighters proved unable to stop the ISIS columns that took over the Iraq's main dam, close to Mosul.

This string of jihadi victories in Iraq was paralleled in Syria, where ISIS conquered the last government pockets in the eastern province of Raqqa (including the Tabqa air base, along with its planes and helicopters). The autocrats of Syria and Iraq had demonstrated their inability to contain ISIS. President Obama ordered limited air strikes to back a successful Kurdish counteroffensive on the Mosul dam. And a spokesman for Ayatollah Khameneï, the Iranian supreme leader, finally called for the designation of a new prime minister in Baghdad.

This Iranian move sealed the fate of Maliki, who had to step down. His successor as Iraqi PM, Haydar al-Abadi, came from the same Daawa party. It took him nearly a month to form a multi-party cabinet in September 2014, without even an agreement on the interior and defence portfolios. Still, Maliki's departure had generated a new dynamic that was crucial to shaping an anti-ISIS international coalition. The beheading of two US hostages prompted Obama into declaring his resolve to 'eradicate a cancer like ISIS'.[22]

This game-changer was even more dramatic when compared with Obama's strong warning to France, in August 2013, not to strike Assad's regime after his mass gas attacks in Damascus. This time, French president François Hollande was able to visit Iraq (both Baghdad and the KRG) before convening in Paris, on 15 September 2014, an international conference dedicated to fighting ISIS. Fouad Massoum, his Iraqi counterpart, co-hosted the conference, excluding any cooperation with the Syrian dictatorship.

*

The evil twins of despotic Mamluk ferocity and jihadi terror have extracted a barbaric toll on the people of Yemen, and even more so of Syria. They have jeopardized the political transition in Yemen and, so far, sabotaged the revolutionary process in Syria. Despite the magnitude of their crimes, Ali Abdullah Saleh and Bashar al-Assad have guaranteed full immunity for their close partners, their family and themselves. On top of that, the Syrian autocrat still controlled around one half of the country and its population in autumn 2014.

This was no small achievement for the Syrian and Yemeni Mamluks, whose oppressive machines seemed to be running out of steam during the summer of 2011. Their dramatic recovery owed a lot to the viciousness of their jihadi gamble that literally caught the popular uprising in a crossfire. But while it is one thing to unleash jihadi fighters on one's own citizens, it is an altogether different matter to allow the jihadi virus spread worldwide.

The Obama administration had turned a blind eye to Saleh as long as AQAP appeared to be kept in check. In autumn 2011, the Yemeni dictator was eventually perceived as part of the problem rather than part of the solution, and he had to withdraw with all undue privileges. It would take another three years for the White House finally to accept that ISIS could not be dealt with if Assad was not side-lined. Side-lined, but not targeted, so the Syrian executioner got away with it, once again.

The Egyptian Mamluks were even more demanding: they would not actively join the anti-ISIS coalition until the 'terrorism' targeted by such an alliance also included the Muslim Brotherhood. President Sisi was obviously hoping to restore the post-9/11 blank cheque that so benefited Mubarak's regime. The USA balked at such a demand but, despite their annual $1.3 billion contribution in military aid to Egypt, they could not force Sisi to join the anti-ISIS caravan.

The Mamluks had scored yet another victory, against their own people as well as against the world's only superpower. Their one problem was the sharp decline in oil prices through the summer of 2014, a trend that could, if sustained, attenuate the income-fuelled violence of their repressive security apparatus. Meanwhile, they had one more commodity to snatch from the Arab people and to trade on their own terms: Palestine.

9

STRANGLING PALESTINE

Arab Mamluks always nurtured a very possessive approach towards Palestine. They knew how little they had achieved in alleviating the plight of the Palestinian people, but they needed the Palestinian decoy to justify the militarization of their own societies under their aegis. The celebration of the Palestinian 'liberation struggle' was also central to Algerian FLN propaganda, which equated the French and Israeli settlers in a pretty far-fetched narrative, divorced from historical truth.

When the Algerian single-party system was rocked by the October 1988 riots, some security officials claimed it was part of an international plot aimed at … undermining Algeria's support for the Palestinian cause.[1] (The PLO symbolically announced the establishment of its 'State of Palestine' during a national council convened in Algiers the following month.) Conspiracy theories abound in such intelligence-run systems, and it was inevitable that the 'Zionist enemy' had a role to play in this delirious cast.

Indeed, some 600 PLO fighters had been evacuated from Beirut to Algiers at the end of August 1982, when Arafat had to leave Lebanon with thousands of his armed supporters, in return for Israel lifting its siege of the Lebanese capital. But Arafat had then moved the PLO's headquarters to Tunis, not to Algiers. He also relocated some 1,100 fedayines to South Yemen and 850 to North Yemen, among other countries of destination.

During the January 1986 civil war that devastated Aden, Palestinian fighters carrying their national flag tried to mediate between the South Yemeni factions, but with limited success. Apart from this baroque episode, in Saleh-run unified Yemen, Palestine became a standard cliché of regime propaganda, beating the drum of its 'unwavering' support for the 'cause'. But in Yemen as in Algeria there were no Palestinian refugees, apart from the fighters' enclaves, so the discourse remained abstract.

This situation differs dramatically from what happened in Syria and Egypt. As we have seen, Hafez al-Assad and Anwar Sadat consolidated their 'corrective movements' by refocusing their military apparatus on their strict national interests. Assad even took power in the context of the betrayal of the PLO insurgency in neighbouring Jordan, during the infamous Black September 1970. After the joint October 1973 offensive, Assad and Sadat diverged on how to regain that part of their national territory that was occupied by Israel.

Sadat chose a US-sponsored peace process with Israel to regain Sinai, while Assad satisfied himself with a US-brokered ceasefire that left the Golan Heights under Israeli occupation. But both leaders considered any Palestinian interference in their plans to be an act of aggression, and dealt with it accordingly. This is why Assad's troops crushed the PLO and its Lebanese allies in the summer of 1976. This also explains the viciousness of the retaliation of Sadat's regime against Gaza when Palestinians opposed the 1979 Camp David peace treaty with Israel.

The Gaza Strip had been under Egyptian administration from 1948 to 1967, with a four-month interlude of Israeli occupation in 1956–7. Cairo never expressed any territorial ambition on this part of British-mandate Palestine, contrary to Jordan, which swiftly annexed East Jerusalem and the West Bank. Egypt granted facilities to the Palestinian residents of the Gaza Strip, especially when it came to admissions and scholarships to Egyptian universities. These facilities were maintained even after the 1967 Israeli occupation.

The Camp David divorce, with the Israeli peace generating a Palestinian crisis, culminated in the Egyptian cancellation of the above-mentioned support to the inhabitants of Gaza. Though this volte-face hit family bonds and trade relations hard, students were the most affected: this led to the establishment of the Islamic University of Gaza as an alternative venue, soon a hotbed for Islamist militants. Sadat's regime launched a propaganda campaign against the 'ungrateful' Palestinians, who had supposedly stolen the blood and bread of generous Egyptians for their petty purposes. This campaign only intensified under Mubarak, in parallel with increasingly xenophobic attacks.

Assad went further in his anti-Palestinian hostility when he fostered 'dissidence' within the mainstream Fatah movement in 1983. PLO loyalists initially kept the upper hand in the refugee camps in Lebanon, but they were progressively rolled back by the Syrian army and artillery from the Bekaa Valley, then besieged in the northern city of Tripoli. Arafat and his guerrilla supporters were pushed by Syria into the Mediterranean for the second time in December 1983 (the first occasion being in August 1982 when Israel expelled them from Beirut).

In Syria, military intelligence monitored the Palestinian refugees, who represented slightly more than 2 per cent of the overall population. A Palestine Branch operated to that purpose, even though it targeted opponents far beyond Palestinian circles. Military conscription was compulsory for young Palestinian males, enrolled in specific Palestinian Liberation Army units, which were in fact auxiliaries of the main Syrian forces.

Palestinians were not granted Syrian nationality (contrary to Jordan), but nor did they suffer the same kind of job restrictions they endured in Lebanon. The refugee camps had become part of Syria's urban fabric, especially with the main Yarmouk camp in southern Damascus. Aleppo, Homs, Hama and Latakia had their camps as well. Syrian security had transferred the direct control of the camps to anti-PLO factions, above all the General Command.[2]

The Nightmare of Yarmouk

From the onset of the Syrian revolution in March 2011, Palestinian refugees were torn between conflicting pressures: the desire to stay neutral dominated among the camp activists,[3] even though young militants shared the Syrian grievances against the security apparatus. Bashar al-Assad's attempt to blackmail Israel into ensuring stability for his regime were to trigger the first stirrings of revolt.

Rami Makhluf, the billionaire cousin of the Syrian president, had issued an unprecedented warning in the *New York Times*: 'If there is no stability here, there is no way there will be stability in Israel.'[4] A few days later, on 15 May 2011, the anniversary of the creation of the state of Israel, Palestinian refugees were bussed by regime loyalists up to the Golan, where two hundred of them tried to cross the 1974 ceasefire line. Four protesters were shot dead by the Israeli army.

Assad was clearly signalling that his Mamluk regime was the sole guarantor of the status quo that had prevailed between Syria and Israel for more than three decades. He reiterated the manoeuvre on 5 June 2011, the anniversary of the Israeli occupation of the Golan Heights. This time, Israeli forces killed twenty-three Palestinians attempting infiltration. The Syrian dictator understood he was playing with Israeli fire, and backed down from further provocation.

However, in the Yarmouk camp, General Command militants were accused of having led Palestinian youngsters to a certain death. Incidents flared between local refugees and the Palestinian auxiliaries of the Syrian security. Never before had the Yarmouk camp been shaken by such violent protest. The regime retaliated with its usual iron-clad repression, which drove even more activists underground.

Tension increased in Yarmouk when the Latakia refugee camp was shelled by government helicopter gunships and artillery in August 2011. The General Command militiamen were then reinforced by Palestinian mercenaries (*shabbiha*), armed and financed by Yasir Qashlak, a Palestinian 'businessman' whose fortune stemmed from his dealings with the Assad regime. Yarmouk activists managed to protect the camp's neutrality for more than a year, despite the breakthrough of the revolutionary insurgency in the neighbouring areas during the summer of 2012.

This delicate balance was upset when the General Command established militarized checkpoints around Yarmouk and started patrolling the camp in December 2012. A few days later, a government fighter-jet bombed Yarmouk, killing tens of civilians. The Free Syrian Army (FSA) and its more radical allies then entered the camp, expelling the General Command and Qashlak mercenaries.

Yarmouk went from being a relatively safe haven in the Greater Damascus area to becoming one of the main battlefields in the struggle for the capital city. The population that had risen to some 150,000 inhabitants due to various influxes of internally displaced people now dropped below 30,000. Hamas, whose policy was never to engage in military activity outside Palestine, believed that divorce with the Assad regime over the Syrian revolution was leaving the refugees unprotected. Consequently, Hamas decided to arm a specific Pact of Umar group in Yarmouk, whose role was to defend the population against government raids and militia looting.

Since July 2013, the regime blockade of the Yarmouk camp had been tightly enforced. Pro-Assad shock troops were positioned at the northern entrances, while Shia militiamen, mostly from Iraq, moved to close the southern rim. In September 2013, government forces fired some seventy mortar shells a day at the camp, half of which was by now either destroyed or uninhabitable. The worst was still to come, when the regime tried to starve Yarmouk into submission, just as it had succeeded in imposing the capitulation of other neighbourhoods of Damascus.

In the last days of 2013, news started to leak from the besieged camp that at least five people had died from hunger.[5] In March 2014, Amnesty International released a special report entitled 'Squeezing the life out of Yarmouk' in which the NGO documented the names of 124 civilians who had starved to death in the besieged camp, a figure that excludes deaths resulting from lack of medical care or victims being shot by snipers while foraging for food.[6]

The regime only selectively authorized United Nations convoys to distribute aid parcels to a population now estimated between 17,000 and 20,000. Armed insurgents agreed to withdraw under the condition that the regime would lift the siege; yet when the government reneged on its promises, at the end of the spring, the revolutionary guerrillas sneaked back into the camp.[7] In August 2014, an UNRWA (United Nations Relief and Works Agency, in charge of the Palestinian refugees) spokesman stated: 'the humanitarian situation in Yarmouk remains desperate'.[8]

The Palestinian refugees have suffered from the Syrian tragedy even more than the rest of the country's population: four camps out of twelve have been razed (in addition to the destruction of half of Yarmouk); more than half of the refugees have been displaced, mostly within Syria[9] (because of the restrictions at the border with Jordan and the overcrowding of the camps in Lebanon). Distressed Palestinian activists lament a new *Nakba*, in echo of the 1948 'catastrophe' that drove them into exile.[10]

Palestinian refugees did not pay such a heavy toll for the Syrian conflict by accident. Yarmouk's descent into hell demonstrated in the most terrible way that neutrality could not be a long-term option in such a polarized environment. But the ferocity of the Assad regime against the Palestinian enclave in Damascus reminded the refugees how vulnerable they were, even after three generations of life in Syria. Among the Palestinians fleeing Syria, a few hundreds managed to make their way into ... the Gaza Strip.

The Prison Warders of Gaza

Contrary to King Hussein of Jordan, and even Nelson Mandela, Husni Mubarak never found time to visit Gaza during the three decades of his presidency (1981–2011). For the chauvinistic Egyptian Mamluk, despising the Palestinians had become a way of life. Gaza was basically a commodity to be traded at the best price with Israel and the USA. It was therefore logical to punish the Palestinians when they dared to alter the terms of such a deal.

The Gaza dossier in Cairo was traditionally handled not by foreign affairs, but by the General Intelligence Department (GID), the very backbone of the regime. General Omar Suleiman, who commanded the GID from 1993 to 2011, devoted a significant part of his time and energy to the dialogue on Palestine with his American and Israeli counterparts. The CIA was then monitoring 'security cooperation' between Israel and the Palestinian Authority (PA), a codename for information-sharing and joint operations against Hamas and other rejectionist armed factions.

De facto, the Egyptian GID was in charge of the back-up to this 'security cooperation'. Suleiman mainly relied on Mohammad Dahlane, appointed chief of Preventive Security, the main Palestinian police, in 1994, when Arafat established the Fatah-led Palestinian Authority in the Gaza Strip. Dahlane was promoted to minister of security in 2003 and consolidated his position as PA police czar (since the Oslo agreements forbid any form of Palestinian army, the police was the only military authorized in the PA-controlled areas).

In September 2005, PM Ariel Sharon implemented the unilateral withdrawal of the Israeli army and settlers from the Gaza Strip. He wanted to relieve the IDF from the burden of direct military occupation of this overpopulated enclave, but this 'unilateral' move was intentionally not negotiated with the PA, since Sharon wanted to close the door to a Palestinian state once and for all.

However, Egypt was a key partner to the Agreement on Mobility and Access (AMA), signed under US auspices two months after the Israeli withdrawal. The Rafah crossing point between the Gaza Strip and the Sinai was to be run jointly by Egypt and the PA, with the support of a European Union Border Assistance Mission (EUBAM), in permanent contact with Israel. This complex mechanism collapsed shortly after the January 2006 Palestinian parliamentary elections: the victory of Hamas led to the formation of an Islamist-run government, which the EU decided to boycott.

Suleiman and the GID, who had kept channels open with Hamas, even though they openly favoured Fatah, were best placed to exploit their contacts in a context of conflict and crisis. Egyptian intelligence was the only one operating openly in the Gaza Strip. When Hamas kidnapped Gilad Shalit, an Israeli tank server, in June 2006, Suleiman himself started mediating between the Islamist movement and Israel. But the Egyptian general suspended his initiative after Israel intensified its raids on Gaza.

The GID officials also worked to ease the growing tensions between Fatah and Hamas. One of them was even injured in May 2007 by a Fatah gunman while hosting a conciliation meeting. But Suleiman was secretly backing, with US support, a military move by Dahlane against Hamas. This offensive was pre-empted by the Qassam brigades, Hamas' military wing, in June 2007, when Dahlane was undergoing knee surgery in an Egyptian hospital. Left leaderless, Fatah loyalists soon lost ground, leaving Hamas as the sole ruler of the Gaza Strip.

Mubarak was furious at this Islamist takeover. He joined Israel in imposing a strict blockade on the Gaza Strip, hoping that an impoverished population would hold Hamas responsible for its plight. In January 2008, Palestinian militants used explosives to destroy parts of the frontier wall with Egypt. Thousands of civilians rushed through the breach and overwhelmed the Egyptian security. But they were eventually stopped at the Suez Canal, if they made it that far west. In less than a week, all the Palestinian 'escapees' had been returned to their open-air prison.

In the meantime, in Cairo, the GID was sponsoring inter-Palestinian talks, supposedly aimed at bridging the gap between Fatah and Hamas. But the Egyptian pro-Fatah bias was so ardent that the talks stalled for years. The Mubarak regime consistently accused Hamas of being responsible of the Israeli blockade, and the Egyptian military added their own pressure in Rafah to this collective sanction on the Gaza population. This Israeli–Egyptian siege had the unexpected result of boosting the tunnel smuggling with Egypt, with two-thirds of the local economy depending on this subterranean trade in 2010.[11]

The Egyptian revolution changed the equation dramatically. Suleiman had the dubious privilege of announcing Mubarak's resignation in February 2011, before disappearing from the public scene himself. Three months later, in Cairo, PA president Mahmud Abbas and Hamas exiled leader Khaled Meshaal agreed on their 'national reconciliation'. This breakthrough was achieved because the GID was at last mediating between the two factions, and not trying to pin Hamas down as it had in the past.

This new Egyptian attitude also allowed the October 2011 prisoner exchange between Israel and Hamas. A total of 1,027 Palestinian detainees were released to secure Shalit's return to Israel. The Qassam brigades and their leader, Ahmad Jaabari, had basically obtained what they had been demanding for the past 2,000 days. Even though German intelligence had played a role in the secret talks, the Egyptian GID was the main broker of the deal, thanks to the bond of trust recently established with Hamas.

The Rafah crossing point remained a challenging ordeal for Palestinians travelling to Egypt. But Mohammad Morsi's victory at the June 2012 presidential election forced the Egyptian military to smooth exit procedures from Gaza. The Sinai security was also ordered to turn a blind eye to most of the smuggling into Palestinian territory, which led to a relative 'real estate bubble', thanks to an unprecedented underground flow of cement and other construction materials.

In November 2012 the Israelis killed Jaabari, which fuelled a new round of hostilities. But this time, Egyptian mediation was proactive and offered a significant diplomatic input. President Morsi succeeded in avoiding an Israeli land offensive and restored the ceasefire in Gaza. The Palestinian enclave remained under siege, yet the breathing space at the border with Egypt made life less difficult for the local population.

In May 2013 an incident revealed how the security forces could undermine Morsi's Gaza policy: the police closed the Rafah crossing point to force Sinai criminals to release seven abducted soldiers. But this ominous blackmail was only a taster of the Egyptian Mamluks' revenge against Gaza after their July 2013 coup against Morsi. While around a thousand people were allowed out from Rafah on a daily basis, the number fell to less than two hundred, with a general ban on men aged 18–40.[12]

The worst was yet to come, with the systematic campaign waged by the Egyptian security forces against the smuggling tunnels. While Hamas and other factions had the capacity to protect their weapons and explosives supply lines, tunnels delivering fuel, cement and consumer goods were hit the hardest. The Gaza Strip, always on the brink of economic collapse, came to a virtual halt, with prices soaring, construction stalled and gas in short supply.

The Egyptian junta went so far as to accuse the deposed president Morsi of being a 'Hamas operative'. They circulated the wildest conspiracy theories, according to which Barack

Obama had offered billions of dollars to buy a large part of the Sinai Peninsula from Morsi's Egypt on behalf of Hamas. In such frantic narratives, the tunnels from Gaza had become a vicious weapon used to dismember Egyptian territorial integrity.[13] Gaza was painted as the focus of such American–Islamist plots against Egypt.

With the wave of murderous and blind violence sweeping Egypt in the summer 2013, those wild theories, hammered out by the junta propaganda machine were increasingly accepted as simple facts.[14] In an echo of the Syrian Mamluks accusing the Palestinian refugees of betraying their 'hospitality', the Egyptian military blamed the Gaza residents for backstabbing and undermining 'friendly' Egypt. The stage was set for a merciless showdown.

The Egyptian justice formally banned the Palestinian Hamas in March 2014. That was only the legal confirmation that any means necessary would be allowed to bring down the rulers of the Gaza Strip. Hamas' incomes fell dramatically and salaries of the government employees in Gaza had to be suspended. This was one of the main reasons why Hamas had to accept the establishment of a unity government under the leadership of the PA.

In the first days of June 2014, Ismaïl Hanyeh resigned after seven years as prime minister of the Hamas government in Gaza. A new Palestinian cabinet was formed for the West Bank and Gaza Strip, without any Hamas members, but with active backing from the Islamist movement. Qatar agreed to transfer to a PA-controlled bank account in Ramallah the funds necessary to pay the wages of the civil servants in the Gaza Strip.

Israel, publicly, and Egypt, more discreetly, vowed to deliver what they believed was the final blow to Hamas. They attacked the unity government as a dangerous manoeuvre to save the Islamist movement. They were dismayed at the readiness expressed by the US and the EU to work with the new Palestinian cabinet. Saudi Arabia, incensed by the Qatari involvement, discussed with Egypt how to sabotage the Palestinian reconciliation.

It did not take long for the Israeli government to launch its anti-Hamas campaign. They accused the Islamist movement of ordering the kidnapping of three young settlers in the Hebron area. The bodies of the murdered teenagers were discovered two weeks later and Hamas responsibility was never documented. But in the meantime, mop-up operations across the West Bank led to the Israeli arrest of hundreds of Hamas activists, including dozens of militants released through the 2011 Shalit deal.

The IDF soon resumed its targeted killings of prominent activists in the Gaza Strip. Hamas and its local allies retaliated with rocket attacks on Israel. On 8 July 2014, the Israeli army launched its Protective Edge offensive on the Gaza Strip. During the following fifty days, more than 2,000 Palestinians were killed, an overwhelming majority of whom were civilians. The final death toll remained inconclusive, since an unknown number of corpses were buried under the ruins (more than 15,000 dwellings had been destroyed).[15]

On the Israeli side, sixty-four soldiers were killed (including five by 'friendly fire'), along with three civilians (two of whom were Israeli nationals). The ratio between Israeli and Palestinian civilian casualties, already set at a mind-boggling 1/100 during previous conflicts, had risen to the 1/1,000 range. Despite this shocking imbalance, the Egyptian GID based its 'mediation' efforts on the Israeli demand for an unconditional ceasefire, while Hamas insisted on the lifting of the blockade and the release of prisoners detained during the recent West Bank sweeps.

After a week of conflict and a phone conversation between the Egyptian president and the Israeli prime minister, Cairo announced a ceasefire with conditions that had not even been discussed with the Palestinians. Hamas rejected the 'offer' and the blame game went in to overdrive against the Islamist movement as shells cascaded on Gaza. The GID resumed its indirect mediation in Cairo, this time between an Israeli delegation and a Palestinian one led by a PA official.[16]

The Egyptian propaganda machine careered out of control against Hamas. Tawfik Okacha, owner and principal anchor of Al-Faraeen TV, the unofficial mouthpiece of the military junta, stated live: 'Gazans are not men. If they were men, they would revolt against Hamas.'[17] A pro-Sisi journalist even tweeted: 'Bless you, Netanyahou, and may God give us more like you to rid us of Hamas.'[18] Never before had an Israeli offensive against Palestinians been greeted by Egypt in such a blatant manner. This belligerent mood was met with approval by the Saudis, given their bias against Qatar and Hamas.

On 5 August 2014, Israeli troops withdrew from the Gaza Strip. But the war was far from over, since Egypt could only sponsor the periodic extension of fragile truces. This was a disaster for the population of Gaza, still besieged from all sides, and bracing itself amid the ruins for mere survival. The GID had forced the Palestinian delegation in Cairo to exclude the issue of the Rafah crossing point from the discussion of an enduring ceasefire. The Sisi regime was therefore keeping this option open in order to squeeze the Palestinian population whenever it wished to do so.

The war went on for three more weeks, with murderous Israeli raids unable to stop the firing of Palestinian rockets. It was now clear that Israel wanted a way out, but the anti-Hamas bias of Egypt forbade the GID from achieving a fully-fledged ceasefire. It took the intervention of the USA, and to a lesser extent of France and the EU, to bring a final end to the fifty-day conflict, on 26 August 2014. The Egyptian grip on Rafah remained as tight as before, contributing to the prolonged nightmare of the people of Gaza.

One non-EU European country, Norway, had opened official channels with Hamas. In the spirit of mediation that had led, two decades earlier, to the Oslo agreements, Norway now took a leading role in the reconstruction of Gaza. It was therefore under the joint presidency of Norway and Egypt that an international conference for the reconstruction of Gaza convened in Cairo, on 12 October 2014. Sisi agreed with Netanyahou that Israel would not be invited. Officially, this was to make the Gulf donors confortable. In fact, it was a devious way of exonerating Israel from compensating at least part of the destruction it had inflicted on Gaza.

As the Israeli press commented, Sisi used the Cairo conference on Gaza as 'a springboard to bring Egypt back to the top of the Arab world's diplomatic pyramid'.[19] State-controlled media broadcast the conference live. John Kerry and Catherine Ashton, who had failed in their August 2013 mediation to prevent the anti-MB bloodbath, were now praising the central role that Egypt could play in this long-awaited peace process. There was no peace in sight, Palestine was still in limbo and Gaza laid in ruins, but Sisi turned this latest Palestinian tragedy into a wonderful PR opportunity to glorify his own dictatorship.

*

The Arab Mamluks had come full circle. They used the collective humiliation of a nascent Israel as a powerful tool to hijack the post-colonial independent states. They then manipulated the Palestinian cause in their merciless power struggles, while abandoning the Palestinians to their terrible fate at every stage in their renewed dispossession. But the barbaric violence that the Arab Mamluks unleashed against the revolution of their own people eventually turned against the Palestinians themselves.

Assad's Syria and Sisi's Egypt besieged and even starved the Palestinian population in the open-air prisons of Yarmouk and the Gaza Strip. The only difference was that Syrian armed forces and militiamen did the killing in Yarmouk, while Egypt let Israel bomb and massacre the Gaza Strip. In the unravelling of the Arab Renaissance, Palestine could only become the ultimate scapegoat for the monsters of the counter-revolution.

Through this campaign against Palestine, its people and its rights, the Deep State has accomplished its final emergence from the dark into the light. There was no longer any need to work behind the scenes, nor to plot complex scenarios and engineer smokescreens. The horror of the carnage is obscene, while the wound of the betrayal is laid bare. For the Arab Mamluks, Palestine should be the graveyard of the Arab dream. No counter-revolution should be complete without the liquidation of the Palestinian cause.

10

THE TUNISIAN ALTERNATIVE

On 24 October 2014, the Egyptian military suffered its worst defeat against the jihadi insurgents in Sinai: at least thirty-three soldiers were killed in two separate and coordinated attacks in El-Arish and its vicinity, involving a sophisticated mix of booby-trapped cars, landmines and ambush techniques. A few hours later, President Sisi chaired a National Council of Defence that pledged to 'avenge the spilled blood'.[1] Three days of national mourning were decreed, while the armed forces, admitting that the guerrillas relied on a strong local base, contemplated the evacuation of entire villages in order to bring about the eventual defeat of the jihadis.

On 26 October 2014, Egypt was still mourning its fallen military and the state propaganda was issuing a retributory rhetoric loaded with the usual vendetta threats and conspiracy theories. (The Rafah checkpoint with Gaza had been sealed, bringing the Palestinian population of the Gaza Strip back to a full and excruciating siege, and more than a thousand families were forcefully displaced from the Egyptian side of the border.)[2] Meanwhile Tunisia held its first free parliamentary elections, and no incident marred this historic polling day.

Some 3.6 million Tunisians went to vote, compared to 4.3 million in the elections for the Constituent Assembly in October

2011 (but the electoral lists had been revised in the meantime, leading to an increase in turnout from 52 per cent to 68 per cent three years later). The Islamist Ennahda party, which had led the polls in 2011 with 37 per cent of the votes and 89 seats (out of 217), fell to 28 per cent of the votes and 69 seats (out of the same number of 217). More troubling for the Islamist party was their loss of one third of their electoral base (from 1.5 million voters in 2011 to fewer than a million three years later).

The main winner of the Tunisian legislative contest was Nidaa Tounes (the Call for Tunisia), a secular catch-all party launched in June 2012 by the 87-year-old Beji Caïd-Essebsi, who had been the first prime minister in post-Ben Ali Tunisia. Nidaa Tounes won 86 seats and led the polls with 37.5 per cent of the vote, a result similar to that achieved by Ennahda three years earlier. In both cases, the majority was only relative and led to coalition governments. Caïd-Essebsi's victory was largely grounded in his talent for rallying round him a patchwork of true revolutionaries, nostalgic for Bourguiba's era, reformed Ben Alists and staunch nationalists.

While Egypt was sinking into the downward spiral of armed conflict, Tunisia was completing a three-year transition from the toppling of its dictator to its first parliamentary elections, based on a new constitution adopted after passionate debate. The Tunisian people and politicians had effectively laid the ground for a functional Second Republic, just when the Egyptian top brass had methodically sabotaged any credible alternative to their Mamluk rule. This military subversion and restoration in Egypt had therefore led to an unprecedented surge in armed violence, while the jihadi threat seemed more or less contained in Tunisia.

The Tunisian Trump Cards

Drawing a parallel between the Egyptian and the Tunisian experiences is tempting since both nations experienced a democratic uprising to oust their dictators in January–February 2011. The Tunisian success story should not be exaggerated and the challenges still facing them remain formidable, but even so the contrast with the Egyptian debacle is striking. To make the comparison follow the general argument of this book, it is worth restating the obvious reality.

Tunisia is not a Mamluk state, and this is the main reason why the Tunisian people were spared the unbridled violence that the vengeful Deep State unleashed on its own citizens in Egypt in order to regain full control of the country. Bourguiba had indeed hijacked Tunisian independence for his own sake, through the elimination of his rival Ben Youssef, along with his supporters, and the establishment of a presidential constitution that eventually led to life presidency. But Bourguiba had been the major champion of Tunisia's liberation struggle from France, while the Egyptian 'Free Officers' moved in after the British had left.

Bourguiba had emasculated the Tunisian armed forces after the failed 1962 plot. His one-party system was security-obsessed, but it acted through the ministry of the interior and the police networks. Ben Ali, a former police general, had refined the repressive apparatus, blending the party's stifling of the population with its security monitoring. The army was kept consistently at the margins, transforming it involuntarily into the main embodiment of a national institution that could not be identified with the ruling regime. (On top of that, the active military personnel represented roughly 0.3 per cent of the Tunisian population, as against 1 per cent in Egypt.)

The Tunisian army refused to fire on protesters in January 2011, forcing Ben Ali to flee, then crushed the last counter-revolutionary strongholds of the presidential guard before returning to their barracks. General Rashid Ammar, the Tunisian chief of staff, went in to Kasbah Square to reaffirm his commitment to the demonstrators to defend the revolution, while Tantawi and the SCAF leaders addressed the Egyptian 'revolutionary youth' in a threatening, paternalistic tone.

Ben Ali drew substantial benefits from his involvement in the 'global war on terror', but those dividends were more geopolitical than financial, since Tunisia was never 'rewarded' by a Camp David-style annual subsidy. Contrary to neighbouring Algeria, Tunisia has no oil reserves and its economy relies essentially on the labours of its citizens. This absence of income was a blessing when it came to redrafting the socio-political pact. Though Tunisia is far from being immune from corruption and nepotism, the negative impact of any such patronage is far less extensive than in Egypt.

The Egyptian Mamluks openly played off the Muslim Brothers against the revolutionary youth during the year following Mubarak's fall. And the Egyptian Muslim Brothers had had half a century of a troubled relationship with the military, starting with their active support for the Free Officers' coup in 1952, through the purges of 1954 and 1965, until the parliamentary partial victory of 2005. Nothing of the kind existed in Tunisia, where Ennahda emerged in 2011 unbesmirched by such murky deals. This Islamist clean slate was key to their success in the first free and fair Tunisian elections.

In Egypt, the transition was monitored by Mubarak's watchdog, the Supreme Constitutional Court (SCC). No wonder that the SCC actively participated in the Mamluk subversion of the democratic process and wholeheartedly supported the July 2013 counter-revolution. On the contrary, in Tunisia, Yadh Ben Achour, chair of the transitional Higher Authority (HA), had resigned from Ben Ali's Constitutional Court as early as 1992, soon after the veteran Caid-Essebsi had stepped down as speaker of the parliament.

This meant that in the so-called Tunisian spring of 2011, both the prime minister and the chair of the transitional authority had severed their links with Ben Ali's regime two decades before the revolution, while the Egyptian SCC had been nominated by Mubarak himself. Ben Achour's HA had the explicit mandate to 'implement the objectives of the revolution, the political reform and the democratic transition'.[3] This rare association between revolution, reform and transition might be the trademark of the Tunisian experience.

The 155 members of the HA who prepared the first post-revolutionary elections from April to October 2011 belonged to the main 12 parties (nicknamed 'G12') or to various NGOs. The Bar association, along with the Judges union, also actively contributed to HA debates. Again, there could be no sharper contrast with Egypt, where the judiciary remained a stronghold of Mubarak nostalgia and where the parties, even when they shared a nationalist vision, proved unable to articulate it into a joint platform.

Apart from the fundamental Mamluk characterization of Egypt against Tunisia, the main difference between the two countries is the vitality of the labour movement in Tunisia. The Tunisian General Union of Labor (known by its French acronym, UGTT)[4] was already 400,000 strong before the revolution, and its ranks swelled after Ben Ali's fall. Its delegates inside the HA managed to impose the strict independence of the electoral commission, along with compulsory gender equality in the party ballot lists.

In Egypt, once the Ultras had been liquidated in the Port Saïd massacre of February 2012, there was no force to counter-balance the heavy weights of the militarized Deep State on one side, and of the Muslim Brothers on the other. Fuelled by the Mamluk subversion, this confrontational dynamic led to the summer 2013 bloodbath. In Tunisia, as we shall see, UGTT repeatedly moved in to mediate the tensions between Islamists and secularists, offering a crucial contribution to the three-year transition.

The Right Moves at (Most of) the Right Times

So non-Mamluk Tunisia had considerable additional assets compared to Egypt from the very beginning of the post-revolutionary period. But the Tunisian process greatly benefited from good decisions made at most of the right moments, sometimes for the wrong reasons, as so often in history. The smartest move was to go for the popular election of a constituent assembly, whose initial mandate was limited to one year. The drafting of a new constitution was largely considered as a prerequisite to the legitimization of new authorities, not as a prize delivered to the winner of the day against his political rivals.

In Egypt, the SCAF, which was supported then by the Muslim Brothers, went for a referendum on specific constitutional amendments just one month after Mubarak's deposition. The revolutionary alliance pushed for a 'no' and was brutally defeated by 77 per cent of the votes. Since this 'new' constitution was only an amended version of Sadat's and Mubarak's, the SCC was consolidated as the supreme watchdog. And in June 2012 it did not shy away from pronouncing the unlawfulness of the parliament elected a few months earlier in the first free and fair elections of modern Egypt.

The Egyptian Mamluks refused from day one to let the Egyptian people have their say, since it was precisely to avoid such an outcome that they had deposed Mubarak. So the parliament elected from November 2011 to January 2012 was deprived of any substantial power long before the SCC dissolved it, since the government remained responsible only to the SCAF. There was no attempt to build a new legitimacy for the rulers of Egypt, who were too busy undermining the democratic credentials of their Islamist challengers.

The Muslim Brotherhood tried to break the stalemate by pushing for a constitution that proved sharply divisive for the country, despite its 64 per cent approval in a referendum held in December 2012. Six months after his anti-Morsi coup, Sisi hoped to reverse the tide with a tailor-made constitution that was approved by 98 per cent of the votes in January 2014. There is no doubt that a significant section of the Egyptian electorate, not restricted to the

Salafi 'swing-voters' (who once supported the Brotherhood, then backed the military), voted in favour of two conflicting and contradictory texts in little more than a year.

This succession of confrontational referendums created what the political scientist Nathan Brown acutely described as 'Egypt's constitutional cul-de-sac'.[5] By contrast, Tunisia waited until October 2011 to hold elections for a constituent assembly, after a three-month postponement from the initial date. This assembly took two and a half years (instead of the expected year) to draft a text whose 146 articles were discussed and approved one by one. The final chart was then approved in January 2014 by 200 MPs against 12.

A referendum could have proved as divisive in Tunisia as it had repeatedly been in Egypt. Instead, the constituent assembly managed to reach a consensus on the most critical issues. The first two articles could not be amended. Article one was the same as in the 1959 constitution: 'Tunisia is a free, independent and sovereign state; its religion is Islam and its language Arabic.' The constructive ambiguity stemmed from the fact that in Arabic the words Tunisia and state are both feminine, so Islam could be considered as the country's or the state's religion.

The second article of the Constitution enshrined the 'civilian' nature of the state (in a parallel refusal of the 'military' and 'religious' options). Articles 40 and 46 were dedicated to the equality between men and women, with an innovative formulation in favour of electoral parity and against domestic violence. The compromise between the secularist support for a presidential system and the Islamist preference for a parliamentary one led to an institutional balance between the head of state (directly elected by the population) and the prime minister (responsible in front of the elected parliament).

Egypt meanwhile, supposedly obsessed with stability and order, had three constitutions in three years without ever reaching a sustained form of domestic consensus. Tunisia, instead, took the necessary time to draft an enduring text and open a new chapter in its national history. The voting system was also markedly different: it forced the leading party to enter coalitions in Tunisia, while it followed a 'winner takes all' rule in Egypt.

Again, instead of bringing stability to Egypt, this majority system only ignited political strife: both Ennahda and the Egyptian Muslim Brothers achieved 37 per cent of the votes in the first free elections held in the autumn and winter of 2011–12, but the Tunisian Islamists reaped only 89 out of the 217 seats, while their Egyptian counterparts filled 235 out of the 508 seats, just 20 seats short of an absolute majority.

The Brothers could rely on the Parliamentary backing of the 121 Salafi MPs every time secular-minded MPs or parties sought to limit the provisions of sharia law. By contrast, Ennahda had to strike a tripartite deal with the nationalist Congress for the Republic (CPR)[6] and the socio-democrat Ettakatol, under which the Islamists chaired and controlled a coalition government, with presidencies of the Republic to the CPR and of the constituent assembly to Ettakatol.

We have seen how the Islamist-dominated parliament was dissolved by the Mubarak-era watchdog only a few months after the vote. In the meantime, the Tunisian assembly went through various and serious crises in the drafting of the January 2014 final text. But Ennahda then agreed to relinquish the presidency of the government in favour of a non-partisan cabinet empowered to organize the first parliamentary elections.

It was only after those elections that the presidential contest was held in December 2014, nearly four years after Ben Ali's downfall. By contrast, the Egyptian Mamluks had drained the parliamentary elections of any substance and had bet on a polarizing presidential contest. Their gamble backfired with Morsi's election in June 2012, but they retaliated with Sisi's coup a year after. The former Field Marshal won the vote in a May 2014 plebiscite with 97 per cent of the vote—nine points more than Bashar al-Assad a few days later!

The Jihadi Challenge in Tunisia

The Tunisian experience is also significant in highlighting an alternative way to fight—and in fact contain—the jihadi menace, with far more convincing results than in the Mamluk states. Tunisian jihadis had been active for a decade and a half through the al-Qaeda associated Tunisian Islamic Fighting Group (GICT).[7] It was in Tunisia that al-Qaeda had struck the first major blow after the 9/11 attacks, with the suicide bombing of a synagogue on the island of Djerba, in April 2002. Additionally, Al-Qaeda in the Islamic Maghreb (AQIM), launched in 2007 in neighbouring Algeria, had attracted a number of Tunisian 'volunteers'.

There was therefore a serious threat from the very beginning of the Tunisian revolution, but it took time for the new leaders to grasp its full. The unconditional release of GICT founder Seifallah Benhassine (aka Abou Iyad) through the general amnesty of February 2011 was a major mistake. Benhassine was certainly no prisoner of conscience, since he had been condemned to 63 years in jail for terrorist activities, including the masterminding of the killing of Ahmed Shah Massoud, Afghan commander of the anti-Taliban resistance, two days before the 9/11 attacks.

Soon after his release, Benhassine founded a radical Salafi group, named Ansar al-Sharia (AS), literally the 'Supporters of Sharia'. Rached Ghannouchi, the charismatic leader of Ennahda, had come back to Tunisia after twenty years in exile, and he believed Salafis could be cajoled back into the ranks of his Islamist catch-all party. Other Ennahda leaders, like Hamadi Jebali or Ali Laarayedh, who had been jailed in Tunisia proper, were less romantic about Salafi hardliners and silently disapproved of Ghannouchi's tolerance towards AS.

After the Islamist relative victory at the October 2011 poll, Jebali was sworn in as prime minister and Laarayedh received the portfolio for the interior. But it took the AS-led assault on the US embassy, in September 2012, to convince Ennahda's leader that a crackdown on AS was urgent. The dissemination of a private American video, considered offensive towards the Prophet Mohammad, led to numerous anti-US incidents in the Muslim world, the worst occurring in Benghazi on 11 September, when the US ambassador was killed; and in Tunis on 14 September, when five demonstrators were shot dead by the presidential guard in order to secure the US embassy.

AS was officially banned as a terrorist organization and Benhassine went underground. The Jebali government even let two AS hunger strikers die in jail, rejecting all their demands. Meanwhile, there were an increasing number of incidents involving armed groups on the Algerian and Libyan borders. Clashes occurred, mines exploded and weapons were seized in unprecedented quantity. It was admitted in early 2013 that AQIM had established a foothold in the Jabal Chambi, a mountain range close to the Algerian border, some 20 km west of the Tunisian city of Kasserine, one of the hotbeds of the January 2011 uprising.

Chokri Belaïd, a prominent leftist activist, was shot dead in front of his home in Tunis, on 6 February 2013. This killing sent shockwaves through a country with very limited experience of political violence. The opposition accused Ennahda of tolerating 'death squads' in order to intimidate, and eventually eliminate, secular and critical voices. Contrary to the nationalist tribute to the 'martyr' Belaïd (*shahîd*), Ennahda soberly eulogized the 'departed' militant (*faqîd*).

The crisis became so intense that Jebali had to step down in favour of Laarayedh. The former minister of the interior imposed a much tougher line against AS in March 2013, brutally suppressing the conference that the Salafi group held every year in Kairouan. Violence also escalated in the Jabal Chambi region, with now dozens of victims on both the security and jihadi sides.

The assassination of a second secular activist, Mohammad Brahmi, on 25 July 2013, precipitated a major showdown between Ennahda and the opposition, led by Nidaa Tounes. The UGTT labour union, whose membership was bigger than both rival parties put together, stepped in with all its might to settle the dispute. This UGTT mediation, supported by the Business union (UTICA),[8] the Bar association and the Tunisian League for Human Rights (LTDH),[9] laid the ground for a 'national dialogue', launched three months after Brahmi's killing.

This dialogue went on for another three months and concluded with the approval of a new constitution and the resignation of the Islamist prime minister Laarayedh. He was replaced by the non-affiliated Mehdi Jomaa, whose technocratic government was bound to prepare the first parliamentary elections. The independent minister of the interior, Lotfi Ben Jeddou, stayed in place and announced in February 2014 that twenty-three jihadis had been killed over recent months, including Belaïd's murderer.[10]

It is therefore wrong to claim that post-revolutionary Tunisia, once AS had been banned, had been more lenient towards jihadism than the Mamluk regimes. But transitional Tunisia had certainly put a distinct emphasis on the due process of law, with 1,343 suspects being tried, according to the minister of the interior, shortly after the approval of the constitution.[11] A jihadi cell retaliated by targeting Ben Jeddou's home in Kasserine, in late May 2014, killing four policemen in their assault.

But the worst jihadi attack occurred that year on 17 July 2014 when 14 soldiers were killed in the Jabal Chambi area. Three days of national mourning were announced but, instead of what had already occurred and what would happen again in Egypt, this terrorist shock consolidated the political consensus on the democratic transition. In October 2014, the first parliamentary vote was not marred by any jihadi provocation and closed effectively a three-year cycle during which an Islamist-led government had been followed by a non-partisan cabinet, both of them accountable towards an elected assembly.

The Libyan Counter-Example

As we have seen, neither Saddam Hussein's Iraq nor Moammar Qaddafi's Libya quite fitted the Mamluk template. Those two regimes were openly totalitarian and did not bother to summon the 'caliph people' in cyclical electoral rites, contrary to the need of the modern Mamluks periodically to rejuvenate their legitimization dramaturgy. Both Iraq and Libya had lived under a strict regime of UN sanctions from 1991 to 2003, which, far from easing the grip of the repressive apparatus, had only aggravated the plight of a very vulnerable population.

George W. Bush's global war on terror (GWT) was designed from the start to target Iraq, through the dubious substantiation of some kind of relation between Saddam and the 9/11 attacks. By contrast, Qaddafi used the GWT to resume his cooperation with the Western intelligence agencies and contribute to the US-led campaign against al-Qaeda. The Libyan nuclear programme became a hot commodity to deal profitably with Washington[12] when no evidence of nuclear capacity could be found in post-Saddam Iraq.

The first decision of the American occupying administration in Iraq, in April 2003, was to dissolve the army and 'de-Baathify' the public service, which led to the effective collapse of the Iraqi state. The US had indeed no colonial antecedent, but such a blank slate only made them more inefficient at state-(re)building in a context of increasing resistance: one year after toppling Saddam, the American contingent was facing both a Sunni insurgency in western Iraq and a Shia one in the south of the country.

The ideological textbook of the neo-conservatives proved useless to sort out this self-inflicted mess. So the US unconsciously amalgamated the worst of two colonial experiences at state-building in the 1920s mandates: the forceful British integration of the three governorates of Baghdad, Basra and Mosul, on one side; and the French sectarian re-partition of power in Lebanon, designed to enshrine the domineering position of the local Christians, on the other.

This disastrous Iraqi process led to the 2005 constitutional impasse and the 2006–8 civil war.[13] The strongest parties in this power struggle were those with the fiercest militias and the most coherent sectarian base. Minorities such as the Christians or the Yezidis would only pay the highest price in this politico-military battle, out of which the Maliki government and the jihadi ISIS emerged as the main players, once the US had completed its military withdrawal in 2011.

Contrary to popular narrative, NATO's campaign in Libya from March to October 2011 stood in sharp contrast to the US invasion of Iraq, eight years earlier. The Obama administration was now 'leading from behind' and had only reluctantly agreed to launch air strikes against Qaddafi. There was no grand design of rebuilding a 'Greater Middle East' after the toppling of the dictator, but a more modest attempt at controlling the damage an infuriated Qaddafi could inflict on neighbouring Egypt and, to a lesser extent, Tunisia.

The Bush administration had destroyed the remaining Iraqi institutions after their 2003 invasion, but Qaddafi had consistently undermined any attempt at collective organization during the forty-two years of his ruthless dictatorship. The challenge was therefore far more daunting than in Cairo or in Tunis. The good news was that the longing for a united Libya was overwhelming. The bad news was that tens of thousands of militia, proud of their revolutionary credentials, were jeopardizing the prospect of a peaceful transition.

The UN had left good memories in Libya through its much-celebrated contribution to the 1951 independence. US and NATO were out, while the European Union had been deeply divided between 'interventionist' France and UK on the one side, and 'neutral' Germany on the other. Even the Arab Mamluks were split between Qaddafi's nostalgic supporters in Algiers and the pro-revolution military in Cairo, backed by the Gulf states. So there seemed to be no competitor to the UN acting as main foreign power broker in Libya.

The National Transitional Council (NTC) led the struggle against Qaddafi and was now running Libya. This pragmatic structure had managed, through co-optation and interaction, to associate various components of such diverse a nation as Libya with a reasonable measure of success: in addition to the colonial triple standard between Tripolitania, Cyrenaica and Fezzan, there were ethnic divisions between Arabs, Berbers and Toubous, against the background of a deeply tribal system (that Qaddafi had entrenched further by promoting his home town of Sirte against neighbouring Misrata).

Unfortunately, the UN fell into the common misapprehension that democratic transitions could only be guaranteed by general elections. As we have seen, the transition from presidents Saleh to Hadi in Yemen was on the contrary secured through a Mamluk-style plebiscite, and a 'national dialogue' was then convened before even conceiving of any general poll. This seems to be the price to pay in countries whose fragmentation had only been aggravated by decades of dictatorship, with the associated 'divide and rule' policies.

So the UN pushed for the premature election of a General National Congress (GNC) in July 2012. NTC cabinet members agreed not to run, and its president pledged to withdraw from political life. The vote was rightfully praised for the popular turnout (61.6 per cent), the technical success (in an immense country) and the absence of major incidents (despite the omnipresence of militias). Algerian and Egyptian Mamluks alike rejoiced at the poor performance of the Libyan Muslim Brotherhood.

The GNC was chaired by nationalist Mohammad Magariaf, who had been fighting Qaddafi's regime for the past three decades. In late October 2012, the liberal Ali Zeidan managed to put together a fairly inclusive government, but the Muslim

Brothers maneuvered against the new authorities, rallying independent members of the GNC. This consistent undermining led, in May 2013, to the passing of the Political Isolation Law that was so excluding of any Qaddafi 'association' that even a veteran revolutionary like Magariaf had to resign (he had been Libyan ambassador to India before his defection in 1980).

The Muslim Brothers carried the major responsibility for this Political Isolation Law that was as disastrous for the future of Libya as the US-imposed 'de-Baathification' had been for Iraq ten years earlier. They supported the new GNC president, Nouri Abusamhain, and incidents flared between him and Prime Minister Zeidan, who was even briefly kidnapped by the militia in Tripoli in October 2013. This paralysis of the revolutionary institutions paved the way for increased warlordism and anarchy.

But the main GNC flaw remained its failure to convene a Constitution Drafting Assembly. Contrary to neighbouring Tunisia, the GNC had no constitutional mandate and should have convened such an assembly as early as September 2012. The power struggles had derailed the constitutional process and it was only in February 2014 that the GNC, eager to prorogate its own mandate, organized the elections for a sixty-member constitutional body (with twenty members each for Tripolitania, Cyrenaica and Fezzan).

This poll was marred by serious incidents and a very low turnout (one third of what had been recorded in July 2012), against the background of a boycott by some Berber and Toubou forces. The number of armed militiamen had swollen from 150,000 in 2012 to 200,000 or even 250,000 one year later,[14] in a country of 6 million people. The so-called revolutionary legitimacy of those armed groups became increasingly questionable, since their recent recruits had never participated in the anti-Qaddafi insurgency.

The main contenders for power in the streets of Tripoli were not indigenous militias, but the rival Misrata and Zintan 'brigades', the first group supporting the Muslim Brotherhood and the second associated with the nationalist forces. None of these militias could have been described as Islamist, even though, as discussed in Chapter 7, the Egyptian and Algerian Mamluks did their utmost to caricature this power struggle as a fight between anti-terrorism and jihadism.

The failure of the GNC soon verged on the catastrophic with the ousting of Prime Minister Zeidan, who fled to Morocco in March 2014. The controversial election of his successor was deemed unconstitutional by the Supreme Court, forcing the GNC to convene parliamentary elections in June. In a country now plagued with unbridled violence, the turnout fell to an abysmal 18 per cent, and 12 out of the 200 seats could not be designated through the polls. Nor could voting take place in the Cyrenaica city of Derna, now under jihadi control. Worse, the new parliament was unable to convene in either Tripoli or Benghazi, and had to take shelter in Tobruk, under de facto Egyptian protection. The GNC refused to transfer power to this 'illegitimate' body, and two competing governments started to operate from Tobruk and Tripoli.

So Libya stood as a sinister illustration of a transition gone astray, especially compared with neighbouring Tunisia. Contrary to popular interpretation in the Western media, the main reason lay not in the 2011 NATO campaign, but in the electoral voluntarism that deepened the political fragmentation instead of favouring a national consensus. Each vote in Libya aggravated the civil strife, while Tunisia voted only twice: for a constituent assembly in October 2011, and a parliament elected on the basis of the new constitution three years later.

Libya still has no constitution to rebuild a polity deeply fractured by four decades of unmitigated dictatorship. The clash of legitimacies between 'revolutionary' Tripoli and 'institutional' Tobruk, each with its own parliament and government, could only be resolved through a 'national dialogue' comparable to those convened in Yemen and Tunisia in 2013. This was the kind of dialogue that the UN had tried and failed to convene one week before the parliamentary elections. But such pleas gained some ground after the Supreme Court deemed the Tobruk parliament unconstitutional, in November 2014.

There is no short cut to democracy, and the comparison between Libya in 2012 and 2014 is appalling in that regard. The Muslim Brothers played a terribly dark game with the Political Isolation Law and its ominous aftermath. But the military interference of the Egyptian Mamluks might have pushed the country over the brink. In a self-fulfilling prophecy that was staged earlier in Yemen, Syria and Egypt itself, the anti-jihadi rallying cry boosted those jihadis it was supposed to combat: in Libya, al-Qaeda and ISIS affiliates became the major long-term winners of the politico-military impasse in late 2014.

*

In Tunisia as well as in Egypt, the prime minister appointed by the dictator before his fall remained in office: Mohammad Ghannouchi in Tunis and Ahmed Shafiq in Cairo. The revolutionary protests therefore targeted this executive legacy of the deposed despot, demanding his unconditional resignation. It took weeks of street unrest and political bickering before the appointment of Béji Caïd-Essebsi in Tunis and, three days later, of Essam Sharaf in Cairo.

The two new prime ministers praised the revolutionary youth, their sacrifices and struggle. But Sharaf soon discovered that the Mamluk SCAF continued to hold real power, while Caïd-Essebsi monitored the transition to the first free and fair elections, never trying to take advantage of his prominent position. Caïd-Essebsi stepped down in favour of authorities legitimized by the popular vote in December 2011, when Sharaf had to bow to military pressure and withdraw on behalf of a SCAF protégé.

Caïd-Essebsi played loyally by the post-revolutionary rules, and his party eventually won the Tunisian parliamentary elections in October 2014. Two months later, the same Caïd-Essebsi was voted in as the first democratically elected president of Tunisia in a poll where the Islamist Ennahda party chose not to run, nor even to support any candidate. By contrast, Sharaf had disappeared from the Egyptian landscape, keeping only honorary titles, such as the presidency of the board of trustees of the Luxor African Film Festival.

The current chapter of the Mamluk-fuelled Egyptian ordeal is only beginning, since Sisi and his clique have no clue about running a country as complex as Egypt, and know just how to fight, preferably their own people, while interfering militarily in neighbouring Libya. Meanwhile, Tunisia has certainly not yet healed all the wounds laid bare between Islamists and secularists, and it remains a long way off from solving its youth unemployment and the regional disparity that sparked the 2010–11 uprising.

But Tunisia paved the way for a Second Republic that fulfils at last the popular demands for self-determination (hijacked under Bourguiba) and emancipation (crushed under Ben Ali). Meanwhile, Egypt is contemplating its future through the rear-mirror of a fantasized Free Officers glorious past. All charges against Mubarak were dismissed in November 2014, a move that erased the last trace of revolutionary trauma in the Mamluk inner circle. Sisi is now contemplating his own version of Nasser's Aswan Dam, with the colossal duplication of the Suez Canal.

Tunisia suffered on 18 March 2015 a terrible blow with the ISIS-inspired attack on the Bardo National Museum, close to Parliament. The two Tunisian terrorists, previously trained in ISIS camps in Libya, went on a shooting rampage that killed twenty foreign tourists and one Tunisian securityman. But this terror attack unexpectedly consolidated Tunisian national unity, while Sisi repeatedly claimed that the increasing toll of jihadi attacks is a reasonable price to pay for the eradication of the Muslim Brotherhood.

Tunis museum was indeed a 'soft target', while the 'hard targets' of the security apparatus are routinely attacked by jihadi groups in Egypt, whether in Sinaï by the ISIS-affiliate ABM or in Cairo itself. Tunisia has reacted collectively and patriotically to the jihadi challenge, while the fourth celebration of the Egyptian revolution against Mubarak was marred, on 25 January 2015, by the killing of eighteen protesters by in live police firing. While Tunisia calls for a UN-sponsored settlement on the Libyan crisis, Sisi is eager to increase his military involvement on behalf of the Tobruk-based alliance, in the same 'eradication' logic that has already nurtured the jihadi escalation in Egypt.

Karl Marx compared Napoléon Bonaparte and his nephew Louis Napoléon, soon to be crowned Napoléon III, with this now famous quote that history has been repeating itself: 'the first time as tragedy, the second time as farce'.[15] We have witnessed the tragedy that Nasser inflicted on Egypt through his intervention in Yemen and the 1967 rout. Sisi is indeed farcical in his pathetic endeavour to emulate his departed role model. But the tragic spiral into which he is dragging Egypt, and possibly Libya, could prove more devastating than all the previous Mamluk adventures.

There was absolutely no inevitability about such a disastrous outcome. Tunisia proved that there was an alternative way out of the legacy of the mythical fathers of the Arab nation and their epigones. But the Deep State had to be neutralized and the Mamluks were bound to lose some of their dearest privileges. Their absolute refusal to relinquish even part of their domineering position had led to the horrors of the black decade twenty years earlier in Algeria. The Arab Mamluks have now already plunged Syria and Yemen into the abyss of civil war. Egypt and Libya are being sucked day after day into such a downward spiral. Welcome to the jihadi nightmare, and give most of the credit to the ruling Mamluks.

CONCLUSION

Four years into the Arab revolution, the depressing realisation prevails that, with the significant exception of vanguard Tunisia, the whole democratic uprising is at best a failure, at worst a fraud. The suicide of a twenty-two-year-old female activist in Cairo, Zeinab al-Mahdi, was as poignant as the last words she left before hanging herself on 13 November 2014: 'There is no justice. Victory will not happen. We lie to ourselves in order to survive.'[1]

That very same day, ISIS disseminated an audio-recording of the now 'Caliph Ibrahim' on the internet, aimed at dispelling recent US reports that he had been injured or killed in a recent strike on northern Iraq. Abu Bakr al-Baghdadi was bragging, 'the agents of the Jews and Crusaders, their slaves and dogs, could not hold out in the face of the Islamic State, and they will never hold out: the Crusaders will indeed be defeated'.[2]

In a move designed to substantiate those threats, ISIS media branch broadcast one of its horror videos on 16 November 2014, showing twenty-two Syrian soldiers having their throats slit, with a final focus on a beheaded American hostage, the third in three months. The executioners appeared to come from various parts of the world, with at least one French jihadi convert identified.

We saw abundantly through this book how Arab Mamluks, especially in Syria, cooperated intimately with jihadi networks. One decade ago, their support was crucial to channel foreign 'volunteers' from Syria to the Iraq-based Zarqawi group, the matrix of today's ISIS. One of those recruits, Boubaker al-Hakim, a dual French–Tunisian citizen, spent several months of 2004 in the Zarqawi-controlled city of Falluja. His brother Redouane was even killed there in a US bombing.[3]

Boubaker al-Hakim sneaked back into Syria, from which he was eventually expelled to France. He was given a a seven-year sentence for his jihadi involvement, and after his release he travelled to post-Ben Ali Tunisia. His 'military' background led him to organize the armed branch of Ansar al-Sharia (AS). Still on the run, Hakim has been accused of participation in the killings of Belaid and Brahmi that nearly derailed the Tunisian transition in 2013.[4] In the last days of 2014, he claimed responsibility for those murders in an ISIS-disseminated video. He warned that he would be returning to Tunisia to carry out further assassinations.

Boubaker al-Hakim is just one illustration of how the evil twins of the Deep State and the Islamic State have been working hand and hand to crush any prospect of democratic progress in the Arab world. Hakim has been accused of masterminding in 2015 both the attacks in Paris in January and the Tunis museum massacre in March. But there are many other Boubaker al-Hakims, dozens, maybe hundreds, working to undermine the painstaking process of institutionalizing pluralism. Caught between a rock and a hard place, Arab revolutionaries have also been abandoned by the West.

A conservative estimate concludes that the Assad regime has killed a hundred times more Syrian civilians than ISIS.[5] Despite this enormous discrepancy, the US-led air campaign has been sparing regime targets since September 2014, while striking the anti-Assad (and anti-ISIS) Nusra front, as well as ISIS. And in America, voices are increasingly calling for a deal with the Syrian despot. A prominent American columnist summarized his concern about such bargaining: 'it is repugnant, but is it wrong?'[6]

One could comment that this kind of 'devil's bargain'[7] would be bound to fail, since it would only nurture the jihadi monster by 'revealing' what ISIS propaganda has been claiming all along: 'Jews and Crusaders' are uniting with the local tyrants to oppress the Arab Muslims, destroy their countries, their homes and their dignity. According to the jihadi narrative, the Western discourse on democracy, freedom and human rights is only a mischievous delusion to enslave the peoples of the Middle East.

The horrendous record of the ruling Mamluks in Algeria, Egypt, Syria and Yemen should have obliterated any illusion about their questionable contribution to domestic and regional 'stability'. But the whole world has kept looking on, not to say-applauding, as non-violent opposition is liquidated. Therefore, the question is not why ISIS has emerged out of this merciless blood bath, but why ISIS has not yet grown stronger.

August 2013 may seem in retrospect to be the turning point when the Arab counter-revolution went from a mass tragedy to a nightmarish hell. The slaughter the modern Mamluks committed then in Cairo is unprecedented in Egyptian contemporary history. One has to go back to the ruthless repression of the Cairo riots by the French expeditionary force, in October 1798, to find a comparable level of urban violence. In the same spirit, some of the neighbourhoods struck by the Assad regime in his August 2013 gas attacks on Damascus had already been the targets of French colonial shelling, during the putting down of the Great Arab Revolt of 1925–6.

So Mamluks treated their own population as cruelly as foreign occupiers did. Bashar's chemical strikes had however a precedent in the Egyptian use of poison gas against Yemeni resistance strongholds, in January 1967. In both instances, hundreds of civilians were gassed because they would not submit to a supposedly 'enlightened' despotism. The main difference lies in the fact that the 1967 gas attacks went largely ignored, while the 2013 Syrian chemical massacre was heavily reported.

The Damascus gas slaughter soon became one of the main jhadi recruiting pitches, with ISIS pretending that Assad was just a pawn in an international conspiracy against Muslims. Scores of aspiring jihadis, in Europe and in North America, fell into this propaganda trap and the flow of 'volunteers' ready to join ISIS significantly increased in autumn 2013. One year later, the US-led bombing campaign against ISIS took great pains to avoid any Assad regime facility, which can only foster the jihadi narrative and its growing popularity.

President and former Field Marshal Sisi stands ready to contribute significantly to the further expansion of ISIS. He has already entrenched in the Sinai mountain ranges the leading jihadi group, Ansar Beit al-Maqdis (ABM), which has pledged allegiance to Baghdadi and extended its terrorist reach far into the Nile Valley. In Libya, Egyptian military interference in support of the Tobruk-based General Haftar has paved the way in neighbouring Derna for the consolidation of an ISIS foothold, under the flag of a local consultative council of the Islamic Youth (Majlis Choura Chabab al-Islam, MCCI).[8]

The Sisi-backed government in Tobruk has for months focused its offensives on Tripoli, 1,250 km away, while its air strikes have spared Derna, only 170 km away. This double-standard bombing is strongly reminiscent of the three years during which the Assad air force spared jihadi targets, even when ISIS might have been nipped in the bud. The Egyptian Mamluks in Libya, like their Syrian counterparts in their homeland in 2012–14, have consistently sabotaged all UN efforts to reconcile a deeply fractured nation before its total collapse. And it took the ISIS massacre in Libya of twenty-one Egyptian Copts, in February 2015, for Sisi finally to hit back against jihadi targets.

Yemen stands as a sinister illustration of how irrelevant it is to oust a despot while keeping his repressive apparatus in place. The modern Mamluks, who had hijacked the Arab independent states two generations ago, are now painting their rabid counter-revolution with 'revolutionary' colours, whether in Cairo or in Sanaa. Saleh's supporters in the Yemeni army are now fighting along pro-Iranian militiamen against the forces loyal to elected president Hadi, forced to flee Aden. In Algiers, the presidential mummy is the embodiment of an old guard that drums its 'revolutionary' struggle against France in the one and only 'revolution' to date. Meanwhile, Bashar al-Assad claims his barbaric killing machine is a beacon of 'resistance'.

The unfolding of such disasters in the Arab world was both predictable and avoidable. It would therefore be stabbing the Arab democrats twice to blame them for such a catastrophe when their deadliest enemies, on the regime and jihadi sides, found enough common ground to unite in hunting them down, even at the cost of burning the nation and its future. But I happen to be one of those famed optimists who answers the pessimist's 'It could not be worse' with a sinister 'Oh yes, it could, it sure could.'

There might be just one ray of hope in this bleak landscape, and it lies in the fact that oil prices fell by 40 per cent in 2014. We have seen how these oil revenues have been—and still are—critical in fuelling the violence unleashed by the Arab Mamluks against their own people, whether the source was domestic, as in Algeria or Yemen, or derived from foreign patrons: Russia and Iran in Syria, Saudi Arabia and the UAE in Egypt. Even ISIS depends to a great extent on the oil it smuggles through the Assad regime and its Turkish partners in crime.

Cheaper oil could alleviate the devastating pressure on Arab society and polities, in the same way that absence of oil was crucial to the success of the Tunisian transition. The Arab revolution is far from over, and the next activist generation will have learned the hardest way possible how to confront such ruthless adversaries. But one can only feel pain and sorrow at all those lives destroyed by the Arab dictators and their jihadi nemesis. Let us hope that their sacrifices will not have been in vain and that their dedication to the cause is remembered.

NOTES

FOREWORD

1. Jean-Pierre Filiu, *The Arab Revolution*, London: Hurst, 2011.
2. Amira El-Azhary Sonbol, *The New Mamluks, Egyptian Society and Modern Feudalism*, New York: Syracuse University Press, 2000.
3. Filiu, *The Arab Revolution*, p. 118.

1. MEET THE DEEP STATE

1. 'Grey Wolves' is the nickname of an ultra-nationalist Turkish group that calls itself 'Young Idealists' (*ülkücü*). See Hamit Bozarslan, 'Network-building, ethnicity and violence in Turkey', Abu Dhabi: ECSSR, 1999, p. 3.
2. Pascal de Gendt, 'La mafia infiltre l'Etat', *Confluences*, Autumn 1997, p. 48.
3. *Milliyet*, 24 December 1996, quoted in Frank Bovenkerk and Yücel Yesilgöz, 'The Turkish mafia and the state', in Cyrille Fijnaut and Letizia Paoli (eds), *Organised Crime in Europe*, Dordrecht: Springer, 2004, p. 587.
4. de Gendt, 'La mafia infiltre l'Etat', p. 48.
5. See for instance Cengiz Candar in *Sabah*, 28 June 1997.
6. Bozarslan, 'Network-building, ethnicity and violence in Turkey', p. 7.
7. Ibid., p. 6.
8. These official data covering the 1984–2010 period have been published in *Milliyet*, 24 June 2011.
9. Bozarslan, 'Network-building, ethnicity and violence in Turkey', p. 17.
10. The widow of the late President Ozal was the first to utter such accusations. Twenty years later, Sabah columnist Rasim Ozan Kutahyali wrote that 'for the majority of the Turkish people, Ozal was killed by the "Deep State"' (*Al Monitor*, 22 August 2013).
11. This conspiracy theory is reproduced as supposed fact in the Wikipedia entry on 'Susurluk scandal'.

12. Fethullah Gülen's official website is http://fgulen.com/en (accessed 8 December 2014). He was a disciple of Said Nursi (1878–1960), who, as often happens with Sufi orders, established his own *tarika* in Izmir after his master's death.

13. BBC, 21 September 2012, http://www.bbc.com/news/world-europe-1967 0530 (accessed 30 April 2014).

14. *Today's Zaman*, 5 August 2013.

15. Ilker Basbug's official website, http://www.ilkerbasbug.com.tr/?p=1942& lang=EN (accessed 30 April 2014).

16. See http://www.theguardian.com/world/2012/sep/25/turkey-sledgeham-mer-coup-trial-verdict (accessed 1 May 2014).

17. European Commission, *Turkey 2012 progress report*, Brussels, 10 October 2012, p. 5.

18. See http://www.worldtribune.com/2012/08/19/erdogan-angered-by-rookie-u-s-ambassadors-criticism-on-freedoms/ (accessed 1 May 2014).

19. *Hurriyet Daily News*, 18 February 2011.

20. The Turkish word that PM Erdogan used on 2 June 2013 was *çapulçu*, which could be translated as 'looter', or 'hoodlum', and was anglicized as 'chapuller'. The verb derived from this neologism, 'chapulling', is supposed to mean 'standing (or fighting) for one's rights'.

21. 'Gülen is thought to have between two and three million followers in Turkey, including as many as sixty members of parliament, about ten per cent of the total' (Dexter Filkins, 'How far will Turkey's Recep Tayyip Erdogan go to stay in power?', *New Yorker*, 12 March 2012).

22. Tim Arango, 'Turkish leader disowns trials that helped him tame the military', *New York Times*, 26 February 2014.

23. See http://www.al-monitor.com/pulse/originals/2014/04/erdogan-mit-interference-authoritarian.html (accessed 1 May 2014).

24. *Today's Zaman*, 7 April 2014.

25. Filiu, *The Arab Revolution*, p. 103.

2. THE MYTHICAL FATHERS OF THE NATION

1. Jean Marcou, 'Le mouvement constitutionnel', in Semih Vaner (ed.), *La Turquie*, Paris: Fayard, 2005, p. 106.

2. Dexter Filkins, 'How far will Turkey's Recep Tayyip Erdogan go to stay in power?', *New Yorker*, 12 March 2012.

3. Eugene Rogan, *The Arabs, A History*, London: Allen Lane, 2009, p. 43.

4. Filiu, *The Arab Revolution*, pp. 141–4.

5. *Daughters of Allah (Allah in Kizlari)* was published in 2008 by Dogan publications (Istanbul), but has not yet been translated into English.

6. Filiu, *The Arab Revolution*, p. 142.

7. Souhayr Belhassen, 'Les legs bourguibiens de la répression', in Michel Camau and Vincent Geisser (eds), *Habib Bourguiba, la trace et l'héritage*, Paris: Karthala, 2004, p. 395.

8. Guy Pervillé, 'La guerre d'Algérie, combien de morts?', in Mohammed Harbi and Benjamin Stora (eds), *La guerre d'Algérie*, Paris: Hachette-Pluriel, 2005, pp. 713–14.

9. Patrick Seale, *The Struggle for Syria*, New Haven, CT: Yale University Press, 1987, pp. 3–4.

10. Ibid., p. 59.

11. Raphaël Lefèvre, *Ashes of Hama: The Muslim Brotherhood in Syria*, London: Hurst & Co., 2013, pp. 33–4.

12. Steven Cook, *The Struggle for Egypt, from Nasser to Tahrir Square*, New York: Oxford University Press, 2012, p. 36.

13. Ibid., p. 11.

14. Ibid., p. 321.

15. George Haddad, *Revolutions and Military Rule in the Middle East, Egypt, the Sudan, Yemen and Libya*, New York: Robert Speller, 1973, p. 371.

16. The major book on the issue is the work by Avi Shlaim, *Collusion across the Jordan: King Abdullah, the Zionist Movement and the Partition of Palestine*, New York: Columbia University Press, 1988.

17. *Le Combattant suprême* (in French) was translated in Arabic as *al-Mujâhid al-Akbar*, with the celebration of the nationalist 'jihad' which Bourguiba had waged for Tunisia's sake.

18. Lazhar Chraïti, one of the executed plotters, had been a charismatic leader of the anti-French insurgency in 1954–6. In 2013, on the anniversary of Tunisian independence, President Moncef Marzouki bestowed upon him posthumously the highest Tunisian distinction (the Grand Order of Independence).

3. THE MODERN MAMLUKS

1. Caterina Bori, 'Théologie politique et Islam, à propos d'Ibn Taymiyya et du sultanat mamelouk', *Revue de l'histoire des religions*, 1, 2007, pp. 31–2.

2. Hazem Kandil, *Soldiers, Spies and Statesmen: Egypt's Road to Revolt*, London: Verso, 2012, p. 37. For a first-hand account of Nasser's relation with the Muslim Brotherhood, see the online excerpt from Khaled Mohieldin, *Memories of a Revolution, 1952*, Cairo: American University of Cairo, 1995, http://english.ahram.org.eg/NewsContent/1/139/48402/Egypt/-July-Revolution/Nasser,-myself-and-the-Muslim-Brotherhood.aspx, accessed 13 December 2014.

3. Kandil, *Soldiers, Spies and Statesmen*, pp. 19–20.

4. Cook, *The Struggle for Egypt*, pp. 55–6.

5. Kandil, *Soldiers, Spies and Statesmen*, p. 38.
6. Ibid., p. 40.
7. Ibid., p. 51.
8. Patrick Seale, *Asad, the Struggle for the Middle East*, Berkeley: University of California Press, 1989, p. 54.
9. Kandil, *Soldiers, Spies and Statesmen*, p. 54.
10. Jesse Ferris, *Nasser's Gamble, How Intervention in Yemen caused the Six-Day War and the Decline of Egyptian Power*, Princeton, NJ: Princeton University Press, 2013, p. 62.
11. Anwar Sadat, *Al-Bahth 'an al-zat*, Cairo: Al-Maktab al-Masry al-Hadith, 1978, p. 220.
12. Eugene Rogan and Tewfik Aclimandos, 'The Yemen war and Egypt's war preparedness', in Roger Louis and Avi Shlaim (eds), *The 1967 Arab–Israeli War: Origins and Consequences*, New York: Cambridge University Press, 2012, pp. 163–4.
13. Cook, *The Struggle for Egypt*, pp. 122–3.
14. Amira El-Azahary Sonbol, *The New Mamlouks*, p. 133.
15. Kandil, *Soldiers, Spies and Statesmen*, p. 170.
16. Ibid., pp. 167–8.
17. Cook, *The Struggle for Egypt*, pp. 158–9.
18. Kandil, *Soldiers, Spies and Statesmen*, p. 180.
19. Hanna Batatu, *Syria's Peasantry, the Descendants of its Lesser Rural Notables and their Politics*, Princeton, NJ: Princeton University Press, 1999, pp. 146–7.
20. Seale, *Asad: the Struggle for the Middle East*, p. 79.
21. David Lesch, 'Syria: Playing with Fire', in Roger Louis and Avi Shlaim (eds), *The 1967 Arab–Israeli War*, p. 86.
22. Jean-Pierre Filiu, *Le nouveau Moyen-Orient, les peuples à l'heure de la Révolution syrienne*, Paris: Fayard, 2013, p. 66.
23. Lesch, 'Syria: Playing with Fire', p. 94.
24. Filiu, *The Arab Revolution*, pp. 74–5.
25. Raphaëlle Branche, *Prisonniers du FLN*, Paris: Payot, 2014, p. 9.
26. Ibid., p. 12.
27. Miriam Lowi, *Oil Wealth and the Poverty of Politics: Algeria Compared*, New York: Cambridge University Press, 2009, p. 66.
28. Lahouari Addi, *L'Algérie et la démocratie, pouvoir et crise du politique dans l'Algérie contemporaine*, Paris: La Découverte, 1994, p. 58.
29. Interview with Colonel Ali Hamlat, *Le Soir d'Algérie*, 24 June 2008.
30. Lowi, *Oil Wealth and the Poverty of Politics*, p. 75.
31. Ibid., pp. 83–4.
32. Ibid., p. 89.
33. Ibid., p. 99.

34. DGPS, with PS standing for 'prevention and security', was thus echoing Merbah's SM 'offices for prevention and security' (BSP) that controlled Algeria under Boumediene.
35. Haddad, *Revolutions and Military Rule in the Middle East, Egypt, the Sudan, Yemen and Libya*, p. 227.
36. Ibid., p. 241.
37. Ferris, *Nasser's Gamble*, p. 60.
38. Haddad, *Revolutions and Military Rule in the Middle East, Egypt, the Sudan, Yemen and Libya*, p. 258.
39. Ferris, *Nasser's Gamble*, p. 188.
40. Stephen Day, *Regionalism and Rebellion in Yemen, A Troubled National Union*, Cambridge: Cambridge University Press, 2012, p. 277.
41. Ibid., pp. 90–93.
42. Ibid., p. 70.

4. THE ALGERIAN MATRIX

1. For an in-depth academic discussion of the FLN–FIS ideological convergences, see Lahouari Addi, *L'Algérie et la démocratie*, ch. 5.
2. Algerians routinely refer, until today, to SM (*Sécurité Militaire*) as an equivalent to DRS (*Département du Renseignement et de la Sécurité*), more than two decades after being revamped into the DRS.
3. Seale, *Asad: the Struggle for the Middle East*, p. 399.
4. Ibid., p. 462.
5. Fanar Haddad, *Sectarianism in Iraq, Antagonistic Views of Unity*, London: Hurst, 2011, p. 66.
6. Ibid., p. 127.
7. Ibid., p. 75.
8. John Entelis, *Algeria: The Revolution Institutionalized*, Boulder, CO: Westview Press, 1986, p. 122.
9. Interview with an anonymous French diplomat, Paris, 5 June 2013.
10. Press conference by François Mitterrand, Luxembourg, 14 January 1992.
11. Statement of gendarmerie chief, General Ghezaiel, to the Algerian press, 15 April 1992.
12. Jean-Pierre Filiu, 'The Local and Global Jihad of Al-Qa'eda in the Islamic Maghrib', *Middle East Journal*, vol. 63, 2, Spring 2009, p. 217.
13. Luis Martinez, *The Algerian Civil War*, London: Hurst, 2000, pp. 148–9.
14. Ibid., p. 213.
15. Ahmed Rouadjia, 'L'Algérie un an après l'élection de Liamine Zeroual', *Confluences*, Winter 1996–7, p. 87.
16. Filiu, 'The Local and Global jihad of Al-Qa'eda in the Islamic Maghrib', pp. 219–20.

17. See for instance, among many other such allegations, Robert Fisk's report in *The Independent*, 30 October 1997.

18. 'Open letter to all governments from the Secretary General of Amnesty International', London, 26 February 1998.

19. International Crisis Group, 'La Concorde civile: une initiative de paix manquée', 9 July 2001, p. 4.

20. Khaled Nezzar, *Le Sultanat de Bouteflika*, Marseille: Transbordeurs, 2003, p. 30.

21. Ibid., pp. 21–5.

22. José Garçon, 'Algérie, l'impossible restauration', *Politique étrangère*, 2/99, p. 343.

23. Amnesty International, 'La libération de milliers de prisonniers politiques est une mesure positive, mais insuffisante', Paris, 6 July 1999.

24. International Crisis Group, 'La Concorde civile', p. 7.

25. Interview with General Mohammad Lamari in *Al-Ahram*, 17 June 2003.

26. Ibid.

27. Ibid.

28. See for instance the 'Open letter to General Mediene', published on 17 February 2013 by Hocine Malti in *Mediapart* (online French media).

29. I collected these remarks during a series of talks I gave on the Arab democratic uprising, in March and May 2012, in Algiers, Oran, Annaba, Constantine and Tlemcen.

30. Statoil, 'The In-Amenas attack', presented to the Board of Directors on 11 September 2013, p. 4.

31. Ibid., p. 70.

32. José Garçon, 'Algérie: l'impossible relève?', in *Politique internationale*, n°145, Fall 2014, p. 136.

33. 26 per cent exactly, according to a study published in March 2012 by the Qatar-based Arab Center for Research and Policy Studies (Arab Opinion Project, *The Arab Opinion Index 2012*, pp. 16–17).

34. Garçon, 'Algérie: l'impossible relève?', p. 130.

35. SIPRI (Stockholm International Peace Research Institute), *Trends in World Military Expenditure, 2013*, April 2014, p. 4. The exact figure is $10.4 billion, with an 8.8 per cent increase from 2012 to 2013 (compared to a 3 per cent estimated growth in GNP during the same period).

5. THE RISE OF THE SECURITY MAFIAS

1. Steven Cook, *Ruling but not Governing: The Military and Political Development in Egypt, Algeria and Turkey*, Baltimore, MD: Johns Hopkins University Press, 2007, p. 14.

2. This is the main thesis, among others, of Batatu, *Syria's Peasantry*, 1999.

3. Charles Tilly, 'War-making and State-making as Organized Crime', in Peter Evans et al. (eds), *Bringing the State Back In*, Cambridge: Cambridge University Press, 1985, p. 170.
4. Ferris, *Nasser's Gamble*, pp. 200–202.
5. Ibid., p. 203.
6. Egypt, Saudi Arabia, Qatar and the United Arab Emirates founded the AOI in 1975 to boost the Arab defence industry on Egyptian soil. After the 1979 Camp David breach, the AOI became an Egyptian conglomerate de facto, with the Gulf partners returning their shares at the beginning of the 1990s.
7. Cook, *Ruling but not Governing*, p. 19.
8. Yezid Sayigh, *Above the State: The Officers' Republic in Egypt*, Beirut: Carnegie Middle East Center, 1 August 2012, p. 5.
9. Ibid., p. 14.
10. Day, *Regionalism and Rebellion in Yemen*, p. 158.
11. Ibid., p. 157.
12. Ibid., p. 158.
13. Martinez, *The Algerian Civil War*, pp. 236–9.
14. Ibid., p. 17.
15. Ibid., p. 17.
16. Ignacio Cembrero, 'Una cicatriz de 1500 kilometros', *El Pais*, 25 May 2008.
17. Cherif Lakhdiri, 'Algérie-Maroc, quand le business ouvre les frontièrcs', *Al-Watan*, 6 February 2012.
18. Cembrero, 'Una cicatriz de 1500 kilometros', *El Pais*, 25 May 2008.
19. Jean-Pierre Filiu, *Le Nouveau Moyen-Orient*, Paris: Fayard, 2013, pp. 123–4.
20. Ibid., p. 97.
21. Assad means 'lion' in Arabic.
22. Filiu, *Le Nouveau Moyen-Orient*, p. 106.
23. For various positions on this debate, see for instance Ola Listaugh, 'Oil Wealth Dissatisfaction and Political Trust in Norway: A Resource Curse?' *West European Politics*, vol. 28, no. 4, 2005; Andrew Rosser, 'Escaping the Resource Curse: The Case of Indonesia', *Journal of Contemporary Asia*, vol. 37, no. 1, February 2007; Jeffrey Sachs, Joseph Stiglitz, Macartan Humphreys (eds), 'What is the Problem with Natural Resource Wealth' in *Escaping The Resource Curse*, New York: Columbia University Press, 2007.
24. Seale, *The Struggle for Syria*, p. 47.
25. Day, *Regionalism and Rebellion in Yemen*, p. 148.
26. Government of Yemen Central Statistics Yearbook, 2009.
27. Day, *Regionalism and Rebellion in Yemen*, p. 103.

28. Peter Salisbury, *Yemen's Economy: Oil, Imports and Elites*, London: Chatham House, MENA Program Paper 2011/2, October 2011, p. 12.
29. Luis Martinez, *The Violence of Petro-dollar Regimes: Algeria, Iraq and Libya*, London: Hurst, 2012, p. 84.
30. Ibid., p. 95.
31. Ibid., p. 90.
32. Ibid., p. 95.
33. Seale, *Asad, the Struggle for the Middle East*, p. 447.
34. Ibid., p. 255.
35. Ibid., p. 263.
36. Henry Laurens, *La Question de Palestine 1967–82*, Paris: Fayard, 2011, p. 699.
37. Michel Seurat, *L'Etat de barbarie*, Paris: Seuil, 1989, p. 43.
38. Seale, *Asad, the Struggle for the Middle East*, p. 398.
39. Cook, *The Struggle for Egypt*, p. 223.

6. THE 'GLOBAL TERROR' NEXT DOOR

1. Cook, *The Struggle for Egypt*, p. 204.
2. Clive Stafford Smith, *Bad Men: Guantanamo Bay and the Secret Prisons*, London: Phoenix, 2008, pp. 79, 245.
3. Jean-Pierre Filiu, *La Véritable histoire d'Al-Qaida*, Paris: Pluriel, 2011, p. 49.
4. Ibid., p. 60.
5. Day, *Regionalism and Rebellion in Yemen*, p. 198.
6. International Crisis Group, *Yemen's Security-Military Reform: Seeds of a New Conflict?*, Middle East Report 139, 4 April 2013, p. 9.
7. Ibid., pp. 7–8.
8. Day, *Regionalism and Rebellion in Yemen*, pp. 198–9.
9. Ibid., p. 255.
10. The best informed and most comprehensive study on this issue is Thomas Hegghammer, *Jihad in Saudi Arabia*, Cambridge: Cambrige University Press, 2010.
11. Jeremy Sharp, *Yemen: Background and US Relations*, Washington: Congressional Research Service (CRS), 6 February 2014, p. 11.
12. Filiu, *La Véritable histoire d'Al-Qaida*, pp. 31–3.
13. This is the title of Abu Musab al-Suri's biography: Brynjar Lia, *Architect of Global Jihad: The Life of Al-Qaeda Strategist Abu Mus'ab Al-Suri*London: Hurst, 2007.
14. Filiu, *La Véritable histoire d'Al-Qaida*, pp. 56–7.
15. *Guardian*, 14 September 2001.
16. George W. Bush, speech to the UN General Assembly, New York, 12 September 2002.

17. United Nations Security Council, Resolution 1441, New York, 8 November 2002.
18. Filiu, *La Véritable histoire d'Al-Qaida*, pp. 190–91.
19. Bernard Rougier, *L'Oumma en fragments*, Paris: PUF, 2011, p. 221.
20. For details about the jihadi cooperation involving Syrian intelligence and Iraqi former officials, see Martin Chulov, 'ISIS: the inside story', *Guardian*, 11 December 2014.
21. Cook, *The Struggle for Egypt*, pp. 222–3.

7. THE STORY OF TWO SQUARES IN EGYPT

1. Samer Suleiman, *Al-Nizâm al-qawî wa al-dawla al-dha'îfa (The Strong Regime and the Weak State)*, Cairo: Dar Merit, 2005, p. 271.
2. Kandil, *Soldiers, Spies and Statesmen*, p. 225
3. Omar Suleiman's address to Egyptian state television, 11 February 2011.
4. Hillel Frisch, 'The Egyptian army and Egypt's "spring"', *Journal of Strategic Studies*, 2013, vol. 36, no. 2, p. 190.
5. Ibid., p. 183.
6. Kandil, *Soldiers, Spies and Statesmen*, p. 237.
7. Rime Naguib, 'A year in review, the SCAF rules in 93 letters', *Al-Masry al-Yom*, 31 December 2011.
8. Ibid.
9. Rana Khazbak, 'Protesters reject "threatening" SCAF statement', *Al-Masry al-Yom*, 12 July 2011.
10. Kandil, *Soldiers, Spies and Statesmen*, p. 232.
11. Ibid., p. 230.
12. http://www.arabist.net/blog/2011/9/16/wael-ghonims-letter-to-tantawi.html (accessed 14 December 2014).
13. Benjamin Barthe, 'En Egypte, l'armée resserre son emprise sur les médias', *Le Monde*, 30 October 2011.
14. The best documented study about the Ultras is James Dorsey, *The Turbulent World of Middle East Soccer*, London: Hurst, 2015.
15. Testimony of one of the revolutionary delegates, who insisted on remaining anonymous, due to the security situation in Egypt.
16. Omar Ashour, 'What do Egypt's generals want?' *Project Syndicate*, 30 January 2012.
17. Claire Talon, 'L'Egypte sous tension après le drame de Port-Saïd', *Le Monde*, 3 February 2012.
18. Alain Gresh, 'De la dictature militaire à la dictature religieuse?' *Le Monde diplomatique*, November 2012.
19. Claire Talon, 'Egypte: l'emprise des Frères inquiète l'opposition', *Le Monde*, 25 August 2012.

20. See http://english.ahram.org.eg/News/55595.aspx (accessed 9 December 2014).

21. Issandr al-Amrani, 'Sightings of the Egyptian Deep State', *MERIP*, 1 January 2012.

22. Agence France Presse, 'Obama calls Egypt's Morsi, commends his truce efforts', Washington, 20 November 2012.

23. Richard Spencer and Magdy Samaan, 'Mohammad Morsi grants himself sweeping new powers in wake of Gaza', *Daily Telegraph*, 22 November 2012.

24. Christophe Ayad, 'Martyr contre martyr, projet contre projet, l'Egypte est coupée en deux', *Le Monde*, 15 December 2012.

25. Human Rights Watch, 'Egypt: Investigate Brotherhood abuse of protesters', New York, 12 December 2012.

26. Information about the documentary film may be found at http://www.imdb.com/title/tt0178909/combined (accessed 9 December 2014).

27. 'At least nine deaths reported, armed forces deployed in Suez', *Al-Masry al-Youm*, 25 January 2013.

28. Ibid.

29. See http://www.sis.gov.eg/En/Templates/Articles/tmpArticles.aspx?ArtID=66098#.VDo4mkuW47s (accessed 9 December 2014).

30. Hélène Sallon, 'Le président égyptien Morsi affaibli par les violences policières', *Le Monde*, 5 February 2013.

31. Benjamin Barthe, 'L'armée revient dans le jeu politique', *Le Monde*, 16 March 2013.

32. Hélène Sallon, 'Les Black Block, nouveau visage de la contestation', *Le Monde*, 3 February 2013.

33. Benjamin Barthe, 'L'armée revient dans le jeu politique', *Le Monde*, 16 March 2013.

34. Charles Levinson and Matt Bradley, 'In Egypt, the "Deep State" Rises Again', *Wall Street Journal*, 19 July 2013.

35. Florence Beaugé, 'L'Egypte, écartelée entre réformes et peur de la rue', *Le Monde*, 5 April 2013.

36. Asma Alsharif and Yasmine Saleh, 'The Real Force Behind Egypt's "Revolution of the State"', Reuters, Cairo, 10 October 2013.

37. Benjamin Barthe, 'Les apprentis sorciers de Tamarrod', *Le Monde*, 18 July 2013.

38. Issandr al-Amrani, 'The de-legitimization of Mohamed Morsi', *The Arabist*, 30 June 2013.

39. See http://www.masress.com/en/ahramweekly/102621 (accessed 9 December 2014).

40. Ibid.

41. Ibid.

42. See http://www.masress.com/en/egyptiangazette/29306 (accessed 9 December 2014).

43. See http://www.thedailybeast.com/articles/2013/07/02/mahmoud-badr-is-the-young-face-of-the-anti-morsi-movement.html (accessed 9 December 2014).

44. Tewfik Aclimandos, 'L'armée va tout faire pour faire tomber Morsi', interview with *Le Monde*, 3 July 2013.

45. Associated Press, Statement by Egypt's Military Chief, Cairo, 3 July 2013.

46. Ibid.

47. Sheera Frankel, 'How Egypt's Rebel Movement Helped Pave the Way for the Sissi Presidency', Buzzfeed, 26 April 2014.

48. Claire Talon, 'Un coup d'Etat planifié par les militaires?' *Le Monde*, 6 July 2013.

49. David Kirkpatrick, 'Ousted General is Back as Islamists' Foe', *New York Times*, 30 October 2013.

50. Christophe Ayad, 'Comment l'armée a récupéré Tahrir', *Le Monde*, 9 August 2013.

51. Ibid.

52. Human Rights Watch, 'Egypt: Security Forces use Excessive Lethal Force', New York, 19 August 2013.

53. See www.lemonde.fr/afrique/article/2013/08/19/en-egypte-plus-de-morts-en-cinq-jours-que-pendant-la-revolution-de-2011_3463410_3212.html (accessed 9 December 2014).

54. Christophe Ayad, 'Les Coptes, cibles privilégiées des représailles des Frères musulmans', *Le Monde*, 19 August 2013.

55. See www.lemonde.fr/afrique/article/2013/08/19/en-egypte-plus-de-morts-en-cinq-jours-que-pendant-la-revolution-de-2011_3463410_3212.html (accessed 9 December 2014).

56. Alistair Beach, 'Now Baradei Faces Wrath of the Army after Resigning from Cabinet', *The Independent*, 20 August 2013.

57. Serge Michel, 'Les généraux égyptiens veulent briser les Frères', *Le Monde*, 20 August 2013.

58. Report of the Arab League meeting, AFP, Cairo, 1 September 2013.

59. Marion Guénard, 'Sissi surfe sur une vague nationaliste', *Le Monde*, 12 October 2013.

60. See https://www.youtube.com/watch?v=du1Xq35b3uY&feature=player_embedded&desktop_uri=/watch%3Ffeature%3Dplayer_embedded%26v%3Ddu1Xq35b3uY&app=desktop (accessed 9 December 2014).

61. See http://weekly.ahram.org.eg/News/4103/44/Catch-the-Al-Sisi-mania.aspx (accessed 9 December 2014).

62. See http://english.alarabiya.net/en/News/middle-east/2014/02/07/In-rare-interview-Mubarak-says-Egyptians-want-Sisi.html (accessed 9 December 2014).

63. See http://www.foreignpolicy.com/articles/2014/02/07/the_crooks_return_
    to_cairo_hussein_salem_egypt (accessed 9 December 2014).
64. Kristina Kausch, 'Recipe for civil war?' FRIDE commentary, n°1, January
    2014.
65. Nathan Brown, 'Egypt's Constitutional Cul-de-sac', *CMI Insight*, March
    2014.
66. David Kirkpatrick, 'Vow of Freedom of Religion goes Unkept in Egypt',
    New York Times, 25 April 2014.
67. Marion Guénard, 'Le maréchal Al-Sissi en "sauveur de la nation"', *Le
    Monde*, 29 January 2014.
68. Maggy Fick, 'Egypt Army Extends Power by Taking Charge of Gulf Aid',
    Reuters, Cairo, 27 March 2014.
69. Ahmed Morsy, 'The Military Crowds out Civilian Business in Egypt',
    Carnegie International Endowment for Peace, 24 June 2014.
70. Zeinab al-Guindy, 'Hot Night, Dark City: how Egyptians cope with
    power cuts', *Al-Ahram*, 28 August 2014.
71. See http://www.al-monitor.com/pulse/originals/2014/09/egypt-water-nile-
    shortage-power-cuts.html (accessed 9 December 2014).
72. Ismail Alexandrani, 'War in Sinai', *Arab Reform Initiative*, March 2014.
73. Quoted in Dina Khawaga, 'From Apparatus State to War State', *Arab
    Reform Initiative*, September 2014.
74. The same militia leader has been accused of the deadly assault on the US
    compound in Benghazi, in September 2012, where the American ambas-
    sador was killed. See David Kirkpatrick, 'A Deadly Mix in Benghazi', *New
    York Times*, 28 December 2013.
75. Patrick Kingsley, Chris Stephen and Dan Roberts, 'UAE and Egypt behind
    Bombing Raids against Libyan Militias, say US Officials', *The Guardian*,
    26 August 2013.
76. http://www.el-balad.com/1164149 (accessed 9 December 2014).
77. Michelle Dunne and Scott Williamson, 'Egypt's Unprecedented Instability
    by the Numbers', Carnegie Endowment for International Peace, Washing-
    ton, 24 March 2014.
78. According to the estimates of the Egyptian Initiative for Personal Rights.
    Marion Guénard, who has covered Egypt for *Le Monde* from 2007 to
    2014, gives even higher numbers, in the absence of official datas: Marion
    Guénard, 'Egypte: Al-Sissi imperator?' in *Politique Internationale*, n°145,
    Autumn 2014, p. 101.
79. Farah Ramzy, 'Le champ de bataille des universités égyptiennes', *Orient
    XXI*, 16 December 2014.
80. http://www.shorouknews.com/news/view.aspx?cdate=22092014&id=
    ff998f19–06f7–4fce-9d4e-d7054c331b39 (accessed 17 December 2014).
81. Dunne and Williamson, 'Egypt's Unprecedented Instability by the
    Numbers'.

8. EVIL TWINS IN YEMEN AND SYRIA

1. Stephen Day, *Regionalism and Rebellion in Yemen*, p. 274.
2. See http://edition.cnn.com/2011/WORLD/meast/05/29/yemen.unrest/index.html?hpt=T2 (accessed 6 December 2014).
3. The memo of the Department of Justice justifying such a killing was published by NBC News in February 2013. See http://investigations.nbcnews.com/_news/2013/02/04/16843014-justice-department-memo-reveals-legal-case-for-drone-strikes-on-americans (accessed 6 December 2014).
4. Agreement on the implementation mechanism for the transition process in Yemen, published in the *Yemen Post*, 19 February 2012.
5. François-Xavier Trégan, 'L'Etat yéménite, otage de la 'révolution' des houthistes', *Le Monde*, 27 December 2014.
6. Laurent Bonnefoy, 'Retour des chiites sur la scène yéménite', *Le Monde diplomatique*, November 2014, p. 4.
7. Ibid.
8. Jean-Pierre Filiu, 'Ansar al-Fatah and the French "Iraqi" network', in Bruce Hoffmann and Fernando Reinares (eds), *The Evolution of the Global Terrorist Threat*, New York: Columbia University Press, 2014, pp. 361–3.
9. Martin Chulov, 'ISIS: the inside story', *The Guardian*, 11 December 2014.
10. See http://syrie.blog.lemonde.fr/2013/10/19/syrie-les-vrais-ennemis-de-bachar-al-assad-pas-les-amis-de-sadnaya-mais-les-revolutionnaires-et-les-democrates/ (accessed 6 December 2014).
11. *Le Monde*, 15 March 2012.
12. Brian Fishman, 'The Islamic State: A Persistent Threat', Testimony to the House Armed Services Committee, Washington, 29 July 2014.
13. Ilina Angelova, 'Rebel-held Suburbs of Damascus, Resilience Mechanisms in the Face of Chemical Attacks', *Arab Reform Initiative*, 17 July 2014.
14. Report of the Arab League meeting, AFP, Cairo, 1 September 2013.
15. Jean-Pierre Filiu, *Je vous écris d'Alep*, Paris: Denoël, 2013, pp. 130–31.
16. International Crisis Group, 'Iraq: Falluja's Faustian Bargain', Middle East report n°150, Baghdad/Brussels, 28 April 2014.
17. Terence McCoy, 'ISIS just stole $425 million', *Washington Post*, 12 June 2014.
18. See http://www.slate.fr/story/87967/bachar-el-assad-syrie-presidentielle (accessed 6 December 2014).
19. Ibid.
20. Alissa Rubin and Rod Nordland, 'Sunnis and Kurds on Sidelines of Iraq Leader's Military plans', *New York Times*, 17 June 2014.
21. Hala Kodmani, 'Un califat lucratif aux mains des jihadistes', *L'Express*, 24 July 2014.

22. Barack Obama, 'Speech to the Nation', White House, Washington, DC, 10 September 2014.

9. STRANGLING PALESTINE

1. Even ten years later, the former chief of the political branch of the Military security (DRS), General Lakehal Ayat, kept playing the same tune. See his contribution to *Octobre, ils parlent*, Alger: Editions Le Matin, 1998, pp. 127–34.
2. The Popular Front for Liberation of Palestine–General Command (PFLP–GC) is a splinter group from the main PFLP, supported by the Syrian intelligence and chaired since its foundation in 1968 by the Palestinian Ahmad Jibril (Abou Jihad), after he served in the Syrian forces.
3. See for instance the fascinating testimony of Nidal Bitari, 'Yarmuk Refugee Camp and the Syrian Revolution: A View from Within', *Journal of Palestine Studies*, vol. XLIII, no. 1, Autumn 2013, pp. 61–78.
4. Anthony Shadid, 'Syrian Elite will Fight Protest till "the End"', *New York Times*, 10 May 2011.
5. See http://blogs.rue89.nouvelobs.com/jean-pierre-filiu/2013/12/28/bachar-el-assad-affame-la-palestine-damas-232003 (accessed 8 December 2014).
6. Amnesty International, 'Squeezing the Life out of Yarmouk', London, pp. 24–34.
7. Ibid., p. 9.
8. Chris Gunness, UNRWA spokesman on Yarmouk camp, 10 August 2014. See http://www.unrwa.org/crisis-in-yarmouk (accessed 8 December 2014).
9. UNRWA, 'Syria crisis regional response, update 77', 11 August 2014.
10. Bitari, 'Yarmuk Refugee Camp', p. 78.
11. Jean-Pierre Filiu, *Gaza: A History*, London: Hurst, 2014, p. 326.
12. Laurent Zecchini, 'La population de Gaza étranglée, victime collatérale de la chute du régime égyptien', *Le Monde*, 20 July 2013.
13. Serge Michel, 'Les généraux égyptiens veulent briser les Frères', *Le Monde*, 20 August 2013.
14. Ibid.
15. The most detailed assessment of the casualties and damages inflicted in the Gaza Strip by the Israeli offensive is the *Gaza Crisis Atlas*, released by the UN Office for the Coordination of Humanitarian Affairs (OCHA) in August 2014. Available at http://www.ochaopt.org/documents/GazaCrisisAtlas_2014.pdf (accessed 8 December 2014).
16. The head of delegation was Fatah Azzam al-Ahmad, assisted by Majed al-Faraj, head of PA intelligence. Representing Hamas was Moussa Abu Marzouk, Meshal's deputy, along with Zyad al-Nakhala for Islamic Jihad.
17. Quoted in Khaled Diab, 'An Insane Alliance: Israel and Egypt Against Gaza', *Haaretz*, 8 August 2014.

18. Ibid.
19. Jack Khoury, 'The Gaza Donor Conference, A Springboard to Sissi?' *Haaretz*, 13 October 2014.

10. THE TUNISIAN ALTERNATIVE

1. Hélène Sallon, 'Sanglante attaque jihadiste dans le Sinaï', *Le Monde*, 26 October 2014.
2. David Kirkpatrick, 'Militant Group in Egypt Vows Loyalty to ISIS', *New York Times*, 10 November 2014.
3. Yadh Ben Achour's interview with *Le Monde*, 20 April 2011.
4. UGTT stands for *Union Générale Tunisienne du Travail*.
5. See http://carnegieendowment.org/2014/03/31/egypt-s-constitutional-cul-de-sac/h7yy (accessed 8 December 2014).
6. CPR stands for *Congrès pour la République* in French.
7. GICT stands for *Groupe Islamique Combattant Tunisien* in French.
8. UTICA stands for *Union Tunisienne de l'Industrie, du Commerce et de l'Artisanat* in French.
9. LTDH stands for *Ligue Tunisienne des Droits de l'Homme* in French.
10. Isabelle Mandraud, 'Les forces spéciales tunisiennes ont tué l'assassin présumé de Chokri Belaïd', *Le Monde*, 6 February 2014.
11. Ibid.
12. In a closed-door meeting I attended with Seif al-Islam Qaddafi, in Washington, the Libyan dictator's heir apparent boasted about how his father 'sold America his yellow cake at the best price', in a reference to the compensation disbursed for the low-enriched uranium stocks (German Marshall Fund, 19 November 2008).
13. A must-read study on this issue is Zeid Al-Ali, *The Struggle for Iraq's Future*, New Haven, CT: Yale University Press, 2014.
14. Luis Martinez, 'Libya from paramilitary forces to militias: the difficulty of constructing a state security apparatus', *Arab Reform Initiative*, May 2014.
15. Opening line of Karl Marx, *The 18th Brumaire of Louis Napoléon*, New York: International Publishers, 1963.

CONCLUSION

1. Hélène Sallon, 'Le suicide de Zeinab al-Mahdi, miroir du rêve perdu de Tahrir', *Le Monde*, 21 November 2014.
2. See http://www.newsweek.com/httpwwwnewsweekcomabu-bakr-al-baghdadi-abu-dua-invisible-sheikh-awwad-ibrahim-284261 (accessed 9 December 2014).

3. Jean-Pierre Filiu, 'Ansar al-Fatah and French "Iraqi" network', p. 362.

4. http://nawaat.org/portail/2013/07/26/qui-est-boubaker-al-hakim-tueur-presume-de-mohamed-brahmi/ (accessed 9 December 2014).

5. http://www.lexpress.fr/actualite/monde/proche-moyen-orient/le-regime-syrien-cent-fois-plus-meurtrier-que-les-djihadistes-de-l-ei_1624707.html#xtor=AL-447 (accessed 9 December 2014).

6. James Traub, 'Bashar al Assad and the Devil's Bargain', *Foreign Policy*, November 2014, available online at http://www.foreignpolicy.com/articles/2014/11/14/bashar_al_assad_and_the_devils_bargain_syria_truce (accessed 9 December 2014).

7. *Ibid.*

8. Rémy Ourdan, 'Derna, premier territoire de l'EI en dehors des "frontières" du califat', *Le Monde*, 13 November 2014.

SELECT ENGLISH BIBLIOGRAPHY

Achcar, Gilbert, *The People Want. A Radical Exploration of the Arab Uprising*, Berkeley: University of California Press, 2013.

Amira El Azhary Sonbol, *The New Mamluks: Egyptian Society and Modern Feudalism*, Syracuse: Syracuse University Press, 2000.

Arjomand, Said (ed.), *The Arab Revolution of 2011: A Comparative Perspective*, Albany: SUNY Press, 2015.

Cole, Juan, *The New Arabs: How the Millennial Generation is Changing the Middle East*, New York: Simon and Schuster, 2014.

Cook, Steven, *The Struggle for Egypt, from Nasser to Tahrir Square*, New York: Oxford University Press, 2012.

Day, Stephen, *Regionalism and Rebellion in Yemen: A Troubled National Union*, Cambridge: Cambridge University Press, 2012.

Dorsey, James, *The Turbulent World of Middle East Soccer*, London: Hurst 2015.

Entelis, John, *Algeria: The Revolution Institutionalized*, Boulder, CO: Westview Press, 1986.

Filiu, Jean-Pierre, *The Arab Revolution. Ten Lessons from the Democratic Uprising*, London: Hurst, 2011.

Hamid, Shadi, *Temptations of Power: Islamists and Illiberal Democracy in the Middle East*, New York: Oxford University Press, 2014.

Haykel, Bernard, Hegghammer, Thomas and Lacroix, Stéphane (eds), *Saudi Arabia in Transition*, Cambridge: Cambridge University Press, 2015.

Kandil, Hazem, *Soldiers, Spies and Statesmen, Egypt's Road to Revolt*, London: Verso, 2012.

Louis, Roger and Avi Shlaim (eds), *The 1967 Arab–Israeli War, Origins and Consequences*, New York: Cambridge University Press, 2012.

Lowi, Miriam, *Oil Wealth and the Poverty of Politics: Algeria Compared*, New York: Cambridge University Press, 2009.

Martinez, Luis, *The Algerian Civil War 1990–1998*, London: Hurst, 2000.

——— *The Libyan Paradox*, London: Hurst, 2007.

——— *The Violence of Petro-Dollar Regimes, Algeria, Iraq, Libya*, London: Hurst, 2012.

Owen, Roger, *The Rise and Fall of Arab Presidents for Life*, Cambridge, MA: Harvard University Press, 2012.

Rogan, Eugene, *The Arabs, A History*, London: Penguin Books, 2011.

Seale, Patrick, *The Struggle for Syria*, New Haven, CT: Yale University Press, 1987.

——— *Asad, the Struggle for the Middle East*, Berkeley: University of California Press, 1989.

Tripp, Charles, *A History of Iraq*, New York: Cambridge University Press, 2007.

——— *The Power and the People, Paths of Resistance in the Middle East*, New York: Cambridge University Press, 2013.

Wedeen, Lisa, *Ambiguities of Domination: Politics, Rhetoric and Symbols in Contemporary Syria*, Chicago: Chicago University Press, 1999.

——— *Peripheral Visions: Publics, Power and Performance in Yemen*, Chicago: Chicago University Press, 2008.

CHRONOLOGY

2011

January

14 Tunisian President Ben Ali flees to Saudi Arabia
17 'National unity' government in Tunisia led by the former Prime Minister Mohammad Ghannouchi
25 First 'Revolution Day' in Egypt; occupation of Tahrir Square in Cairo
27 Tunisian cabinet reshuffle and violent dispersal of the protesters rallying on Government Square (Kasbah I)
28 Mubarak appoints Ahmed Shafiq as his new prime minister
29 Omar Suleiman sworn in as Egyptian vice president

February

 2 Pro-Mubarak mobs on the rampage against Egyptian protesters. Yemeni president Ali Abdullah Saleh promises to step down at the end of his term in office in 2013
 6 'National dialogue' between Suleiman and the Egyptian opposition, including the Muslim Brotherhood
11 'Farewell Friday' in Egypt; Mubarak steps down
12 Crackdown on demonstrations in Algeria
13 The Supreme Council of the Armed Forces (SCAF) suspends the Egyptian constitution and dissolves the parliament. Renewed protest in Yemen
18 'Victory Friday' in Egypt; clashes in Yemen

19 General amnesty in Tunisia
20 Launch of a 13-day mass sit-in in Tunisia's Government Square (Kasbah II)
24 State of emergency officially lifted in Algeria after nine years
27 Béji Caïd-Essebsi new Tunisian prime minister. Arrest of eighteen teenage graffiti taggers in the Syrian city of Deraa

March

1 'Day of Rage' in Yemen
2 Essam Sharaf appointed new Egyptian prime minister
3 Constitutional elections scheduled in Tunisia for 24 July
4 Popular occupation of State Security offices in Alexandria
7 Dissolution of State Security in Tunisia
15 First revolutionary protests in Damascus
18 'Bloody Friday' in Sanaa, 'Dignity Friday' in Deraa
19 77 per cent approval in the SCAF-sponsored constitutional referendum in Egypt
21 Continued riots in Deraa
22 Defection of high-ranking officials in Yemen

April

1 'Salvation Friday' in Yemen
2 Launch of 'Martyrs' Week' in Syria
4 Brutal crackdown in the Yemeni city of Taez
8 Mass protest against corruption in Egypt
11 Demonstrations on Damascus city university campus
15 Joint tribal statement against the Yemeni president. Algerian President Bouteflika's address to the nation on constitutional reforms
23 Transition plan in Yemen (suspended eight days later)
25 Army deployment in the Syrian city of Deraa

May

5 Current Algerian budget increased by 25 per cent ($23.8 billion)

9   Establishment of the electoral commission in Tunisia
11 Tanks shell the Syrian city of Homs
20 Syrian 'Freedom Friday' results in 44 deaths
25 Lebanese Hezbollah leader gives his public support to the Syrian president
27 Rally for a 'second revolution' on Tahrir Square, Cairo. Jihadi takeover of the Yemeni city of Zinjibar

June

3   Saleh badly injured in a bomb attack inside the Yemeni presidential palace, and evacuated from Sanaa to Riyad. Sixty people killed in the Syrian city of Hama
8   Three-month postponement of the Tunisian constitutional elections
15 Pro-Assad mass rally in Damascus
18 Launch of a mop-up campaign in the Syrian border zones with Turkey

July

1   Mass protests in Hama, Syria (also on 8th)
8   'Determination Friday' in Cairo, Alexandria and Suez
15 One million protesters gather all over Syria
23 On Egyptian national day, clashes occur between protesters and pro-SCAF mobs
30 Establishment of a Free Syrian Army (FSA)
31 Launch of a government offensive against Hama (Syria)

August

1   Tahrir Square cleared of protesters by the Egyptian army
7   Launch of a government offensive against Deir Ezzor (Syria)
21 After the insurgent takeover of the Libyan capital, popular attacks against the Algerian embassy in Tripoli
29 Moammar Qaddafi's wife and sons flee to Algeria, which closes its border with Libya

31 Public warning of the Syrian revolutionary committees against the 'trap' of armed action

September

6 Arab League mediation plan in Syria

10 Coalition of Yemeni loyalist and rebel military units retakes the jihadi stronghold of Zinjibar

15 Signing of a transition code of conduct by 12 Tunisian parties (nicknamed 'G12')

23 Return of recovering President Saleh to Sanaa

27 Demand by the revolutionary committees for a 'no-fly zone' over Syria

30 US drone strike in Yemen kills the Yemeni–American jihadi Anwar al-Awlaki

October

1 Fifteen Egyptian parties (including the Muslim Brotherhood) publicly support the SCAF

2 Official founding of a Syrian National Council (SNC) in Istanbul

4 Veto by Russia and China in the UN Security Council in support of the Syrian regime

9 'Maspero massacre' of Christian protesters in front of Egyptian state TV in Cairo

23 Ennahda leads the poll at the elections for the National Constituent Assembly (NCA)

November

12 Syria suspended from the Arab League

18–20 Violent anti-SCAF protests in downtown Cairo

21 Tripartite agreement between Islamist Ennahda, Ettakatol (socialist) and nationalist CPR (Mustapha Ben Jaafar, from Ettakatol, elected as NCA president on 22nd)

23   In Riyad, Saleh signs an agreement on transfer of power

28   First round of the Egyptian parliamentary elections (until 11 January 2012)

30   Turkey imposes sanctions against the Syrian regime

December

7   Kamal Ganzouri replaces Essam Sharaf as Egyptian prime minister

11 General strike against the Syrian regime

12 Moncef Marzouki (CPR) elected as Tunisian President of the Republic

14 Hamadi Jebali (Ennahda) designated Tunisian prime minister

27 Beginning of the mission of the Arab League observers in Syria

2012

January

11 End of the Egyptian parliamentary contests with a sweeping Islamist victory (37 per cent for the MB, 25 per cent for the Salafi)

22 Arab League call for a power transfer in Syria

24 First communiqué of the Nusra Front, a Syrian jihadi group

28 'Freedom marches' in Tunis and Sfax

February

1 Massacre at the Port Saïd soccer stadium (74 killed)

4 More than 200 civilians killed in the Syrian government bombing of Homs. Russian and Chinese vetoes at the UNSC against any condemnation of the Assad regime

21 Abd Rabbo Mansour Hadi sole candidate, by consensus, for the Yemeni presidential elections (99.8 per cent of the votes)

27 Power transfer in Sanaa from Saleh to Hadi

March

2 Army reconquest of the rebel stronghold of Baba Amr in the Syrian city of Homs

4 Massacre of 185 Yemeni soldiers in a jihadi raid against Al-Kawd (Zinjibar province)

7 Outrage in Tunisia after a Salafi desecration of the national flag

10 'Summit meeting' in Tunisia between Ennahda and the UGTT

16 Demonstration in favour of the Sharia in front of the Tunisian parliament

20 Mass demonstrations in Tunisia in support of a 'civil and democratic state'

21 Endorsement by the UNSC of the six-point plan drafted by Kofi Annan, UN and Arab League special envoy for Syria

April

5 In Gao (Mali), 7 Algerian consular officials abducted by a jihadi group

12 UN-sponsored (limited) ceasefire in Syria

29 First UN observers in Damascus

May

18 Unprecedented protests in Aleppo

21 In Yemen, 100 military killed in a jihadi terror attack on the National Day parade; president Hadi reacts by demoting two of Saleh's nephews

23–24 First round of the Egyptian presidential elections

25 Massacre in the Syrian village of Houla (Homs province)

June

14 Dissolution of the Egyptian parliament by the Supreme Constitutional Court (SCC)

16 Suspension of the UN observers' mission in Syria. Launch of the Nidaa Tounes (Call for Tunisia) party by Beji Caïd-Essebsi

17 Mohammad Morsi elected Egyptian president with 51.7 per cent of the votes

26 'State of war' declared by Syrian President Bashar al-Assad

30 Morsi sworn into office by the Egyptian SCC

July

7 Libyan elections for the General National Congress (GNC), to be presided over by Mohammad Magariaf

13 Popular protests against Annan and the UN in Syrian rebel-held areas

17 FSA launch of 'the battle to liberate Damascus'

18 Death of the Syrian minister of defence and his deputy in a bomb attack in Damascus

21 Insurgent breakthrough in Aleppo

August

2 Hesham Qandil replaces Kamal Ganzouri as Egyptian prime minister

12 Morsi reshuffles the military hierarchy, with General Abdel-fattah Sisi new minister of defence

14 Pro-Saleh military storm the ministry of defence in Sanaa

17 Annan resigns, replaced by Lakhdar Brahimi as UN and Arab League special envoy for Syria; end of the UN observers' mission

26 Massacre in the Damascus suburb of Daraya

September

8 Regime air raids in Aleppo (until 13th)

11 Death of the US ambassador in the attack on the American consulate in Benghazi

14 Deadly assault on the US embassy in Tunis

29 The old city of Aleppo is burning

October

26   Failure of a UN-sponsored truce in Syria
29   Regime air raids against Damascus suburbs
30–31 Vote of the Libyan GNC on Ali Zeidan's government

November

1   FSA conquest of the city of Saraqeb (Idlib province)
2   Peace talks under Algerian auspices between Bamako and the Malian jihadi insurgency
11   Syrian National Council (SNC) integrated in Doha into a wider 'National Coalition' of the opposition forces
21   Ceasefire in Gaza under Egyptian auspices between Israel and Hamas
22   Morsi issues a 'constitutional declaration' granting him unprecedented powers
27   Mass anti-MB protests in Egypt

December

5   Clashes around the Egyptian presidential palace
16   Regime air raid on the Palestinian refugee camp of Yarmouk in Damascus
19   In Yemen Hadi dissolves both the pro-Saleh Republican Guard and the pro-opposition Firqa
21   Launch of an Iraqi Sunni protest movement against Nouri al-Maliki's government sectarian policy
22   Referendum approving the MB-drafted (and Salafi-supported) Egyptian constitution by 63.8 per cent

2013

January

12   Algerian public support of the French-led anti-jihadi campaign in Mali
16   Jihadi attack on the Algerian oil facilities of In Amenas

25 Violent anti-MB protests on the second anniversary of the Egyptian revolution; army deployed in Suez

26 In Port Saïd, thirty people are killed in anti-MB riots

27 Curfew imposed in the Suez Canal region

February

6 Assassination of the Tunisian leftist Chokri Belaïd

March

9 Egyptian army deployed in Port Saïd

13 Ali Laarayedh (Ennahda) new Tunisian prime minister

18 Opening of the 'national dialogue' in Yemen

April

9 Abu Bakr al-Baghdadi, leader since 2010 of the Islamic State in Iraq (ISI), announces his expansion into an Islamic State in Iraq and Syria (ISIS), but this merger is rejected by the Nusra front

23 Massacre of Sunni protesters in the Iraqi town of Hawija, leading to the radicalization of an anti-Maliki 'uprising'

24 Government bombing of the minaret of the Omeyyad mosque in Aleppo, Syria

27 Bouteflika enters a Parisian hospital and is treated in France for two and a half months

28 Launch of the Egyptian Tamarod (Rebellion) movement

May

5 'Political isolation law' in Libya

15 Five public messages by the Egyptian minister of defence Sisi

28 Resignation of Libyan GNC President Magariaf

June

12 First images shown of the Algerian president in France receiving chief of staff Ahmad Gaïd Salah

29 Tamarod announces it has gathered 22 million signatures to impeach Egyptian president Morsi

30 Human wave protests against the MB in Egypt

July

1 Sisi's 48-hour ultimatum to Morsi in Egypt

3 Sisi takes power in Egypt, Adly Mansour interim president, Morsi held incommunicado

8 In front of the Cairo Officers Club fifty-one protesters are killed; Mansour issues 'Constitutional declaration'

14 Beginning of the regime's siege of the Palestinian refugee camp of Yarmouk in Damascus

16 Bouteflika returns to Algiers

25 Assassination of the Tunisian leftist Mohammad Brahmi

26 'Anti-terrorism' marches in Egypt

August

7 Termination by the Egyptian authorities of US and European mediation to solve the internal crisis

14–18 All over Egypt, around 1,000 people killed in repression of the MB sit-ins and protests

21 Regime mass gas attacks of the Damascus suburbs lead to an estimated 1,400 killed

29 Amr Saadni becomes secretary general of the ruling FLN party in Algeria

September

5 Failed jihadi attack against the Egyptian minister of the interior.

11 Gaïd Salah appointed deputy Algerian minister of defence (with Bouteflika formally in charge of the portfolio)

18 ISIS takes over Azaz from the FSA, in the Syrian province of Aleppo

23 Egyptian MB declared illegal and its properties seized

24 Defection of several FSA brigades to a new Syrian Islamic Front

October

25 Beginning of the 'national dialogue' in Tunisia

November

8 The Nusra front becomes officially al-Qaeda branch for Syria

December

5 Jihadi attack on the military hospital in Sanaa (53 killed)
24 Jihadi attack by Ansar Beit al-Maqdis (ABM) in the Egyptian city of Mansoura
25 Egyptian MB declared a 'terrorist' organization

2014

January

3 Launch of the 'second revolution' of the Syrian insurgency, this time against ISIS, soon expelled from Aleppo (some 3,000 killed in the following two months)
14–15 Egyptian referendum approves by 98.6 per cent the Sisi-inspired constitution
18 UN first aid delivery to the Yarmouk camp in Damascus, after a six-month siege; over 100 dead by starvation
24 Sisi promoted by the Egyptian interim president to field marshal
25 End of the ten-month long 'national dialogue' in Yemen, with the adoption of a final outcomes document (refused by the Houthis)
27 SCAF endorses Sisi's eventual candidacy for the Egyptian presidency
29 Mehdi Jomaa new Tunisian head of a non-partisan government

February

3 Saadni calls publicly for the Algerian intelligence czar Mediene to step down

18 Ultimatum issued by the Zintani brigades against the GNC in Tripoli

20 Libyan elections for the constitution drafting assembly

22 Bouteflika announces his candidacy for a fourth term in office; a protest movement 'Barakat' (Enough) rises against it

28 FSA retakes Azaz from ISIS, in the Syrian province of Aleppo

March

11 GNC vote of non-confidence in the Libyan PM Zeidan

22 The criminal court in Minya (Egypt) issues 529 death sentences (37 confirmed) against pro-MB dissenters

26 Sisi resigns from Egyptian army to run officially for president

April

17 Bouteflika, voting in a wheelchair, is re-elected with 81 per cent of the counted votes (his main contender, former PM Ali Benflis, declares that he has won the contest himself)

28 The criminal court in Minya (Egypt) issues 683 death sentences (183 confirmed) against pro-MB dissenters

29 Unprecedented offensive against jihadi strongholds in the Yemeni provinces of Abyan and Shabwa

May

7 Evacuation of insurgent fighters from their last stronghold in the Old City of Homs, Syria

9 Jihadi attack on the presidential palace in Sanaa (5 killed)

26–28 Presidential elections in Egypt with 97 per cent votes to Sisi

27   Jihadi attack on the home of Tunisian minister of the interior (4 killed)

June

3   Presidential 'elections' in Syria (with officially 88.7 per cent for Bashar al-Assad); this prompts Brahimi's resignation and his replacement by Steffan di Mistura as UN special envoy for Syria

10 ISIS blitzkrieg in northern Iraq, with takeover of Mosul

15 Showdown in Sanaa between loyalist military and pro-Saleh militia

25 For his first foreign visit as Egyptian president, Sisi meets Bouteflika in Algiers. Parliamentary election in Libya

29 ISIS, now plain 'Islamic State', announces the re-establishment of the 'caliphate'

July

4   First public appearance of Abu Bakr al-Baghdadi, now 'caliph Ibrahim', in a Mosul mosque

8   Launch of an unprecedented Israeli offensive on Gaza (Protective border), to last 50 days (until 26 August)

15 Evacuation to Tunis of the UN mission personnel in Libya

17 Jihadi attack on the Tunisian army (14 killed)

August

8   First US air strikes against ISIS in Iraq, soon joined by French and British strikes

11 Maliki steps down as Iraqi prime minister in favour of Haydar al-Abadi

17 Emirati air raid on Misrata militia positions in Tripoli, Libya, with Egyptian support (also on 23rd)

19 ISIS releases video of beheading of an American hostage

24 ISIS conquers the Syrian regime air base of Tabqa (Raqqa province)

CHRONOLOGY

September

2 ISIS releases video of beheading of a second American hostage (and of a British hostage on 13th)

12 USA officially 'at war' with ISIS

16 ISIS launches its assault on the Syrian Kurdish city of Kobani, exit to the Turkish border (over 800 killed in one month)

21 UN-sponsored ceasefire in Yemen between President Hadi and the leader of the Houthi rebellion (Ansarullah)

22 Extension of the US-led air campaign to Syria, with GCC and Jordanian participation

24 Beheading of a French hostage by an Algerian jihadi group

October

3 Launch of a Syrian regime offensive against the jihadi-free section of Aleppo. ISIS releases video of beheading of a second British hostage

16 Egypt accused of having bombed Benghazi

24 In Sinaï, 33 Egyptian military killed in jihadi attacks

26 Victory of the main secular party in the first Tunisian parliamentary elections

November

6 Libyan Supreme Court deems unconstitutional the parliament elected in June 2014

7 UN sanctions against former Yemeni president Saleh

10 Ansar Beit al-Maqdis (ABM), the leading Egyptian jihadi group, pledges allegiance to Baghdadi

13–15 Bouteflika hospitalized in the French city of Grenoble

16 ISIS releases video of beheading of a third American hostage

29 Charges against Mubarak dismissed by Egyptian justice

CHRONOLOGY

December

6 Two Western hostages killed in a failed US attempt to release them in Yemen

21 Béji Caïd-Essebsi elected president of the Tunisian Republic with 55.7 per cent of the votes (and 60 per cent turnout)

2015

January

7–9 17 people killed in a string of jihadi attacks in Paris

11 Four million protesters in the streets of France against jihadi terror

25 Eighteen protesters killed in the police repression of the celebration of the fourth anniversary of the Egyptian revolution

27 ISIS ousted from the Syrian Kurdish city of Kobani, on the border with Turkey, after four months of fighting and some 700 US airstrikes

29 At least twenty-six killed in series of jihadi attacks in Sinaï

February

14 Two persons killed in two separate jihadi attacks in Copenhagen

16 Egyptian air raids on Libya, in retaliation for ISIS killing twenty-one Egyptian Copts in the Western part of the country

21 President Hadi flees Houthi-controlled Sanaa and moves to Aden, soon proclaimed the new Yemeni "capital city"

March

1 Syrian opposition rejects a UN-sponsored truce in Aleppo

7 Boko Haram pledges allegiances to ISIS

16 Syrian government gas attack on the rebel city of Sarmin (Idlib), with six civilians killed

18 ISIS attack on Tunis National museum, killing twenty foreign tourists and one Tunisian securityman
20 ISIS bombing of Zaydi mosques in Sanaa, killing at least 142 people
24 Five protesters killed in Taez, after an offensive on the city jointly waged by Houthi militiamen and former President Saleh's supporters

INDEX

INDEX